25/2/25

THE CAMPAIGN OF SEDAN.

THE CAMPAIGN OF SEDAN:

THE DOWNFALL OF THE SECOND EMPIRE

AUGUST-SEPTEMBER, 1870

BY GEORGE HOOPER

Author of
"Waterloo: the Downfall of the First Napoleon:
a History of the Campaign of 1815."

WITH MAPS AND PLANS

WORLEY PUBLICATIONS
1998
with Brigade Library

Facsimile Edition Published 1998
by Worley Publications
10, Rectory Road East
Felling
Tyne & Wear NE10 9DN
Telephone: (0191) 469 2414

Originally Published 1887

This Edition © Worley Publications

ISBN 1 869804 49 X

Printed and Bound in Great Britain by
Antony Rowe Ltd., Bumper's Farm,
Chippenham, Wiltshire.

PREFACE.

The War of 1870-71 was opened by a campaign of thirty days, complete in itself, and the author must plead the dramatic unity of the great event as a reason for treating it in a separate form. Although the foundation of those ulterior successes which enabled the Germans to proclaim the King of Prussia Emperor in Germany, and to do so in the palace of Louis XIV., yet, from a historical point of view, the astonishing series of battles and marches which ended in the Investment of Metz, and the Capitulation of Sedan may be regarded as standing apart, because they carried with them the Downfall of the Second Empire. The Campaign of Sedan, in this respect, is the supplement of the Campaign of Waterloo; but, of course, there is no resemblance between Napoleon III. and Napoleon I., nor in the political and military conditions and results of the two catastrophes.

The materials at the disposal of any author who ventures to narrate the campaign are abundant and yet incomplete. The History of the War prepared by the German Staff is minute even to weariness, but it must always stand as the authentic foundation of every narrative. Unreadable to the general public, it is invaluable to the soldier-student, and to all who wish to know what the German Army is like, and how it wages war.

It need scarcely be said that the Staff narrative is the
basis of this book, which is an endeavour to present its
essence in a succinct and readable form. Unhappily,
the French accounts are wanting in precision, so that it
is difficult to comprehend how they fought their battles,
and impossible to ascertain accurately what was their
numerical strength at any moment. The deficiency is
serious, because it mars the completeness of the story,
and frustrates every attempt to do them full justice.
For, if the Army, as an Army, was wasted by incapable
commanders, the soldiers fought well and did nothing
to derogate from their old renown. They had to encounter better commanders, more numerous and better
soldiers, and they were beaten, but they were not dis-
graced. The whole lesson of the war is lost, if the fact
is ignored that the German Army, from top to bottom,
was superior in every way to that of Napoleon III., as
well as more numerous; and that what made it superior
was the spirit of Duty, using the word in its highest
sense, which animated the host, from the King, who was
its shining exemplar, to the private who was proud to
rival his King.

The contrast, which this war exhibited, between the
French and German methods of making and using an
Army is so violent, that it becomes painful, and imparts
an air of one-sidedness to the narrative. But the facts
must be stated, although the bare statement suggests
partiality in the narrator. I have, nevertheless, tried
to be impartial, and in doing my best, I have found it
impossible to read the abounding evidence of Imperial
neglect, rashness and indecision, without feeling pity
for the soldiers and the nation which had to bear the
penalties. The French Army has been re-modelled and
increased enormously; the secular quarrel between
Germany and France is still open; and some day it may

be seen whether the Republicans, out of the same materials, have been able to create an Army such as the Imperialists failed to produce. Whether they have succeeded or not, it may be fervently hoped that the deep impression which the examples of thoroughness, revealed by the wars of 1866 and 1870, made on our own country will never be effaced; and that the public will insist that our small Army, in every part, shall be as good as that which crossed the French frontier in 1870, and triumphed in the Campaign of Sedan.

KENSINGTON, *April 6th, 1887.*

CONTENTS.

MAPS AND PLANS.

" *The policy of your Government will bring you to Jena,*" *said*
M. de Moustier to Herr von Bismarck during the Crimean War.
" *Why not to Waterloo?*" *was the prompt and prophetic reply.*

Wo Kraft und Muth in deutscher Seele flammen.

INTRODUCTION.

In July, 1870, fifty-five years after the Allied Armies, who had marched from the decisive field of Waterloo, entered Paris, a young diplomatist, Baron Wimpfen, started from the French capital, for Berlin. He was the bearer of a Declaration of War, from the Emperor Napoleon III., to William I., King of Prussia; and the fatal message was delivered to the French Chargé d'Affaires, M. le Sourd, and by him to the Prussian Government on the 19th of July. Thus, once again, a Napoleon, at the head of a French Empire, was destined to try his strength against the principal German Power beyond the Rhine.

Yet, under what different conditions! The Emperor was not now the Napoleon who surrounded the Austrians at Ulm, broke down the combined forces of Austria and Russia at Austerlitz, and extorted a peace which set him free to overthrow, at Jena and Auerstadt, the fine army left by Frederick the Great, and allowed to crystallize by his weak successors. Nor did the late Emperor find in his front a divided Germany, and the mere survival of a great military organization. He found a united people, and an army surpassing in completeness, as it did in armaments—the victors of Prague,

Rosbach, and Leuthen. The Germany known to the
Congress of Vienna had disappeared—the deformed had
been transformed. The little seed of unity, sown early
in the century, had grown into a forest tree. The
spirit of Arndt had run through the whole Teutonic
nation, which, after the turmoil of 1848 had subsided,
and the heavy hand of Russia had been taken off by
the Crimean War, found a leader in the strongly-
organized kingdom of Prussia. When the weak and
hesitating will of Frederick William IV. ceased, first,
by the operation of a painful disease, and then by ex-
tinction, to disturb the course of his country's fortunes,
Prussia, in a few years, became practically a new
Power. King William I., who crowned himself with
his own hands at Königsberg, began his task, as a ruler,
in a grave and earnest spirit, holding that kingship was
not only a business, but a trust, and taking as his
watchwords, Work and Duty. No monarch in any age,
no private man, ever laboured more assiduously and
conscientiously at his *métier*, to use the word of Joseph
II., than the King of Prussia. He became Regent in
1858, when Napoleon III. was engaged in preparing
for his Italian campaign against the House of Austria.
French policy, with varying watchwords, had run that
road for centuries; and, during the summer of 1859,
it was the good fortune of the Emperor to win a series
of victories which brought his army to the Mincio, and
before the once famous Quadrilateral. The German
Bund had taken no part in the fray, but the rapid successes of the French aroused some apprehensions in
Berlin, and there went forth an order to mobilize a
part of the army, which means to put each corps on a
war-footing, and to assemble a force in Rhenish Prussia.
Whatever share that demonstration may have had in
producing the sudden arrangement between the rival

Emperors, who made peace over their cigarettes and coffee at Villafranca, the experiment tried by the Berlin War Office had one important result—it brought to light serious defects in the system then practised, and revealed the relative weakness of the Prussian army. From that moment, the Regent, who soon became King by the death of his brother, began the work of reforming the military system. For this step, at least from a Prussian standpoint, there was good reason; since the kingdom, although it was based on a strong and compact nucleus, was, as a whole, made up of scattered fragments lying between great military Powers, and therefore could not hope to subsist without a formidable army. The relative weakness of Prussia had, indeed, been burnt into the souls of Prussian statesmen; and King William, on his accession, determined that so far as in him lay, that grave defect should be cured. A keen observer, a good judge of character and capacity, his experience of men and things, which was large, enabled him at once to select fit instruments. He picked out three persons, two soldiers and a statesman, and severe ordeals in after years justified his choice. He appointed General von Roon, Minister of War, and no man in modern times has shown greater qualities in the organization of an army. He placed General von Moltke at the head of the General Staff, which that able man soon converted into the best equipped and the most effective body of its kind known to history. It rapidly became, what it now is, the brain of the army, alike in quarters and in the field. Finally, after some meditation, he called Herr Otto von Bismarck from the diplomatic service, which had revealed his rare and peculiar qualities, and made this Pommeranian squire his chief political adviser, and the manager of his delicate and weighty State affairs.

Thenceforth, the long-gathering strength of Prussia, the foundations of which were bedded deep in the history of its people, began to assume a form and a direction which great events revealed to astonished and incredulous Europe. The experiment undertaken by the King and his chief councillors was rendered less difficult by that effect of the Crimean War which so materially lessened the influence of Russia in Germany. The intimate and friendly relations subsisting between the two Courts remained unbroken, and to its preservation in fair weather and foul, Prussia owed, to a large extent, the favourable conditions surrounding the application and development of her policy. It seemed as necessary to Prussian, as it now does to German interests, that the Russian Government should be, at least, benevolently neutral; and probably the art of keeping it so was profoundly studied by Herr von Bismarck when he filled the post of Ambassador to the Court of St. Petersburg. The large military reforms designed by the King and his advisers aroused an uncompromising opposition in the native Parliament, which was only overcome by the firmness with which King William supported his outspoken and audacious Minister. The victory was secured by methods which were called, and were, unconstitutional. The control of the Chamber over the Budget was placed in abeyance, by a clever interpretation of the fundamental law. It was held that if the Deputies could not agree with the Government respecting the estimates of the current year, the law which they had sanctioned in the preceding year still remained valid. Thus the taxes were collected, appropriated and expended, just the same as if the Chamber had not virtually "stopped the supplies" in order to defeat the measures which were intended to give the army stability, numbers, efficiency and cohesion. The whole transaction ran counter to English maxims and customs; but it should be remembered that Parliamentary Government, and especially government by party, were never, and are not even now established in Berlin. The net result of the contest was the renovation and the strengthening of the National Army to an extent which, while it did not exceed, perhaps, the expectations of those who laboriously wrought it out, left some Powers of Europe ignorant, and others incredulous respecting its value.

Not that the military institutions of Prussia, dating back from the " new model," devised during the stress of the Napoleonic Wars, had been fundamentally altered. Nothing was done except to increase the numbers, close up and oil the machinery, render its working prompt and easy by prudent decentralization, give it a powerful brain in the General Staff, and impart to the whole system a living energy. The art of war, if the phrase may be allowed, was, in accordance with venerable traditions rooted in the Hohenzollern House, taken up as a serious business; and that deep sense of its importance which prevailed at the fountain head, was made to permeate the entire frame. That is the real distinguishing characteristic of the Prussian, now the German army, as contrasted with the spirit in which similar labours were undertaken by some other Powers. The task was a heavy one, but the three men who set about it were equal to the task. King William, with a large intelligence, a severe yet kindly temper, and a thorough knowledge of his work, threw himself heart and soul into the business, and brought to bear upon its conduct that essential condition of success, the "master's eye." General von Roon framed or sanctioned the administrative measures which were needed to create an almost self-acting and cohesive organism, which could be set in motion by a telegram, as an engineer starts a complicated piece of machinery by touching a lever. Von Moltke, as chief of the General Staff, supplied the directing intellect, and established a complete apparatus for the collection and classification of knowledge, bearing upon military affairs, which might be applied wherever needed. These men, working with " unhasting, unresting " diligence, founded a school of war, not based on " the law of the Medes and Persians which altereth not," but upon the vital principle that a good army should possess in itself such a power of adaptation, as will make it always abreast with the latest genuine discoveries in tactics, arms, material appliances, and discipline. Also the army was treated as a great school in which officers and men alike were teaching and learning from dawn to sunset, throughout the allotted period of service. The principal trio had other and able helpers, but they were the main springs moving and guiding the marvellous product of constant labour applied by rare capacity.

The ultimate, although not the immediate, effect of the French successes at Magenta and Solferino, was the creation of an Italian kingdom, which included within its boundaries, Naples, Sicily, the States of the Church, except Rome, and of course the Duchies on the right bank of the Po. The price of compliance, exacted by the Emperor Napoleon, whose plans had been thwarted, was the cession to him of Nice and Savoy. Venice and the territory beyond the Mincio remained Austrian for several years. While the map of Italy was in course of reconstruction, the political conflict in Berlin raged on with unintermitted violence. Simultaneously the Austrian Emperor was induced to assert his claims to predominance in Germany, but the plans laid, in 1863, were blighted by the prompt refusal of William I. to take any share in them. It was the first symptom of reviving hostility between the two Powers, although a little later, on the death of the King of Denmark, they were found, side by side in arms, to assert the claims of the German Bund upon Holstein, Schleswig and Lauenburg, and avert the occupation of those countries by the troops of Saxony and other minor States alone. The campaign which ensued brought the new model of the Prussian army to the test of actual experiment. But the brave adversaries they had to encounter, if stout in heart, were weak in numbers; and Europe did not set much store by the victories then achieved by Prussia. The public and the Governments were intently occupied with the Secession War in the United States of America, and the astounding expedition to Mexico, which was designed to place an Austrian Archduke on "the throne of the Montezumas," under illustrious French patronage. Thus the quality of the troops, the great influence of the famous "needle-gun," the character of the staff, and the excellent administrative services escaped the notice of all, save the observant few. The political aspects of the dispute were keenly discussed. Lord Palmerston and Lord Russell were, at one moment, disposed to fight for the Treaty of 1851; but the Danish King committed grave blunders; Russia stood aloof, the Emperor Napoleon III. distinctly refused to enter the lists, and the House of Commons was decidedly averse to war. Here it should be noted that the French Emperor, meditating on the value to him of the rival Powers in Germany, had determined to stand well with both. He hoped to please Austria by making the brother of Francis Joseph Emperor of

Mexico, and to keep open the possibilities of an alliance with Prussia, by throwing no obstacles in her way on the Eider.

Then began the great strife between the two Governments which had wrested the Elbe Duchies from the Dane. When the short war ended, certain divisions from each army were posted in the conquered country, and the rivalry which animated the two Courts was carried on by diplomats and statesmen. Prussian policy, since the days of Frederick II., had leaned always towards, if not an alliance with Russia, yet the maintenance of a solid understanding with that growing Power. Herr von Bismarck, who was a deep student in the history of his own country, and who had always nourished large ideas, kept steadily on the well-trodden path, but imparted to his methods a boldness, an inventiveness, and an energy most unusual in Prussian statescraft. The Polish insurrection of 1864 gave him an opportunity which he did not neglect, and while the poor patriots were assisted from the side of Galicia, on the Posen frontier they were ruthlessly repressed, the Russian and Prussian troops making common cause, and crossing the frontier whenever that step seemed needful. The ill-fated Poles, of course, were defeated; Prussia had recorded a fresh claim upon the benevolent neutrality of Russia, while Austrian "ingratitude," never forgiven in St. Petersburg, took a deeper tinge in the eyes of the Czar. The Prussian Government had not long to wait for their reward. During the summer of 1865, the abiding quarrel between Vienna and Berlin, respecting the future status of the conquered or restored Duchies, nearly came to an open rupture. Neither side, however, was ready for a blow, and the "Convention of Gastein," which Bismarck, in a letter to his wife, defined as a mode of "pasting together the cracks in the building," was devised to gain time. The Prussian army, still incomplete from the royal and the military point of view, had been augmented after the Danish war, and the new levies of horse and artillery had not acquired the requisite instruction. So the summer and autumn of 1865 wore away, revealing the spectacle of King William and Herr von Bismarck battling fiercely with the Parliament, and not so clearly displaying Von Moltke and Von Roon labouring hourly to bring the machine entrusted to their charge up to the highest attainable efficiency. There were other reasons for delay. As it was more than probable that the South Germans, and possible that the King of Hanover would not rank themselves with Prussia, but go with Austria and the Bund, an ally was wanted who would divide the forces of the largest Power. That ally was found in the newly united kingdom of Italy.

But before the Italian envoy astonished the diplomatic world by his apparition at Berlin, in March, the controversy between Austria and Prussia had gone on rapidly, step by step, nearer towards a rupture. Count Mensdorff, on behalf of the Emperor Francis Joseph, set up a claim to full liberty of action in the Duchy of Holstein, and began openly to favour the pretensions of the Duke Frederick of Augustenburg to the Ducal Chair. That position was vigorously contested by Herr von Bismarck, who put an opposite construction on the Treaty, which created what was called the "condominium." The consequence was a frequent and animated exchange of despatches, containing such "arguments" as seemed proper to the occasion. Into the merits of this dispute it is needless to enter now, since the whole drift of the verbal struggle shows that while Prussia was intent on providing a solid ground on which to fight out a long-standing quarrel—"inevitable," said Von Moltke, "sooner or later,"—Austria was by no means inclined to shrink from a test directly applied to her position in Germany. Whatever line she had taken her rival would have discovered, or tried to discover, an opposing course; but, it so happened, that, whether by chance or miscalculation, Count Mensdorff, the Austrian Foreign Minister, managed his case so as to give advantages to his abler antagonist. In the last days of February a great council was held in Berlin. Not only the King and his chief Minister, but General von Moltke and General von Manteuffel, from Schleswig, took part in its deliberations. It was the turning point in the grave debate, so far as Prussian action was concerned; for the decision then adopted unanimously, was, that Prussia could not honourably recede, but must go forward, even at the risk of war. No order was given to prepare for that result, because the organization of the army was complete, and moreover, because "the King was very adverse to an offensive war." Nevertheless, from that moment such an issue of the dispute became certain to occur at an early day. Yet neither party wished to fight over the Duchies; each felt that the cause was too paltry. The Austrians, therefore, extended the field, by appealing to the Bund, a move which gave Herr von Bismarck the advantage he so eagerly sought. He answered it by resolving to push, in his own sense, the cause of federal reform. Learning this determination early in March, M. Benedetti observed to Herr von Bismarck that it would ensure peace. "Yes," answered the Minister President,—"for three months," a very accurate forecast by a prophet who could fulfil his own prediction, and who desired to fight the adversary promptly, lest a reconciliation should be effected between Vienna and Pesth, and Hungary, from a source of weakness, should thus become a tower of strength.

A few days later, March 14th, General Govone, from Florence, arrived in Berlin. His advent had been preceded by attempts, on the part of Bismarck, to discover how the French would look on a Prusso-Italian alliance. The subject was delicate, and even after the General's arrival, it was officially stated that he had come, exclusively, to study the progress in small arms and artillery! The pretence was soon abandoned, and the negotiations were avoided ; but the conclusion of a treaty was delayed for some days, because no specific date could be fixed on for the outbreak of war, Prussia having determined, at least to make it appear, that she was not the aggressor. At length a form of words was devised, which satisfied both Powers, stipulating that Italy was to share in the war, providing it began within " three months," and the Convention was signed on the 8th of April. Not, however, before it had been well ascertained that France had really helped on the Prussian alliance and desired to see war ensue, although, avowedly, she did not interfere, giving out that she stood neuter, and that the understanding which might be ultimately come to between France and Prussia would be determined by the march of events, the extension of the war, and the questions to which it might give rise. This language foreshadowed the policy which the Emperor, if not M. Drouyn de Lhuys desired to follow ; and as Russia, recently obliged in the Polish troubles, was friendly, if not allied, Herr von Bismarck was convinced that no foreign Power would array itself on the side of Austria, unless the campaign were prolonged.

Henceforth, the aim of each disputant was to secure a vantage-ground in Germany. Austria had partially collected troops in Bohemia and Moravia, and had secretly stipulated with several States to call out four Federal corps d'armée; while Prussia, who could wait, being always ready, had only carried her preparations forward to a certain extent. M. von Beust, the Saxon Minister, then intervened with a proposal that the Diet should name arbiters, whose decision should be final; a suggestion instantly rejected by the principals in the quarrel. The Emperor Napoleon III., towards the end of May, when Prussian mobilization had practically been completed in eight corps, produced his specific— the characteristic proposal that a Conference should be held in Paris to study the means of maintaining the peace. Prussia accepted the offer, but Austria put an end to the hopes of Napoleon, by stipulating that no arrangement should be discussed which would augment the territory or power of any party of the Conference, and in addition that the Pope should be invited to share in any deliberations on "the Italian Question." These pretensions, by excluding, what everyone wanted, the cession of Venetia to Italy, decided the fate of the Conference. "They desire war at Vienna," said Von Bismarck to Count Benedetti. "These conditions have been conjured up solely for the purpose of giving the States in South Germany time to complete their military preparations." And when the news came officially from Paris that the Austrian answer had killed the project, the Minister President shouted in the French Ambassador's presence "Vive le Roi!" The solution was war. The Prussian army, for once, had been mobilized by slow degrees. More than a month elapsed between the first precautionary and the final steps, but by the 12th of May the entire active army had been summoned to arms. The Conference project was a last attempt, made, indeed, after all hope of arresting the conflict had vanished, alike in Vienna and Berlin; and it was followed by events in Holstein, which put an end to the period of suspense, and formed a prelude to the war. Practically, but without actual fighting, General von Manteuffel compelled the Austrian brigade, under Field-Marshal von Glablenz, to retreat swiftly over the Elbe. The pretext for this strong measure was the fact that Austria, by her sole will, had summoned the Estates to meet at Itzehöe, and had thus infringed the rights of King William! Thereupon Austria requested the Diet at Frankfort to call out all the Federal Corps; and her demand was complied with, on the 14th of June, by a majority of nine to six. The Prussian delegate protested, and withdrew, leaving Austria, Bavaria, Saxony, Wurtemburg, the two Hesses, and several minor States, in open combination against Prussia. But the same stroke which isolated the latter, also destroyed the German Bund, invented by the kings and statesmen of 1815, to preserve internal tranquillity, and safeguard the Fatherland against France. The arrangement implied the co-operation of two Powers; one purely German, yet subordinate; the other parcel German, and mainly consisting of divers peoples outside Germany; and it fell to pieces at a blow, because the time had arrived when one of the two must attain supremacy. Side by side with the secular dynastic conflict arose in the nation that longing for unity which could only be accomplished by a thoroughly German Power.

That Power was Prussia, trained for the task by the steadfast labours of two hundred years. The army she had formed did its work swiftly. Pouring through Saxony and over the Silesian Mountains, the King and his son, July 3rd, crushed the Austrian, on the memorable field of Sadowa, near Königgrätz. The Hanoverian troops, after winning the fight at Langensalza, had been obliged to surrender, and in South Germany the army employed to overcome the Confederates was equally victorious. On the 22nd of July, so swiftly had the main body moved, the Prussians were in front of Vienna and Presburg on the Danube. Four days afterwards, the Emperor Napoleon having struck in with an offer of mediation, which was accepted, the preliminaries of a peace were signed at Nickolsburg, on the 26th of July, and the final treaty was settled and ratified at Prague, on the 23rd of August, long after King William and his formidable Minister were once more in Berlin. By this instrument, Austria was excluded from Germany; a Northern Confederation, reaching to the Main, was founded; Hanover, the Elbe Duchies, Hesse-Cassel, and other territories, were annexed to Prussia; and a formal statement was inserted, declaring that Napoleon III., to whom Austria had ceded Venetia, had acquired it in order to hand over the city and Terra Firma, as far as the Isonzo, to Victor Emmanuel, when the peace should be re-established. Prussia thus became the acknowledged head of Germany, at least as far as the Main; and the national longing for complete unity was about to be gratified in a much shorter time than seemed probable in 1866.

Naturally, the astonishing successes won by Prussian arms against the Federal Corps, as well as the Austrians, compelled the South German States to sue for peace, and accept public treaties, which, while leaving them independent, brought them all, more or less, within the limits of a common German federation. But something more important was accomplished at Nikols-

burg. Herr von der Pfordten, the Bavarian Prime
Minister, repaired thither towards the end of July, and
Bismarck was in possession of information, including
a certain French document, which enabled him to
state the German case in a manner so convincing and
terrifying, that the Bavarian agreed to sign a secret
treaty, bringing the army within the Prussian system,
and stipulating that, in case of war, it should pass at
once under the command of King William. That
which Von der Pfordten conceded the Ministers of
Wurtemburg and Hesse Darmstadt could not refuse,
and thus provision was made, on the morrow of
Sadowa, for that concentration of armed Germany
which overwhelmed France in 1870-71. So that,
although nothing formally constituting a United
Germany had been done, Prussia, by securing the
control of all her forces, and knowing that a strong
and deeply-rooted public sentiment would support her,
was satisfied that, providing time could be gained in
which to arm, instruct and discipline upon the Prussian
model the South Germans and the troops raised from
the annexed provinces, she would be more than a
match for France. South Germany, indeed, had long
known her relative helplessness against the French.
Perhaps it would be more correct to say that the real
peril was more perceptible to the soldiers and statesmen
than to the people, many of whom were strongly
imbued with democratic ideas of the French type.
Yet, although they hungered for what they understood
as liberty and independence, they were still German,
and did not fail to see that their cherished desires could
not be gratified either under French patronage or
French prefects. The soldiers and statesmen had
early perceived the full secret of South German depend-
ence. The Archduke Charles, who had great knowledge

and harsh experience to guide him, pointed out that
the French posts on the Rhine had placed the country
south of the Main at the mercy of France. " As long
as the Rhine frontier from Huningen to Lauterbourg
remains in her hands," wrote a Prussian staff-officer at
a later period, " Germany is open on the Rhine frontier
to an invasion directed upon the Southern States."
No stronger testimony to the sense, if not to the reality
of insecurity could be adduced, than the remarkable
fact that, even so far back as the Crimean War, the then
King of Wurtemburg, in conversation with Herr von
Bismarck, set forth, significantly, the feelings, the
hopes and the dread of South Germany. " Give us
Strassburg," he said, " and we will unite to encounter
any eventuality . . . . for until that city shall become
German, it will always stand in the way of Southern
Germany, devoting herself unreservedly to German
unity and to a German national policy." Hence it will
be seen that, beyond the Main, there were traditional,
yet very real fears of French invasion; and that these
apprehensions had no small share in facilitating the
acceptance of the secret military treaties, and in
shaping the course of subsequent events.

    Thus much it seems needful to state, in order that some
portion of the earlier transactions which had a great influence in bringing on the war of 1870, may be recalled
to the reader's mind. The short, sharp and decisive
duel fought between Austria and Prussia for leadership
in Germany, created a profound impression throughout
Europe. Austria was irritated as well as humbled;
Russia, although the Czar remained more than friendly,
was not without apprehensions; but the French ruler
and his Ministers were astounded, indignant and bewildered. The telegram, which reported the Battle
of Sadowa, wrenched a "cry of agony " from the Court

of the Tuileries, whose policy had been based on the conjecture or belief that Prussia would be defeated, and would call for help. The calculation was, that Napoleon III. would step in as arbiter, and that while he moderated the demands of Austria, he would be able to extort territorial concessions from Prussia as the reward of his patronage. M. Drouyn de Lhuys would have had his master strike in, at once, and cross the Rhine, or occupy the Palatinate; but the Emperor was not then in the mood for heroic enterprises ; he feared that his army was not "ready," and, besides, he still thought that by arrangement he could obtain some sort of "compensation" from Prussia, at the expense of Germany. But all he did was to pose as mediator at Nikolsburg; and Herr von Bismarck, who had done his utmost to keep him in a dubious frame of mind, regarded it as "fortunate" that he did not boldly thrust himself into the quarrel. The "golden opportunity" slid by; M. Drouyn de Lhuys resigned; and Imperial France acquiesced, publicly, in the political and territorial arrangements which, for the first time, during the lapse of centuries, laid broad and deep the foundations of German Unity, and, as a consequence, rendered inevitable a Franco-German War.

c

CHAPTER I.

THE CAUSES OF THE WAR.

THE Treaty of Prague, the secret military conventions signed at Nikolsburg, the ascendency secured by von Bismarck, now elevated to the dignity of a Count, together with the complete removal of alien Powers from Italy, wrought a radical change in the political relations of the European States. Excluded from Germany, although including powerful German elements, the dominions of Austria still extended to the verge of Venetia and the Lombard plains ; but as the Prussian statesman had already hinted, her future lay Eastward, and her centre of gravity had been removed to Buda-Pesth. In the South German Courts, no doubt, there was a bias towards Vienna, and a dislike of Prussia; yet both the leaning and the repugnance were counterbalanced by a deeper dread of France rooted in the people by the vivid memories of repeated and cruel invasions. Russia, somewhat alarmed by the rapid success of King William, had been soothed by diplomatic re-assurances, the tenour of which is not positively known, although a series of subsequent events more than justified the inference made at that time, that promises, bearing on the Czar's Eastern designs, were tendered and accepted as a valuable consideration for the coveted boon of benevolent neutrality, if not something more substantial. Like Russia, France had lost nothing by the campaign of 1866 ; her territories were intact ; her ruler had mediated between Austria and Prussia ; and he had the honour of protecting the Pope, who, as a spiritual and temporal Prince, was still in possession of Rome and restricted territorial domains. But the Napoleonic Court, and many who looked upon its head as a usurper, experienced, on the morrow of Sadowa, and in a greater degree after the preface to a peace had been signed at Nikolsburg, a sensation of diminished magnitude, a consciousness of lessened prestige, and a painful impression that their political, perhaps even their military place in Europe, as the heirs of Richelieu, Louis XIV., and Napoleon, had been suddenly occupied by a Power which they had taught themselves to contemn as an inferior.   Until the summer of 1866 the Emperor Napoleon fancied that he was strong enough to play with the Prussian Minister a game of diplomatic finesse ; indeed, he seems to have thought that the Pomeranian gentleman would be an easy prey; but having thus put it to the proof, he did not concur in the maxim that it is as pleasant to be cheated as to cheat, especially when the result is chiefly due to complaisant self-deception.   On the other hand, Herr von Bismarck had no longer any delusions concerning Louis Napoleon. If, at an early period, when the English Radicals were considering whether the new Emperor was " stupid," a proposition they had taken for granted theretofore, he had over-estimated the capacity of the self-styled " parvenu," later experience had reduced the estimate to just proportions, and had produced a correct judgment upon the character of one who, down to the last, was always taken for more than he was worth.   If any one knew him well, it was probably his cousin, the Duc

de Morny, and M. St. Marc Girardin has preserved a
sentence which is an illuminative commentary upon so
many curious transactions during the Second Empire.
" The greatest difficulty with the Emperor," said De
Morny, "is to remove from his mind a fixed idea, and
to give him a steadfast will." His fixed ideas were not
always compatible one with another. He professed
great devotion to the " principle of nationalities ;" yet
he desired to carry the French frontiers as far as the
Rhine, adding further German populations and Flemish
towns whose inhabitants are not French to those
acquired by Louis XIV. He wished for peace, no
doubt, when he said that the Empire was synonymous
with that word, but he also hungered for the fruits of
war; and, knowing that his internal position and his
external projects required, to uphold the one and realize
the other, a strong and complete army, he had neither
the wit to construct a trustworthy instrument, nor the
ceaseless industry needed to make the most of an
inferior product, nor that absolute independence of the
party whose audacity gave him his crown, which would
have enabled him to select, in all cases, the best officers
for the higher and highest commands. Before, and
during the war of 1866, he wavered between two lines
of policy, hoping to combine the advantages of both ;
and when it was over he demanded compensation for
his " services " as an alarmed spectator, although he had
made no bargain for payment, but had stood inactive
because he conjectured that it would be the more profitable course.

FRENCH DEMANDS FOR THE RHINE.

In making that calculation he erred profoundly. M. Benedetti, the French Ambassador to the Court of Berlin, was instructed as early as the first week in August, 1866, to claim the left bank of the Rhine as far as, and including the important fortress of Mainz. " Knowing the temper of the Minister-President," and knowing also, as he had repeatedly told his Government, that all Germany would resist any proposal to cede the least portion of territory, he first sent in a copy of M. Drouyn de Lhuys' despatch, and afterwards called on the Minister. Prince von Bismarck, in 1871, published in the official newspapers his account of the famous interview, which shows that Benedetti, as he had pledged himself to do, resolutely pressed the large demand. He was told that it meant war, and that he had " better go to Paris to prevent a rupture." Unmoved, he replied that he would return home, "but only to maintain a proposition the abandonment of which would imperil the dynasty." " The parting words " of the Prussian statesman to Count Benedetti, as nearly as they could be remembered by the man who spoke them, were calculated to suggest grave reflections. " Please to call his Majesty's attention to this," said Herr von Bismarck. " Should a war arise out of this complication, it might be a war attended by a revolutionary crisis. In such a case the German dynasties are likely to prove more solid than that of the Emperor Napoleon." It was a menace and a prophetic warning, which touched a sensitive fibre in the heart of the French ruler, who, after a conversation with Count Benedetti, wrote, on the 12th of August, a remarkable letter to M. de Lavalette, who became the *ad interim* successor of M. Drouyn de

Lhuys. Expressing his fears lest " the journals " should taunt him with the refusal of his demand for the Rhine provinces, he directed that the report should be con- tradicted, flatly ; and he added, " the true interest of France is not to obtain an insignificant increase of territory, but to aid Germany in constituting herself after a fashion which will be most favourable to our interests and those of Europe." Neither Dodona nor Delphos could have been more oracular Alarmed as he was, he did not altogether recede from his position, but occupied it in a different way. On the 16th of August a fresh set of proposals was forwarded to Count Benedetti, comprising a regular scale of concessions— the frontiers of 1814 and the annexation of Belgium, or Luxemburg and Belgium, or the Duchy with Belgium, without Antwerp, which was to be " declared a free city." The last-named device was designed " to obviate the intervention of England " when the projected act of violence was committed. " The *minimum* we require," wrote the French Government to M. Benedetti, "is an ostensible treaty which gives us Luxem- burg, and a secret treaty which, stipulating for an offensive and defensive alliance, leaves us the chance of annexing Belgium at the right moment, Prussia engaging to assist us, by force of arms, if necessary, in carrying out this purpose." If Herr von Bismarck asked what he should gain by such a treaty, the answer was to be that he would secure a powerful ally, and that " he was only desired to consent to the cession of what does not belong to him." The official papers on which these statements are founded were discovered and ac- quired by the Germans in Cercay, M. Rouher's chateau, during the war of 1870 ; neither their authenticity nor the construction put on them have ever been contested ; and they show, plainly, what was the kind of projects

nourished by the French Court in 1866-67.   The precise
manner in which Count von Bismarck actually dealt
with them has not been revealed, but he kept a rough
copy of the project drawn up by Benedetti, which was
handed to him by the French Ambassador in 1867, and
the boxes of papers found at Cercay gave him the
draft treaty itself annotated by the Emperor.   Practically, the secret negotiation dropped, was not renewed
for several months, and was only " resumed, subsequently, at various times," without producing any other
result than that of letting Bismarck know the plans
which were conceived in Paris, and inducing him to
keep the Napoleonic Government in play.   There can
be no doubt on one point.   The Prussian statesman did,
at various periods, probably at Biarritz in 1865, when
he captivated Prosper Merimée, and afterwards, while
refusing point-blank to cede an inch of German soil, ask
his interested auditors why they could not indemnify
themselves by seizing Belgium.   But a grim smile of
irony must have lighted up his face when he pointed to
a prey which would not have to be ceded, but caught
and overpowered by main strength.   He was tempting,
probing, playing with the Frenchman, employing what
he called the "dilatory" method, because he wanted
time to equip the new and still imperfect Germany;
and, considering their own dark schemes, can it be said
that they deserved better treatment?

Having direct knowledge of the steps taken by France
in August, 1866, the earliest recorded formal attempt to
procure secret treaties on the basis of territorial concessions, with what searching comment must Bismarck
have read the astonishing diplomatic circular, signed by
M. de Lavalette, and sent out on the 2nd of September,
at the very time when the dark proceedings just briefly
sketched were in full swing!   It was a despatch framed

for public consumption, and intended to present the
Imperial policy in a broad, generous, and philosophic
light, having no relation to the course which, either then
or afterwards, the French ruler followed. Louis
Napoleon told the whole world that France could not
pursue " an ambiguous policy," at the moment when he
was meditating the forcible acquisition of Belgium.
The Emperor painted himself as one who rejoiced in the
change effected by the war, perhaps because it shattered
the treaties of 1815. Prussia, he said, had insured the
independence of Germany; and France need not see in
that fact any shadow cast over herself. " Proud of her
admirable unity, and indestructible nationality, she
cannot oppose or condemn the work of fusion going on
in Germany." By imitating, she took a step nearer to,
not farther from, France; and the Imperial philosopher
professed not to see why public opinion " should recognize adversaries, instead of allies, in those nations
which—enfranchised from a past inimical to us—are
summoned to new life." But there was consolation for
those alarmed patriots who could read between the
lines. Petty states, they were assured, tended to disappear and give place to large agglomerations; the
Imperial Government had always understood that
annexations should only bring together kindred populations; and France, especially, could desire only such
additions as would not affect her internal cohesiveness
—sentences which, like finger-posts, pointed to the
acquisition of Belgium. The war of 1866, it was
admitted, showed the necessity of perfecting the organization of the army; yet smooth things were predicted
by the Imperial soothsayer, for, on the whole, the
horizon, in September, as scanned from Paris, seemed to
be clear of menacing possibilities, and a lasting peace
was secure! The despatch was, in fact, prepared and

administered as a powerful anodyne. By keeping the
French moderately quiet, it suited the purposes of
Bismarck, who, well aware of the uneasiness which it
covered, felt quite equal to the task of coping with each
fresh attempt to obtain "compensation" as it might
arise. Perhaps Louis Napoleon was sincere when he
dictated this interesting State paper, for it is not devoid
of some "fixed ideas" which he cherished; yet probably
it may take rank as a curious example of the subtle
tactics which he often applied to deceive himself, as
well as to cajole his people and his neighbours. At all
events, his will, if he willed peace, did not endure, for
he soon sanctioned and set in motion renewed projects,
for he intended to push forward the boundary posts of
France.

LUXEMBURG.

As he found Prussia polite yet intractable, and
prompt to use plain language, if concessions were
demanded, the Emperor Napoleon formed, or was
advised to form, an ingenious plan whereby he hoped
to secure Luxemburg. He entered into secret negotiations with Holland for the purchase of the Duchy.
The Queen of Holland, a Princess of the House of
Würtemberg, was a keen partizan of France. She
it was who, in July, 1866, uttered a cry of warning
which reached the Tuileries. " It is the dynasty," she
wrote, " which is menaced by a powerful Germany and
a powerful Italy, and the dynasty will have to suffer
the consequences. When Venetia was ceded, you
should have succoured Austria, marched on the Rhine,
and imposed your own conditions. To permit the
destruction of Austria is more than a crime, it is a
blunder." Perhaps the notion that Luxemburg could
be acquired by purchase came from this zealous, clear-

sighted, and outspoken lady. Wherever it may have
originated, the scheme was hotly pursued, negotiations
were opened at the Hague, the usual Napoleonic operations were actually begun to obtain a plébiscite from
the Duchy; Count von Bismarck was discreetly
sounded by M. Benedetti, with the usual indefinite
result, and the consent of the King of Holland was
obtained without much difficulty. At the same time
there was a strong current of opposition in the Dutch
Government, and Prince Henry, the Governor of
Luxemburg, made no secret of his hostility. The
King himself was subject to recurring tremors caused
by his reflections on the possible action of the Prussian
Court; and his alarms were only mitigated or allayed
from time to time by assurances based, in reality, on
M. Benedetti's "impressions" that the Chancellor was
not unfavourable to the plan of cession. The truth is
that M. Benedetti did not accurately perceive the
position which Bismarck had taken up from the outset.
It might be thus expressed : " Luxemburg belongs to
the King of Holland. It is his to keep or give away.
If you want the Duchy, why don't you take it, and with
it the consequences, which it is for you to forecast."
The French Court and its Ministers still laboured
under the belief that they could manage the Berlin
Government, and they put their own interpretation on
the vague, perhaps tempting language of the Chancellor.
At a certain moment, the fear, always lurking in the
King of Holland's breast, gained the mastery, and he
caused the secret to be disclosed to the public. " He
would do nothing without the consent of the King of
Prussia ;" and by revealing the negotiations he forced
on a decision. The incident which terrified the King
of Holland was, no doubt, startling. M. Thiers had
made a strong anti-German speech in the Chamber, and

M. Rouher had developed his theory of the "trois tron-
çons," or triple division of Germany.   The Chancellor,
who had acquired full knowledge of French pretensions
from French Ministers, answered both statesmen by
printing, in the foreground of the "Official Gazette,"
the treaty which gave King William the control of the
Bavarian army, in case of war.   That fact also produced a decisive effect upon the Dutch monarch, who
saw in this characteristic indirect retort to the French
parliamentary display a menace specially directed
against himself.   Hence the revelation sufficed to thwart
the bargain, then so far finished that signatures were
alone wanting to render it binding.   The German
people fired up at the bare mention of such a proposal
as the cession of a German province.   M. de Moustier,
vexed and taken aback, called on Bismarck to restrain
the passions of his countrymen, and vainly urged the
Dutch monarch to sign the treaties.   On the morning
of the day when he was to be questioned in the Reichstag, Bismarck asked Benedetti whether he would
authorize the Minister to state in the Chamber that the
treaties had been signed at the Hague.   The Ambassador could not give the required authority, seeing
that although the King, under conditions, had pledged
his word to the Emperor, the formal act had not been
done, because Prussia had not answered the appeal for
consent from the Hague.   On April 1, 1867, while
Napoleon was opening the Exhibition in Paris, Herr
von Bennigsen put his famous question respecting the
current rumours about a treaty of cession.   If the
French were not prepared for the fierce outburst of
Teutonic fervour, still less could they relish the question put by Herr von Bennigsen and the answer which
it drew from the Chancellor.   The former described
the Duchy as an "ancient province of the collective

Fatherland," and the latter, while "taking into account the French nation's susceptibilities," and giving a brief history of the position in which Luxemburg stood towards Germany, made his meaning clear to the French Court. " The confederate Governments," he said, " are of opinion that no foreign power will interfere with the indisputable rights of German States and German populations. They hope to be able to vindicate and protect those rights by peaceful negotiations, without prejudicing the friendly relations which Germany has hitherto entertained with her neighbours." Napoleon and his advisers were not likely to misconstrue language which, although it lacked the directness of Von Bennigsen's sentences, obviously meant that the French scheme could not be worked out. Indeed, a few days earlier, the Chancellor had used a significant phrase. Answering a question in the Chamber, he said :— " If the previous speaker can manage to induce the Grand Duke (of Luxemburg) to come into the North German Confederation, he will be able to say that he has called an European question into existence ; what more, Time alone can show." The phrase could hardly have escaped the notice of M. de Moustier, and coupled with the second reply, already quoted, gave rise to indignation not unmixed with alarm. At first the Emperor seemed determined not to recede, and he took counsel with his generals, who could not give him encouragement, because they knew that the Government was absolutely without the means of making even a respectable defence against an invasion. The period of suspense at the Tuileries did not endure long. Shortly after the scene in the Reichstag, the Prussian Minister at the Hague brought the matter to a crisis by a message which he delivered to the Dutch Government. The King of the Netherlands, he is reported to

have said, can act as he pleases, but he is responsible
for what he may do. If he had believed that the
meditated cession was a guarantee of peace, it was
the Minister's duty to destroy the illusion. "My
Government," he added, "advises him in the most
formal manner, not to give up Luxemburg to France."
The blow was fatal ; the King, of course, took the
advice to heart, and such a stroke was all the more
deeply felt in Paris because there the Emperor, who
had considered the end gained, now knew from Marshal
Niel that it would be madness to provoke a war. Yet,
unless a loophole of escape could be found, war was
imminent. M. de Moustier discovered a safe and digni-
fied line of retreat. The Chancellor had referred to the
treaty of 1839 which governed the status of Luxemburg ; M. de Moustier took him at his word, and virtually brought the dispute within the purview of
Europe, by formally demanding that the Prussian
garrison should be withdrawn. He held that since the
German forces were practically centred in the hands of
Prussia, Luxemburg, no longer a mere defensive post,
had become a menace to France. In this contention
there was much truth, seeing that the new Confederation of the North, and its allies in the South, constituted a political and military entity far more formidable
and mobile than the old Bund. When the Chancellor
refused a demand, which his adversaries assert he was
at one time prepared to grant, the French Government,
declaring that they had no wish for other than friendly
relations with Berlin, appealed to Europe. The dispute
ended in a compromise arranged as usual beforehand,
and settled at a conference held in London. The
garrison was withdrawn, the fortifications were to be
razed, and the Duchy, like Belgium, was thenceforth to
be neutral ground, covered by a collective guarantee of

the Powers ; but it still remained within the German Zollverein.

There were at work several influences which largely operated to determine a peaceful issue. The French possessed no real army, and the Emperor had only just begun to think about the needful military organization on a new model ; he had, besides, on hand an International Exhibition, by which he set great store ; and in addition a summons to withdraw a garrison did not provide a *casus belli* certain to secure the support of public opinion. Nor did the Prussian Government consider the moment opportune, or the question raised a suitable ground on which to determine the inveterate cause of quarrel between France and Germany. Upon this subject Dr. Busch has recorded some characteristic observations made by the Chancellor, at Versailles, in 1870. "I remember," he said, "when I was at the Paris Exhibition of 1867, I thought to myself 'how would it have been by now, if we had fought out the Luxemburg quarrel? Should I be in Paris, or the French in Berlin?' We were not nearly as strong then as we are now. The Hanoverians and Hessians of that day could not have supplied us with so many good soldiers as to-day. As for the Schleswig-Holsteiners, who have lately been fighting like lions, they had no army at all. The Saxon army was broken up, and had to be entirely reconstructed. And there was but little to be expected from the South Germans. What splendid fellows the Würtembergers are now, quite magnificent ! but in 1866 no soldier could help laughing at them, as they marched into Frankfort like a civic guard. Nor was all well with the Baden forces ; the Grand Duke has done a great deal for them since then. Doubtless public opinion throughout Germany was with us, if we had chosen to make war about Luxemburg.

But that would not have made up for all those short-comings." It is plain, from this retrospective comment, which comes in aid of other evidence, that the great conflict, deferred to 1870, was nearly brought about in 1867, and that France was saved from utter rout, at that early period, by the operation of a set of influences over which neither of the principal actors had full control. The Franco-Dutch negotiation was the last attempt which the Emperor Napoleon made to obtain territory by direct or furtive diplomatic processes.   In the early stages of the risky business he had full confidence in his own ascendency, not to say " preponderance " in Euro-pean councils. He was rudely undeceived. Herr von Bismarck had tempted him with all kinds of sugges-tions, but the Emperor himself, his Ministers and Ambassadors had been content to take the " impres-sions," which they derived from confidential conversa-tions, for definite, binding promises.   One French agent correctly described the fact when he said that " Herr von Bismarck is ready, not to offer us compensa-tions, but to allow us to take them ; " he might have added, " if we can and at our own risk."   There is no published evidence that the Prussian statesman ever offered to cede Luxemburg, or sanction the annexation of Belgium, or preclude himself from adopting, at any conjuncture, the line which appeared most accordant with German interests. On the contrary, long after the interviews at Biarritz and in Paris, and the battle of Sadowa, Napoleon III., to use his own terms, wanted, at least, " une certitude relative " that the Prussian Government would not interpose any obstacle in the way of French "aggrandizement" in the North. He asked, not for words, but an act which he could never obtain ; and the Luxemburg incident proved to him conclusively that nothing could be gained by

making demands on the Court of Prussia. In 1867 and
afterwards in November, 1870, according to Dr. Busch,
Bismarck described with his usual frankness the hesitation of the Emperor. He had not understood his
advantages, in 1866, when he might have done a good
business, although not on German soil, was the earlier
commentary. The later was more illuminative. "In
the summer of 1866," said Bismarck, "Napoleon had
not the pluck to do what was the right thing from his
point of view. He ought—well, he ought to have taken
possession of the subject of Benedetti's proposal [Bel-
gium], when we were marching against the Austrians,
and have held it in pawn for whatever might happen.
At that time we could not stop him, and it was not
likely that England would attack him—at least he
might have waited to see." On this it may be observed
that the influence of Lord Cowley and Lord Clarendon
would probably have sufficed to turn him from such a
plan had it entered into the Emperor's mind; and had
he delivered the blow, in defiance of their protests, or
without consulting them, England, at that time, would
have been enraged at the treachery, and would have
certainly occupied Antwerp. The Emperor was a man
who caressed audacious projects which he had not
always the nerve and courage to carry out. What is
more astonishing, he did not or could not provide the
means essential to the accomplishment of his desires.
Thus the precedent afforded by his conduct in 1866
was followed in 1867, and in each case the result was
the same—vexatious failure.

AN INTERLUDE OF PEACE.

The war-clouds sank below the horizon, the Paris
Exhibition was duly opened; sovereigns and princes,
statesmen and generals, journeyed to the French

capital, and the Court of the Tuileries gave itself up to amusement, gaiety, and dissipation, neglecting nothing which could give pleasure to its illustrious guests. It was the last hour of splendour, the sunset of the Empire. Yet the brilliant scenes, which followed each other day by day, were even then flecked with dark shades. If politics were evaded or ignored in the palace, they were not absent from the highways. Polish hatred found vent in the attempt of Berezowski to slay the unfortunate Emperor Alexander II., and M. Floquet shouted in his ear as he passed through the Courts of Justice, "Vive la Pologne!" The crime and the insult augured ill for the future of that Franco-Russian alliance which Charles X. endeavoured to establish and certain French statesmen have always sighed for. M. Hansen records a sharp observation made by Prince Gortchakoff during the Polish insurrection which the Western Powers regarded with friendly eyes. The Vice-Chancellor held that France and Russia were natural allies, because their interests were the same. "If the Emperor Napoleon will not admit it," he roughly said, "so much the worse for him. Governments vanish, nations remain." Still, in 1867, he did not find the nation more favourable than the Government had been in 1864. Twenty years later, although Russia had become less unpopular, at least with the politicians, and a yearning for a Russian alliance had gathered strength, the ultras proved how little they understood some conditions essential to its gratification by clamoring for the pardon and liberation of Berezowski! The Prussian King and Queen were not exposed to any outrage, and the Parisians gazed with curiosity upon "Bismarck" and "Moltke," whom they admired, and had not yet learned to detest; but the sparkling and joyful assemblies, although the actors,

on both sides, were doubtless sincere at the time, nevertheless suggests a famous incident in the French Revolution which figures on historical pages as " le baiser de
l'amourette." And underneath the shining surface
were concealed gnawing anxieties and fears. The
Emperor Napoleon had dreamed that he could found a
Mexican Empire, and he had induced the Austrian
Archduke Maximillian to accept at his hands an
Imperial crown. The enterprise, which was pushed on
by French troops, not only failed, but irritated England,
who had been deceived, and offended the United States,
whose Government, victors in a civil war, would not
tolerate the establishment of the " Latin race" in the
centre of the huge continent. Not only had it become
necessary to recall the troops, but to bear a still deeper
misfortune—if the word may be applied to the consequences of a reckless and unscrupulous adventure. It
was while opening the Exhibition that the earliest hints
reached the Emperor of an event which dealt him a
heavy blow ; and, on the eve of the day fixed for the
distribution of prizes to the competitors he had
assembled, came the confirmation of the dreaded intelligence, whispered weeks before. The gallant Archduke
and Emperor Maximilian, who had fallen into the hands
of the triumphant and implacable Mexicans, had been
tried and shot, a deed which his French patron was
powerless to avenge.

THE SALZBURG INTERVIEW.

The tragedy of Quaretaro reacted upon European
politics, and incidentally emphasized afresh the peren-
nial antagonism between France and Germany. Still
smarting from the wounds of 1866, Austria hungered
for an ally, and the Saxon Count von Beust, whom the
Emperor Francis Joseph had made his Chancellor, was

eager to try one more fall with Count von Bismarck.
Swayed by political reasons, the Austrian Emperor not
only did not resent the death of his brother, but was
even willing to welcome as his guest Louis Napoleon,
who had so successfully seduced the Archduke by dang-
ling before him the bait of an Imperial Crown. The
French Emperor and his Empress, therefore, travelled
in state through South Germany to Salzburg, where
they met their Austrian hosts. The occasion was,
nominally, one of condolence and mourning, and the
vain regrets on both sides were doubtless genuine.
Yet it so chanced that the days spent in the lovely
scenery of Salzburg were given up to gay mirth and
feasting—not to sorrow and gloom; and that the irre-
pressible spirit of politics intruded on the brilliant company gathered round an open grave. Both Emperors
felt aggrieved; one by the loss of his high estate in
Germany and his Italian provinces, the other because
his demand for the Rhenish territory had been rejected,
and he had not been allowed to take Belgium or buy
Luxemburg. The common enemy was Prussia, who
had worsted Austria in battle, and France in diplomacy;
and at Salzburg, perhaps earlier, the ground plans were
sketched for an edifice which the architects trusted
might be built up sufficiently large and strong to con-
tain, at least, two allies. The sketch was vague, yet it
was definite enough at least to reveal the designs of the
draughtsmen; and the Emperors returned home still in
jubilation.

Perhaps the Emperor Napoleon suffered some pangs
of disappointment. " Austria was his last card," says
M. Rothan, who, from the French standpoint, has so
keenly studied the period preceding the war of 1870.
He wanted an offensive and defensive alliance, which
Austria would not accord, Count von Beust fearing

that so grave a fact would never escape the lynx-eyes of Bismarck, who, when it came to his knowledge, would not fail to provoke a war before either ally had fully, or even partially, completed his military preparations, then so much in arrear. Not only were they backward in 1867, but Austria, at all events, was still unprovided in 1870. The Archduke Albert, who visited Paris during the month of February of that year, impressed the fact on the Emperor Napoleon. " The story runs," says M. Rothan, " that, after having quitted the study of his Majesty, the Archduke returned, and, through the half-opened door, exclaimed, ' Sire, above all things do not forget, whatever may happen, that we shall not be in a fit state to fall into line before a year.' " Hence, it may well be that the Austrian Chancellor was even then determined, in case of a conflict, to shape his policy in accordance with the first victories; and that the meditations of the Emperor Napoleon, as he re-crossed the Rhine, were tinged with bitter reflections on his political isolation. A little later, when he knew that Bismarck had discovered the drift of the conversation at Salzburg, his anxieties must have become more poignant. That Chancellor, who had secured afresh the goodwill of Russia, and beheld with satisfaction the effect of the Imperial display on Germany, enlarged, in a circular despatch, on the proof thus once more afforded that German national feeling could not endure " the mere notion " of " foreign tutelage " where the interests of the Fatherland were concerned. Germany had a right to mould her own fortunes and frame her own constitution. So that, as von Beust had foreseen, the dreaded Chancellor had promptly turned to account even the colloquies of Salzburg. " France, with one hand," he said, " presents us with soothing notes, and with the other permits us to see the point of

her sword." There was no open quarrel between the
two antagonists, but each suspected and closely watched
the other. M. Rothan, himself a vigilant and zealous
official, furnishes an amusing example. In November,
1866, he learned from "a Foreign Minister accredited
to a South German Court," what was to him the
appalling fact, that the Imperial work of mediation at
Nikolsburg had been counteracted, "even before it had
been sanctioned by the treaty of Prague." He referred
to the now famous military treaties. M. de X——, his
informant, he says, obtained his knowledge of the secret
by a sort of inquisitorial method, "a la façon d'un juge
d'instruction," that is, he affirmed the existence of the
documents, and thus extorted confessions, express or
implied. "The Bavarian Foreign Minister," he said,
blushed; "the Minister of Würtemberg was confused;
the Minister of Baden did not deny it, and the Minister
of Hesse avowed everything." Further, M. de X——
asserted that, when it was no longer necessary to keep
France in good humour, Prussia would enforce the
clauses which gave her supreme command, and would
bring the Southern armies into harmony with her own
organization. Apparently, this authentic information
did not obtain a ready belief in the autumn of 1866;
but it alarmed and disturbed the French Court, and the
public confirmation of the unwelcome report, less than a
year afterwards, visible to all men in the actual re-
organization of the Southern armies, together with the
failure to purchase Luxemburg, still further increased
the suspicion, deepened the alarm, and aroused the
indignation of the Emperor at the slights inflicted on
France, who, as the "predominant" Continental power
and the "vanguard of civilization," always considered
that she ought to have her own way.

THE EMPEROR SEEKS ALLIES.

In the beginning of 1868 the principal parties were
engaged in preparing for a conflict which each considered to be inevitable; and the other Powers, great
and small, more or less concerned, were agitated by
hopes and fears. Russia desired to recover her freedom
of movement in the East, and especially to throw off
what Prince Gortchakoff called his "robe de Nessus,"
the clause in the treaty of Paris which declared the
Euxine to be a neutral sea. Austria aimed at the
restoration of her authority in Germany, and was not
yet convinced that her path lay eastward. Italy had
many longings, but her pressing necessity was to seat
herself in the capital of the Cæsars and the Popes, once
again occupied by the French, who had re-entered the
Papal States to expel the Garibaldians. It was in the
skirmish at Mentana that the new breech-loading rifle,
the Chassepot, "wrought miracles," according to
General de Failly, and established its superiority over
the "needle gun." Holland, Belgium, and even Switzerland were troubled by the uncertain prospect which
the Imperial theory of "large agglomerations" had laid
bare ; Spain was in the throes of a revolutionary con-
vulsion; and England—she had just mended her constitution, and had begun to look on Continental politics
with relative indifference, except in so far as they
affected the fortunes of "parties," and might be used
strategically as a means of gaining or holding fast the
possession of power. Yet so strained were the relations of France and Prussia that General von Moltke
actually framed, in the spring of 1868, the plan of campaign which he literally carried out in 1870—a fact
implying that even then he considered that his Govern-

ment was sufficiently prepared to encounter the new
and imperfectly developed scheme of army organization
and armament originally devised by the Emperor and
Marshal Niel, and modified to satisfy the objections and
suspicions raised in a deferential Senate and an oblig-
ing Chamber of Deputies. For while the Opposition
distrusted the Emperor, the whole body shrank from
the sacrifices which Cæsar and his Minister of War considered necessary to the safety of the State from a defensive, and absolutely indispensable from an offensive
point of view. The prime actors in the drama expressed a love of peace, perhaps with equal sincerity:
but as Germany thirsted for unity, all the more because
France, true to her traditional policy, forbad it, the
love so loudly avowed could not be gratified unless
Germany submitted, or France ceased to dictate. " I
did not share the opinion of those politicians," said
Bismarck in July, 1870, " who advised me not to do
all I could to avoid war with France because it was inevitable. Nobody," he added, " can exactly foresee
the purposes of Divine Providence in the future; and I
regard even a victorious war as an evil from which
statesmanship should strive to preserve nations. I
could not exclude from my calculations the possibility
that chances might accrue in France's constitution and
policy which might avert the necessity of war from two
great neighbour races—a hope in connection with which
every postponement of a rupture was so much to the
good." The language is a little obscure, but the
meaning will be grasped when it is remembered that
his remark on the " chances " referred to the probable
grant of increased freedom to the French Parliament,
which he thought would fetter the Court and thwart
the politicians. That forecast was not justified by the
event, since it was the partially-liberated Chamber and

the Liberal Ministry which so hastily sanctioned the declaration of war. The truth is, however, that each rival nationality inherited the liabilities contracted in the past. The French had been accustomed for more than two hundred years to meddle directly in Germany and find there allies, either against Austria, Prussia, or England; and the habit of centuries had been more than confirmed by the colossal raids, victories, and annexations of Napoleon I. A Germany which should escape from French control and reverse, by its own energetic action the policy of Henri IV., Richelieu, Louis XIV., his degenerate grandson, Louis XV., and of the great Napoleon himself, was an affront to French pride, and could not be patiently endured. The opposing forces which had grown up were so strong that the wit of man was unable to keep them asunder; and all the control over the issue left to kings and statesmen was restricted to the fabrication of means wherewith to deliver or sustain the shock, and the choice of the hour, if such choice were allowed.

To that end the adversaries had, indeed, applied themselves after the last French failure to obtain any material compensation, not even what M. Rouher called such a rag of territory as Luxemburg. Thenceforth, keeping an eye on Prussia, the French Government sought to gain over Austria and Italy, and form a defensive alliance which, at the fitting moment, might be converted into an offensive alliance strong enough to prevent the accomplishment of German unity, win campaigns, and enable each confederate to grasp the reward which he desired. Carried on during more than two years, the negotiations never got beyond a kind of vague preliminary understanding which signified the willingness of the three Courts to reach a definite, formal treaty if they could. But obstacles always

arose when the vital questions lying at the root of the
business had to be solved. Italy demanded and Austria was willing that she should have Rome. To that
France steadfastly demurred, even down to the last
moment, as will presently be seen. Austria also, besides being unready, in a military sense, was visited by
the chronic fear that, if she plunged into war against
Germany, Russia would at once break into her provinces from Lithuania and the Polish Quadrilateral,
and settle the heavy account opened when Prince
Schwarzenberg displayed his " immense ingratitude "
during the Crimean war. Nor was the Court of
Vienna exempt from apprehensions growing out of
the possible, even probable conduct of half-reconciled
Hungary. Count von Beust also deluded himself
with the notion that the Prussian treaties with the
South German States were mere " rags of paper,"
and nourished the fond belief, except when he had
a lucid interval, that the South German people would
not fight for the Fatherland. Waiting on Providence, the would-be confederates, at the same time,
counted on the fortune of war, arguing that France was
certain to win at first, and that one victory under the
tricolor would bring the inchoate alliance instantly to
maturity, and the armies it controlled into the field.
Based on such conjectural foundations, and opposed by
such solid obstacles, the grand design was doomed to
fail; indeed it never got nearer to completion than an
exchange of letters by the Sovereigns; grounded on the
very eve, and went to pieces on the day of battle.

Diverted from Luxemburg, the French Government
did not relax its efforts to pave the way for the annexation of Belgium. During the spring and summer of
1869 a successful effort was made to secure political,
commercial, and strategic advantages by obtaining a

certain control over the Belgian railways, notably the
line which runs from Luxemburg to Liege, and thence
to the North Sea ports.   These proceedings, of course,
did not escape notice at Berlin, where the ends in view
were perfectly appreciated; but they form only a petty
incident in the great struggle, and can only be mentioned with brevity in order to indicate its growth.   It
may be stated here that, in 1873, the German Chancellor reversed the process, and secured for his Government the control of the Luxemburg lines.   Another
railway question which cropped up in May, 1870, was the
famous railway which, by means of an ingenious tunnel
within the Alps near St. Gothard, placed Germany in
direct communication with Italy through neutral territory.   Count von Bismarck openly said it was a
Prussian interest, and the Northern Confederation paid
a part of the cost, which aroused indignation in France.
At one moment it seemed possible that this enterprise
would serve as a *casus belli;* but the French Government, after careful deliberation, decided, in June, 1870,
that they could not reasonably oppose the project,
although it certainly was regarded at the Foreign
Office in Paris as a further proof of German antagonism,
and a sort of bribe tendered to Italy.   Since the beginning of the year France had been in the enjoyment of
certain Liberal concessions made by the Emperor, and
confirmed, in May, by the famous " plébiscite," which
gave him a majority of more than five millions.   Now,
although the Emperor's reflections on this triumphant
result of an appeal to universal suffrage were embittered
by the knowledge that large numbers of soldiers had
helped to swell the million and a half of Frenchmen who
voted " No," still the Foreign Minister and his agents,
according to M. Ollivier, were so elated that they
exclaimed with pride, " Henceforth, all negotiations are

easy to the Government," since the world thoroughly understood that, for France, peace would never mean " complaisance or effacement." Yet Prince Napoleon, in his brief sketch of these critical months, says plainly that the Government concerned itself less with fore-seeing the political complications which might lead up to war, than with the best mode of proceeding when war arrived. So true is this, that a General was sent to Vienna to discuss the bases of a campaign with the Austrian War Office. But in the spring of 1870 for-tune seemed to smile on official France; and on the last day of June M. Ollivier, instructed by the Foreign Minister, considered himself authorized to boast before the admiring Deputies that the peace of Europe had never been less in danger than it was at the moment when he delivered his optimistic declaration. In Eng-land, also, the Foreign Secretary could not discern " a cloud in the sky."

THE HOHENZOLLERN CANDIDATURE.

One week later, not only M. Ollivier and Lord Gran-ville, but Europe, nay, the whole world, saw plainly enough the signs and portents of discord and convul-sion. On the 3rd of July the Duc de Gramont learned from the French Minister at Madrid that Prince Leopold of Hohenzollern-Sigmaringen, with his own full consent, had been selected as a candidate for the vacant throne of Spain, and that, at no distant date, the Cortes would be formally requested to elect him. The French Govern-ment quivered with indignation, and the political atmosphere of Paris became hot with rage. Not that the former were unfamiliar with the suggestion. It had been made in 1869, considered, and apparently aban-doned. Indeed, the Emperor himself had, at one time, when he failed to obtain the Rhenish provinces, pro-

posed that they should be formed into a State to be
ruled by the King of Saxony, and at another, that the
Sovereign should be the Hereditary Prince of Hohenzollern-Sigmaringen; the very Prince put forward by
Marshal Prim. He had been grievously hampered and
perplexed in the choice of a Sovereign of Spain by some
Powers, especially by France; but now the Imperial
Government turned the whole tide of its resentment,
not upon Madrid, but Berlin, which, it was assumed,
aimed at establishing an enemy to France beyond the
Pyrenees. Explanations were demanded directly from
the Prussian Government, but M. Le Sourd, the chargé
d'affaires, could extract no other answer than this—that
the Prussian Government knew nothing about the
matter. The Duc de Gramont, who had succeeded
Lavalette, in May, as Minister for Foreign Affairs,
regarded the statement as a subterfuge, and forthwith
determined to fasten on the King a responsibility which
he could not fasten on the Government. The Duc de
Gramont was not a wise counsellor; he was deep in
negotiations having for their object an offensive and
defensive alliance against Prussia, and he was hardly
less moved by a noisy external opinion than by his own
political passions. He ordered M. Benedetti, who had
only just sought repose at Wildbad, to betake himself at
once to Ems, whither King William, according to
custom, had repaired to drink the waters. The French
Ambassador reached the pleasant village on the Lahn
late at night on the 8th of July, and the next day began
a series of interviews with the King, which take rank
among the most curious examples of diplomacy recorded
in history.

Before the ambassador could commence his singular
task, an event had occurred in Paris which seemed to
render a war unavoidable. The politicians of the

French capital had become feverish with excitement.
Not only did a species of delirium afflict the immediate
advisers of the Emperor, but the band of expectants,
who, more ardent Imperialists than he was, still believed
that nothing could withstand the French army; while
the opposition, loving France not less, but what they
called liberty more, were eager to take advantage of an
incident which seemed likely to throw discredit on the
Bonapartes. Wisdom would have prevented, but party
tactics demanded a movement in the Chamber which
took the innocent-looking form of an inquiry. The
Government dreaded, yet could not evade, the ordeal,
and M. Cochery put his question on the 6th of July.
Had the Duc de Gramont been a clever Minister, or
had he represented a Government strongly rooted in the
national respect and affection, he would have been able
to deliver a colourless response, if he could not have
based a refusal to answer upon public grounds. The
truth is, he was carried off his feet by the sudden storm
which raged through the journals and society, and it
may be surmised that, even then, despite the plébiscite,
fears for the stability of the dynasty had no small share
in determining his conduct. Yet, it must be stated,
that he was only one of the Council of Ministers who
sanctioned the use of language which read, and still
reads, like an indirect declaration of war. After expressing sympathy with Spain, and asserting, what was not
true, that the Imperial Government had observed a
strict neutrality with regard to the several candidates
for the crown, he struck a note of defiance: " We do
not believe," he exclaimed, " that respect for the rights
of a neighbouring people obliges us to endure that a
foreign State, by placing one of its princes on the throne
of Charles V., should be able to derange, to our injury,
the balance of power in Europe, and to imperil the

interests and honour of France." The pacific sentences uttered by M. Ollivier on this memorable occasion were forgotten ; the trumpet-blast of the Duc de Gramont rang through the world, and still rings in the memory. Prussia was not named by the Minister, but everyone beyond the Rhine knew who was meant by the " German people," and a " foreign Power;" while, as Benedetti has stated in a private despatch to Gramont, the King deeply felt it as a " provocation."

Not the least impressive characteristic of these proceedings is the hot haste in which they hurried along. M. Benedetti, neither in that respect nor in the swiftness and doggedness which he imparted to the negotiations, is to blame. The impulse and the orders came from Paris; he somewhat tempered the first, but he obeyed the second with zeal, and, without overstepping the limits of propriety in the form, he did not spare the King in the substance of his demands. Nor, in the first instance, were they other than those permitted by diplomatic precedent; afterwards they certainly exceeded these limits. The first was that the King himself should press Prince Leopold to withdraw his consent: indeed, direct him so to do. The answer was that, as King, he had nothing to do with the business; that as head of the Hohenzollern family he had been consulted, and had not encouraged or opposed the wish of the Prince to accept the proffered crown; that he would still leave him entire freedom to act as he pleased, but that his Majesty would communicate with Prince Antoine, the father of Prince Leopold, and learn his opinion. With this reply, unable to resist the plea for delay, the ambassador had perforce to be content. Not so the Imperial Government. The Duc de Gramont sent telegram on telegram to Ems, urging Benedetti to transmit an explicit answer from the King, saying that he had ordered Prince Leopold to give up the project, and alleging, as a reason for haste, that the French could not wait longer, since Prussia might anticipate them by calling out the army. The ambassador, to check this hurry, prudently warned his principals, saying, that if they ostentatiously prepared for war, then the calamity would be inevitable. " If the King," wrote De Gramont, on the 10th of July, " will not advise the Prince to renounce his design—well, it is war at once, and in a few days we shall be on the Rhine." And so on from hour to hour. A little wearied, per-- haps, by the pertinacity of the ambassador, and nettled by the attempt to fix on him the responsibility for the Spanish scheme, the King at length said that he looked every moment for an answer from Sigmaringen, which he would transmit without delay. It is impossible, in a few sentences, to give the least idea of the terrier-like obstinacy displayed by M. Benedetti in attacking the King. Indeed, it grew to be almost a persecution, so thoroughly did he obey his importunate instructions. At length the King was able to say that Prince Antoine's answer would arrive on the 13th, and the ambassador felt sure of a qualified success, inasmuch as he would obtain the Prince's renunciation, sanctioned by King William. But, while he was writing his despatch, a new source of vexation sprang up in Paris—the Spanish Ambassador, Señor Olozaga, announced to the Duc de Gramont the fact that Prince Antoine, on behalf of his son, had notified at Madrid the withdrawal of his pretensions to the crown. It was reasonably assumed that, having attained the object ostensibly sought, the French Government would be well content with a diplomatic victory so decisive, and would allow M. Benedetti to rest once more at Wildbad. He himself held stoutly that the " satisfaction " accorded to the wounded interests and honour of France was not insufficient. The Emperor and the Duc de Gramont thought otherwise, because, as yet, no positive defeat had been inflicted, personally, upon King William. The Foreign Minister, therefore, obeying precise instructions from St. Cloud, directed Benedetti to see the King at once, and demand from him a plain declaration that he would not, at any future time, sanction any similar proposal coming from Prince Leopold. The Duc de Gramont's mind was so constructed that, at least a year afterwards, he did not regard this demand as an ultimatum! Yet how could the King, and still more Bismarck, take it in any other light? Early on the 13th the King, who saw the ambassador in the public garden, advanced to meet him, and it was there that he refused, point blank, Louis Napoleon's preposterous and uncalled-for request, saying that he neither could nor would bind himself in an engagement without limit of time, and applying to every case; but that he should reserve his right to act according to circumstances. King William brought this interview to a speedy close, and M. Benedetti saw him no more except at the railway station when he started for Coblenz. Persistency had reached and stepped over the limits of the endurable, and King William could not do more than send an aide-de-camp with a courteous message, giving M. Benedetti authority to say officially that Prince Leopold's recent resolution had his Majesty's approval. During the day the ambassador repeated, unsuccessfully, his request for another audience; and this dramatic episode ended on the 13th with the departure of the King, who had pushed courtesy to its utmost bounds.

During that eventful 13th of July Count Bismarck, recently arrived in Berlin from Pomerania, had seen and had spoken to Lord Augustus Loftus in language which plainly showed how steadfastly he kept his grip on the real question, which was that France sought to gain an advantage over " Prussia," as some kind of compensation for Königgrätz. The Duc de Gramont also conversed with Lord Lyons in Paris, and induced him to set in motion Lord Granville, from whose ingenious brain came forth a plausible compromise wholly unsuitable to the exigency, and promptly rejected at Berlin, but having an air of fairness which made it look well in the pages of a Blue Book. It was a last effort on the part of diplomacy, and served well enough to represent statesmanship as it was understood by the Cabinet to which Lord Granville belonged. On the evening of that day Count Bismarck entertained at dinner General von Moltke and General von Roon; and the host read aloud to them a telegram from Ems, giving an account of what had occurred, and the royal authority to make the story public. " Both Generals," writes Dr. Moritz Busch, " regarded the situation as still peaceful. The Chancellor observed—that would depend a good deal upon the tone and contents of the publication he had just been authorized to make. In the presence of his two guests he then put together some extracts from the telegram, which were forthwith despatched to all the Prussian Legations abroad, and to the Berlin newspapers in the following form:— ' Telegram from Ems, July 13th, 1870. When the intelligence of the Hereditary Prince of Hohenzollern's renunciation was communicated by the Spanish to the French Government, the French Ambassador demanded of His Majesty the King, at Ems, that the latter should authorize him to telegraph to Paris that His Majesty would pledge himself for all time to come never again to give his consent, should the Hohenzollerns hark

back to their candidature. Upon this His Majesty refused to receive the French Ambassador again, and
sent the aide-de-camp in attendance to tell him that
His Majesty had nothing further to communicate to
the Ambassador.'"

Substantially, it was the grotesque pile of misrepre-
sentation built up on this blunt telegram—M. Benedetti
read it next morning in the "Cologne Gazette," and
took no exception whatever to the brief and exact narrative it contained—which set the Parisians on fire.
Travestied in many ways by calculating politicians, as
well as gossips, the message became a "Note," or a
"despatch," imputing the extreme of intentional rudeness
to King William, and imposing the depth of humiliation,
publicly inflicted, upon France through her representative, who, all the time, was not only unconscious of
any insult, but emphatic in his acknowledgments of the
King's courtesy, kindness, and patience. Probably
Count Bismarck wrote his telegram for Germany, but
its effect in satisfying the Fatherland, was not greater
than its influence upon the fiery French, who never read
the text until months afterwards, and in July, 1870,
were set a-flame by the distorted· versions freely supplied by rumour's forked tongue.

THE FRENCH GOVERNMENT AND THE CHAMBER.

War was now plainly inevitable, yet the decisive
word still rested with the Imperial Government. In
Paris there were two currents running strongly in
opposite ways, and, for a moment, it seemed possible
that the tide which made for peace would overpower
the surging stream which drove onwards towards war.
More than one-half the Ministry believed, and some, M.
Ollivier for one, said that the retreat of Prince Leopold,

with the consent of the King, a great diplomatic victory
for France, was enough, and had, indeed, brought the
quarrel to an end.   At midday, on the 13th, M. Robert
Mitchell, meeting M. Paul de Cassagnac, said, " I have
just left Ollivier, and, thank God, peace is secured."
" My father," was the reply, " has just quitted the
Emperor; war is resolved on."   The statement was
not then exact, but it may be accepted as a forecast.
For, in truth, it was only at noon the next day that the
Ministers assembled in council at the Tuileries to
answer the momentous question which so profoundly
agitated their minds.   They sat six hours; they were
divided in opinion; yet, although Marshal Lebœuf was
authorized to call out the reserves—he had threatened
to resign unless that were done—the Ministers separated with the understanding that a peaceful line of
action should be adopted, based on a demand for a Congress of the Powers to sanction the principle that no
member of any reigning house should accept a foreign
throne.   The Duc de Gramont's brief account of this
notable Council shows that the hankering after war was
powerful therein; since he says that " the Government
decided, not without hesitation, but influenced by a
love of peace, to propose this pacific solution."   But
all, or some of the Ministers, and still more the Emperor,
stood in dread of two things: they were alarmed lest
the " dynasty " should be injured by a course which
bore the semblance of a forced retreat, and they could
not rely with confidence on the sober opinion of the
Chambers.   The Court war-party operated upon the
Senators and Deputies through M. Clément Duvernois,
a schemer, and M. Jérôme David, by birth and training
a fanatical Bonapartist, the second accentuating the
questions of the first, and giving to his own language a
substance which made retreat almost impossible.   Both

these men had a double object. They intended to extort a declaration of war and, at the same time, expel
Emile Ollivier, together with what they called the Parliamentary element, from the Ministry. The energetic,
aggressive and relentless group were really the mouth-
pieces of the Emperor and Empress, and in a less degree of M. Rouher, who had been deposed by the new
Imperial constitution, and of the Duc de Gramont, who
all through the business desired to secure a prolonga-
tion of peace, solely because it would give him time to
ripen the projects of alliance with Austria and Italy,
and also to make war, lest " la Prusse," aware of his
design, should choose her own hour for battle. It so
chanced that Marshal Lebœuf, after despatching the
orders calling out the reserves, received a note from the
Emperor, which, he says, seemed to suggest a regret
at the decision adopted by the Council ; and thinking,
innocent man, that some constitutional scruples had
sprung up in the Imperial mind, the Marshal begged
that the Ministers might be summoned once more.
That night they met again, talked for an hour, and had
nearly resolved that the mobilization of the army should
be deferred, when papers were placed in the hands of
the Duc de Gramont. The exact contents of these
documents have not been described, but they seem to
have contained some report of language held by Count
Bismarck which exasperated the war party ; and, in
an instant, the Council resolved on war. That same
night, M. Robert Mitchell, walking in the garden of
the Foreign Office, asked M. Ollivier why he did not
resign ? The Minister gave a host of plausible reasons
having no real weight ; adding these prophetic words :
" Whatever happens, I am sacrificed ; for the war will
sweep away the régime to which I have attached my

name. If we are beaten, God protect France! If we are victorious, God protect our liberties !"

So that, having a clear perception of the future, this Minister, at least, met the Chambers on the morrow. The exciting events of the past week, imperfectly understood and carelessly or purposely misrepresented, had aroused a tempest of passion in Paris and France, which,by its violence and uproar, overpowered, but could not wholly silence, the voices of sagacity and sober judgment. The Senate was unanimous for war. In the Chamber the opposition waged courageously a desperate contest, so desperate from the outset, that even M. Thiers, perhaps because he told unpleasant truths, could not command an unbroken hearing, while M. Gambetta only secured one by making a rare display of forensic tact, basing himself on Parliamentary ground, and tempering his appeal for " more light " with evidences of his indisputable patriotism. The Duc de Gramont favoured the Senators with a version of the facts, which was neither complete nor candid. M. Emile Ollivier allowed an unhappy phrase to escape from his lips—he went into the war " *à cœur leger.*" A committee was appointed to inspect the diplomatic documents on which the Court relied ; it was easily satisfied, and late in the night, sustained by a large majority, the policy of the Government was amply sanctioned.

Perhaps a sentence spoken by M. Guyot Montpayroux best illustrates the predominant feeling. " Prussia," he said, " has forgotten the France of Jena, and the fact must be recalled to her memory." Thus was war declared by these infuriated legislators on the night of July 15th. M. Thiers, who desired a war with Prussia " at the proper time," has left on record his judgment that the hour then selected was " detest-

ably ill-chosen." Yet even he and M. Gambetta were
both anxious that " satisfaction " should be obtained for
Sadowa ; while the thought which animated the Court
is admirably expressed in the phrase imputed to the
Empress who, pointing to the Prince Imperial, said,
"This child will never reign unless we repair the misfortunes of Sadowa." Such was the ceaseless refrain.
The word haunted French imaginations incessantly,
and it was the pivot on which the Imperial policy
revolved, and it exercised a spell scarcely less powerful
and disastrous upon Monarchists like M. Thiers, and
Republicans like Gambetta and Jules Favre. Still, it
may be said that France was divided in opinion. Consulted through the Prefects, only sixteen departments
were for war ; no fewer than thirty-four were adverse,
and the remainder could not be said to hold with the
one or the other. Nor should it be overlooked that
these estimates of popular feeling were transmitted by
functionaries who have always a wish to please the
superior Powers. Germany, on the other hand, was
united as it had never been since 1813. King William
was applauded everywhere. When he reached Berlin
on the evening of the 15th, he was met at the railway
station by the Crown Prince, Count von Bismarck,
General von Moltke, and General von Roon. There
the decision was formally taken to accept the challenge,
the fact was repeated to the crowd who had assembled,
and whose shouts were loud, deep, and prolonged ; and
that same night went forth the brief telegraphic orders
which from one centre touched a thousand springs, and
called into instant being an army, perfectly organized,
equipped, trained and supplied. So that when Baron
Wimpfen, a secretary of legation, entered Berlin on the
19th of July, and handed to M. Le Sourd the French
declaration of war—the sole official document on the

subject received by Prussia, as Von Moltke bluntly
remarks—that work had already begun which finished in
little more than a fortnight, enabled the King to break
into France at the head of more than three hundred
thousand soldiers.

Only one word more need be said on this subject—the
causes of the war. Clearing away the diplomatic mist
which hides the realities, the student will discover two
deadly opposites ; on one side the determination of
France to insist on a right of meddling with internal
German affairs, and even of prescribing the form or
forms which the national aggregate should assume ; on
the other, the fixed resolve of the German people that
the French should no longer dictate or pretend to
dictate beyond the Rhine, that an end should be put to
the policy of seeking political profits by fomenting the
spirit of discord in the petty German Courts ; and that,
if possible, by dint of "kraft and muth," Germany
should secure palpable safeguards against French
invasions, and resume possession of the strongholds
and dependent territories which were acquired, in
times of adversity and disunion, by Louis XIV. Thus,
the causes of war were deeply rooted in essential facts.
The moment to be chosen, if it can be said to have
been chosen, was for statesmen to decide. The
Imperial Government, down to the last hour, sought
to form a combination adverse to Prussia, intending to
wage war at its own time. Prussia refused to be made
the victim of a triple alliance, and taking a fair advantage of the imperious conduct of the French Court,
seized the golden opportunity, promptly answered the
declaration of war, and struck down the French
Empire before its hesitating and unprepared allies could
move a finger to avert a defeat which neither attempted,
nor dared attempt to repair. Austria, the unready,

stood in fear of Russia : Italy, the ambitious, demanded the right to enter Rome. " We can grant nothing of the kind," said the over-confident Duc de Gramont, so late as July 30. If Italy will not march," he exclaimed, " let her sit still." Abundant evidence exists to prove that war between France and Germany was solely a question of time, and Prussia cannot be blamed justly for selecting or seizing the hour most suitable to her and least suitable to her adversaries. The Duc de Gramont asserts that neither the Emperor nor the Government nor France, desired war—certainly not just then ; but they intended to make war at a time and under conditions chosen by themselves. He admits that it was the duty of the Imperial Government to evade a war, but also prepare for a war as much as possible ; and, failing to do the former, he further confessed many months afterwards, that too much confidence in the army and in its untested military virtues, and the dazzling splendour of a glorious past dragged France, its Government and its representatives, into an unequal struggle. " We believed ourselves too strong to stoop," he says, " and we knew not how to resist the system of provocations so ably combined and directed by the Cabinet of Berlin." A frank confession, especially from the pen of a statesman who was himself endeavouring to combine a system of alliances, and who was anticipated by the Power against whom his plans were directed. M. Prevost Paradol, who in a moment of weakness had accepted from the Emperor the post of Minister at Washington, saw more clearly into the future than the Duc de Gramont and some of his colleagues. On the very afternoon of the day when the unhappy journalist killed himself, he saw a countryman, the Comte d'Hérisson, and his language to the young man showed how deeply he was moved, and with what sagacity he estimated the near future. In his opinion, expressed on the 10th of July, war was even then certain, because not only "la Prusse" desired war, but because, as he said, "The Empire requires war, wishes for it, and will wage it." The young Frenchman to whom he spoke made light of the peril, and said he should like to travel in Germany, and study in the libraries of her conquered cities. But the Minister checked his natural exultation, saying, "You will not go to Germany, you will be crushed in France. Believe me, I know the Prussians. We have nothing whatever that is needed to strive with them. We have neither generals, men, nor *matériel*. We shall be ground to powder. *Nous serons broyés*. Before six months are over there will be a Revolution in France, and the Empire will be at an end." Mourning over the error he made in laying down his sharp critical pen to put on a diplomatic uniform, and maddened by the retrospect and prospect, Paradol, a few hours after uttering his predictions, escaped from unendurable misery by a pistol-shot. It was like an omen of the coming catastrophe.

CHAPTER II.

THE GATHERING OF THE HOSTS.

GERMAN MOBILIZATION.

THE great contest, thus precipitated by the formal defiance which Baron Wimpfen bore from Paris to Berlin,
excited deep emotion all over the world. The hour
had at length struck which was to usher in the
deadly struggle between France and Germany. Long
foreseen, the dread shock, like all grave calamities,
came nevertheless as a surprise, even upon reflec-
tive minds. Statesmen and soldiers who looked on,
while they shared in the natural feelings aroused by
so tremendous a drama, were also the privileged
witnesses of two instructive experiments on a grand
scale—the processes whereby mighty armies are brought
into the field, and the methods by means of which they
are conducted to defeat or victory. The German plan
of forming an Army was new in regard to the extent
and completeness with which it had been carried out.
How would it work when put to the ultimate test?
Dating only from 1867, the French scheme of organization, a halting Gallic adaptation of Prussian principles,
modified by French traditions, and still further by the
political exigencies besetting an Imperial dynasty,

having little root in the nation, besides being new and
ricketty, was in an early stage of development; it may
be said to have been adolescent, not mature.   No greater
contrast was ever presented by two parallel series of
human actions than that supplied by the irregular,
confused, and uncertain working of the Imperial arrangement of forming an Army and setting it in motion
for active service, and the smoothness, celerity, and punc-
tuality which marked the German "mobilization." The
reason is—first, that the system on which the German
Army was built up from the foundations was sound
in every part, and that the plan which had been designed
for the purpose of placing a maximum force under arms
in a given time, originally comprehensive, had been
corrected from day to day, and brought down to the
last moment.   For example, whenever a branch or
section of a railway line was opened for traffic, the
entire series of time-tables, if need be, were so altered
as to include the new facility for transport.   The labour
and attention bestowed on this vital condition was also
expended methodically upon all the others down to the
most minute detail.   Thus, the German staff maps of
France, especially east of Paris, actually laid down
roads which in July, 1870, had not yet been marked
upon any map issued by the French War Office.   The
central departments, in Berlin, exercised a wide and
searching supervision; but they did not meddle with
the local military authorities who, having large discretionary powers, no sooner received a brief and simple
order than they set to work and produced, at a fixed
time, the result desired.

When King William arrived in Berlin, on the evening
of July 15, the orders already prepared by General von
Moltke received at once the royal sanction, and were
transmitted without delay to the officers commanding

the several Army Corps. Their special work, in case
of need, had been accurately defined; and thus, by
regular stages, the Corps gradually, but swiftly, was
developed into its full proportions, and ready, as a
finished product, to start for the frontier. The reserves
and, if needed, the landwehr men filled out the battalions, squadrons, and batteries to the fixed strength;
and as they found in the local depôts arms, clothing,
and equipments, no time was lost. Horses were bought,
called in, or requisitioned, and transport was obtained.
As all the wants of a complete Corps had been ascertained and provided beforehand, so they came when
demanded. At the critical moment the supreme directing head, relieved altogether from the distracting duty
of settling questions of detail, had ample time to consider
the broad and absorbing business problems which should
and did occupy the days and nights of a leader of
armies. The composition of the North German troops,
that is, those under the immediate control of King
William, occasioned no anxiety; and there was only a
brief period of doubt in Bavaria, where a strong minority
had not so much French and Austrian sympathies, as
inveterate Prussian antipathies. They were promptly
suppressed by the popular voice and the loyalty of the
King. Hesse, Würtemberg, and Baden responded so
heartily to the calls of patriotism that in more than one
locality the landwehr battalions far exceeded their
normal numerical strength, that is, more men than
were summoned presented themselves at the depôts.
The whole operation of bringing a great Army from a
peace to a war footing, in absolute readiness, within the
short period of eighteen days, to meet an adversary on
his own soil, was conducted with unparalleled order
and quickness. The business done included, of course,
the transport of men, guns, horses, carriage, by railway

chiefly, from all parts of the country to the Rhine and the Moselle; and the astonishing fact is that plans devised and adopted long beforehand should have been executed to the letter, and that more than three hundred thousand combatants—artillery, horse, infantry, in complete fighting trim, backed up by enormous trains—should have been brought· to specified places on specified days, almost exactly in fulfilment of a scheme reasoned out and drawn up two years before. The French abruptly declared war; the challenge was accepted; the orders went forth, and "thereupon united Germany stood to arms," to use the words of Marshal von Moltke. It is a proud boast, but one amply justified by indisputable facts.

FRENCH MOBILIZATION.

How differently was the precious time employed on the other side of the Rhine. When the Imperial Government rushed headlong into war, they actually possessed only one formed Corps d'Armée, the 2nd, stationed in the Camp of Chalons, and commanded by General Frossard. Yet even this solitary body was, as he confesses, wanting in essential equipments when it was hurriedly transported to St. Avold, not far from Saarlouis, on the Rhenish Prussian frontier. Not only had all the other Corps to be made out of garrison troops, but the entire staff had to be provided in haste. Marshal Niel, an able soldier, and the Emperor, had studied, at least, some of Baron Stoffel's famous reports on the German Army, and had endeavoured to profit by them; but the Marshal died, the Corps Législatif was intractable, favouritism ruled in the Court, the Emperor suffered from a wearing internal disease, and the tone of the Army was one not instinct with the spirit of self-sacrificing obedience. In time it is possible

that the glaring defects of the Imperial military
mechanism might have been removed, and possible,
also, that the *moral* and discipline of the officers and
men might have been raised. Barely probable, since
Marshal Lebœuf believed that the Army was in a state of
perfect readiness, not merely to defend France, but to
dash over the Rhine into South Germany. His illusion
was only destroyed when the fatal test was applied.
Nominally, the French Army was formidable in
numbers; but not being based on the territorial system,
which includes all the men liable to service in one Corps,
whether they are with the colours or in the reserve,
and also forms the supplementary landwehr into local
divisions, the French War Office could not rapidly
raise the regiments to the normal strength. For a
sufficient reason. A peasant residing in Provence
might be summoned to join a regiment quartered in
Brittany, or a workman employed in Bordeaux called
up to the Pas de Calais. When he arrived he might
find that the regiment had marched to Alsace or
Lorraine. During the first fortnight after the declaration of war thousands of reserve men were travelling
to and fro over France in search of their comrades.
Another evil was that some Corps in course of formation were split into fragments separated from each other
by many score miles. Nearly the whole series of Corps,
numbered from One to Seven, were imperfectly supplied
with a soldier's needments; and what is more astonishing,
the frontier arsenals and depôts were sadly deficient in
supplies, so that constant applications were made to
Paris for the commonest necessaries. There were no
departmental or even provincial storehouses, but the
materials essential for war were piled up in three or
four places, such as Paris and Versailles, Vernon and
Chateauroux. In short, the Minister of War, who said

and believed that he was supremely ready, found that, in fact, he was compelled almost to improvise a fighting Army in the face of an enemy who, in perfect order, was advancing with the measured, compact, and irresistible force of a tidal wave.

The plan followed was exactly the reverse of the German method. East of the Rhine no Corps was moved to the frontier, until it was complete in every respect, except the second line of trains ; and consequently, from the outset, it had a maximum force prepared for battle. There were some slight exceptions to the rule, but they were imposed by circumstances, served a real purpose, and disappeared when the momentary emergency they were adapted to meet had been satisfied. West of the Rhine, not one solitary Corps took its assigned place in a perfect state for action. All the battalions of infantry, and of course the regiments, were hundreds short of their proper strength. Before a shot had been fired, General de Failly, at Bitsche, was obliged to send a demand for coin to pay the troops, adding notes won't pass— "les billets n'ont point cours." General Frossard, at St. Avold, reported that enormous packages of useless maps had been sent him—maps of Germany—and that he had not a single map of the French frontier. Neither Strasburg, Metz, Toul, Verdun, Thionville, nor Mézières, possessed stores of articles—such as food, equipments, and carriage—which were imperatively required. The Intendants, recently appointed to special posts, besieged the War Office in Paris, to relieve them from their embarrassments—they had nothing on the spot. The complaints were not idle. As early as the 26th of July, the troops about Metz were living on the reserve of biscuits ; there were sent only thirty-eight additional bakers to Metz for

120,000 men, and even these few practitioners were sadly in want of ovens. "I observe that the Army stands in need of biscuit and bread," said the Emperor to the Minister of War at the same date. "Could not bread be made in Paris, and sent to Metz?" Marshal Lebœuf, a day later, took note of the fact that the detachments which came up to the front, sometimes reserve men, sometimes battalions, arrived without ammunition and camp equipments. Soldiers, functionaries, carts, ovens, provisions, horses, munitions, harness, all had to be sought at the eleventh hour. These facts are recorded in the despairing telegrams sent from the front to the War Office. The very Marshal who had described France as "archi-prête," in a transcendent state of readiness for war, announced by telegram, on the 28th of July, the lamentable fact that he could not move forward for want of biscuit— "Je manque de biscuit pour marcher en avant." The 7th Corps was to have been formed at Belfort, but its divisions could never be assembled. General Michel, on the 21st of July, sent to Paris this characteristic telegram : "Have arrived at Belfort," he wrote : "can't find my brigade ; can't find the General of Division. What shall I do? Don't know where my regiments are"—a document probably unique in military records. Hardly a week later, that is on the 27th, Marshal Lebœuf became anxious respecting the organization of this same Corps, and put, through Paris, some curious questions to General Félix Douay, its commander. "How far have you got on with your formations? Where are your divisions?" The next day General Douay arrived at Belfort, having been assured in Paris by his superiors that the place was "abundantly provided" with what he would require. After the War, Prince Georges Bibesco, a Roumanian in the French Army, attached to the 7th Corps, published an excellent volume on the campaign, and in its pages he describes the " cruel deception " which awaited Douay. He writes that, for the most part, the troops, had " neither tents, cooking pots, nor flannel belts; neither medical nor veterinary canteens, nor medicines, nor forges, nor pickets for the horses— they were without hospital attendants, workmen, and train. As to the magazines of Belfort—they were empty." In the land of centralization General Douay was obliged to send a staff and several men to Paris, with instructions to explain matters at the War Office, and not leave the capital without bringing the articles demanded with them. Other examples are needless. It would be almost impossible to understand how it came to pass that the French were plunged into war, in July, 1870, did we not know that the military institutions had been neglected, that the rulers relied on old renown, the " glorious past" of the Duc de Gramont, and that the few men who forced the quarrel to a fatal head, knew nothing of the wants of an army, and still less of the necessities and risks of war.

WAR METHODS CONTRASTED.

As the story is unfolded, it will be seen that the same marked contrast between the principles and methods adopted and practised by the great rivals prevailed throughout. The German Army rested on solid foundations; the work of mobilization was conducted in strict accordance with the rules of business; allowing for the constant presence of a certain amount of error, inseparable from human actions, it may be said that " nothing was left to chance." The French Army was loosely put together; it contained uncertain elements; was not easily collected, and never in formed

F

bodies; it was without large as well as small essentials;
it "lacked finish." And similar defects became rapidly
manifest in the Imperial plan for the conduct of the
war. Here the contrast is flagrant. The Emperor
Napoleon, who had lived much with soldiers, who had
been present at great military operations, and had
studied many campaigns, could not be destitute of
what the French call "le flair militaire." He had,
also, some inkling of the political side of warfare; and
in July, 1870, he saw that much would depend upon
his ability to make a dash into South Germany, because,
if he were successful, even for a brief time, Prussia
might be deprived of South German help, and Austria
might enter the field. There was no certainty about
the calculation, indeed, it was almost pure conjecture;
seeing that Count von Beust and the Archduke Albert
had both warned him that, "above all things," they
needed time, and that the former had become frightened
at the prospect of Hungarian defection, and a Russian
onfall. Yet it was on this shadowy basis that he
moved to the frontier the largest available mass of
incomplete and suddenly organized batteries, squadrons
and battalions. He and his advisers were possessed
with a feverish desire to be first in the field; and the
Corps were assembled near Metz, Strasburg, and Belfort,
with what was called a reserve at Chalons, on the
chance that the left might be made to join the right
in Alsace, and that the whole, except the reserve which
was to move up from Chalons, could be pushed over
the Rhine at Maxau, opposite Carlesruhe, and led with
conquering speed into the country south of the Main.
Before he joined the head-quarters at Metz, on the
28th of July, the Emperor may have suspected, but
on his arrival he assuredly found that the plan, if ever
feasible, had long passed out of the range of practical

warfare. He reaped nothing but the disadvantages which spring from grossly defective preparation, and "raw haste half-sister to delay." He knew that he was commander-in-chief of a relatively weak and ill-found Army, and he acquired the certainty at Metz, that, unless he were conspicuously victorious, neither Austria nor Italy would move a man.

His mighty antagonist, on the other hand, was advancing to the encounter with such large resources, and so thoroughly equipped, that no fewer than three Army Corps were left behind, because even the admirably managed and numerous German railway lines were not able to carry them at once to the banks of the Rhine. Moreover, General von Moltke, the Chief of the Great Staff, had, in 1868-69, carefully reasoned out plans, which were designed to meet each probable contingency, either a march of the French through Belgium, an early irruption into the Rhenish provinces, or the identical scheme upon which the Emperor founded his hopes; while, if the French allowed the Germans to begin offensive operations on French soil, then the method of conducting the invasion, originally adopted, would come into play. The memorandum on this great subject, the essential portions of which have been published by its author, von Moltke, is, for breadth, profundity, and insight, one of the most instructive to be found in the records of war. This is not the place to deal with its general or detailed arguments. For present purposes, it is sufficient to set forth the main operative idea. The contention was, that an army assembled on the Rhine between Rastadt and Mainz, and on the Moselle below Treves, would be able to operate successfully, either on the right bank of the main stream, against the flank of a French Army, which sought to invade South Germany; or,

with equal facility, concentrate on the left bank, and
march in three great masses through the country
between the Rhine and Moselle, upon the French
frontier. Should the French make a precipitate dash
into the German country towards Mainz, then the
Corps collected near that fortress would meet them in
front, and those on the Moselle would threaten their
communications or assail them in flank. The soundness of the reasoning is indisputable; its application
would depend upon the prompt concentration of the
Armies, and that had been rendered certain by careful
and rigorously enforced preparations. The great
Prussian strategist had calculated the movement of
troops and railway trains to a day; so that he knew
exactly what number of men and guns, within a given
area, he could count upon at successive periods
of time; and, of course, he was well aware that the
actual use to be made of them, after the moment of
contact, could not be foreseen with precision, but must
be adapted to circumstances. But he foresaw and
prepared for the contingency which did arrive. " If,"
he said, " the French desired to make the most of their
railways, in order to hasten the assembly of all their
forces," they would be obliged to disembark, or as we
now say, "detrain" them, "at Metz and Strasburg,
that is, in two principal groups separated from each
other by the Vosges." And then he went on to point
out how, assembled on the Rhine and Moselle, the
German Army would occupy what is called the
"interior lines" between them, and "could turn
against the one or the other, or even attack both at
once, if it were strong enough."

The grounds for these conclusions, succinctly stated,
were the conformation of the frontier, an angle flanked
at each side by the neutral states of Switzerland and

Luxemburg, restricting the space within which operations could be carried on; the possession of both banks
of the Rhine below Lauterbourg; the superior facility
of mobilization secured by the Germans, not only as
regards the rapid transition of Corps from a peace to a
war footing, but by the skilful use of six railway lines
running to the Rhine and the Moselle; and, finally, the
fact that, fronting south between those rivers, the
advancing German Army would be directed against an
adversary whose line of retreat, at least so far as railways were concerned, diverged, in each case, to a flank
of any probable front of battle. The railway from
Strasburg to Nancy traversed the Vosges at Saverne;
the railway from Metz to Nancy on one side, and
Thionville on the other, followed the valley of the
Moselle; and as the important connecting branch from
Metz to Verdun had not been constructed, it follows
that the French Army in Lorraine had no direct railway
line of retreat and supply. The railway from Metz to
Strasburg, which crossed the Vosges by the defile of
Bitsche and emerged in the Rhine valley at Hagenau,
was, of course, nearly parallel to the German front,
except for a short distance west of Bening. The
frontier went eastward from Sierck, on the Moselle to
Lauterbourg on the Rhine, and thence southerly to
Basle. The hill range of the Vosges, starting from the
Ballon d'Alsace, overlooking the Gap of Belfort, runs
parallel to the river, and extends in a northerly direction beyond the French boundary, thrusting an irregular
mass of uplands deep into the Palatinate, ending in the
isolated Donnersberg. It follows that the main roads
out of, as well as into, France were to the east and west
of this chain, and it should be observed that the trans-
verse passes were more numerous south than north of
Bitsche, and that, practically, while detachments could

move along the secluded valleys, there was no road available for large bodies and trains through the massive block of mountain and forest which occupies so considerable a space of the Palatinate. Thus, an army moving from Mainz upon Metz would turn the obstacle on the westward by Kaiserslautern and Landstuhl ; while if Strasburg were the goal, it would march up the Rhine valley by Landau, and through the once famous Lines of the Lauter. If two armies, as really happened in 1870, advanced simultaneously on both roads, the connection between them is maintained by occupying Pirmasens, which is the central point on a country road running from Landau to Deux Ponts, and another going south-east to Wissembourg.

The influence of this mountain range upon the offensive and defensive operations of the rival armies will be readily understood. The French could only unite to meet their opponents in the Prussian provinces at or north of Kaiserslautern ; while the Germans, assuming that their adversaries assembled forces in Alsace, as well as in Lorraine, would not be in direct communication until their left wing had moved through the hill-passes and had emerged in the country between the Sarre and the Meurthe.

It has been seen that the available French troops, including several native and national regiments from Algeria, had been hurried to the frontier in an imperfect state of organization and equipment. There were nominally seven Corps d'Armée and the Guard; but of these two, the 6th and 7th, were never united in the face of the enemy. Marshal Canrobert, commanding the 6th, was only able to bring a portion of his Corps from Chalons to Metz; and General Douay, the chief of the 7th, had one division at Lyons, and another at Colmar, whence it was sent on to join the 1st Corps assembling under Marshal MacMahon near Strasburg. The principal body, consisting of the 2nd, 3rd, and 4th Corps, ultimately joined by the greater part of the 6th, and the Guard were posted near and north of Metz; while the 5th occupied positions on the Saar, and formed a sort of link, or weak centre, between the right and left wings. Nothing indicated cohesion in this array, which, as we have shown, was adopted on the vain hypothesis that there would be time to concentrate in Alsace for the purpose of anticipating the Germans and crossing the Rhine at Maxau.

No such error was made on the other side. The German troops were divided into three armies. The First Army, consisting of the Seventh and Eighth Corps, under the veteran General von Steinmetz, formed the right wing, and moved southward on both banks of the Moselle. The Second Army, composed of the Guard, the Third, Fourth, and Tenth Corps, commanded by Prince Frederick Charles, was the central body, having in rear the Ninth and Twelfth Corps as a reserve. They were destined to march on the great roads leading from Manheim and Mainz upon Kaiserslautern. The Third Army, or left wing, under the Crown Prince, was made up of the Fifth and Eleventh and the two Bavarian Corps, together with a Würtemberg and a Baden Division. Each Army had one or more divisions of cavalry, and, of course, the due proportion of guns. By the 31st of July, the whole of these troops, except the Baden and the Würtemberg Divisions, were on the west of the Rhine, with foreposts on the Saar, below Saarbrück, in the mountains at Pirmasens, and on the roads to the Lauter; the great mass of troops being close to the Rhine. The advantages, in point of concentration, were already secured by the German Staff; the First Army alone. one-half at Treves, and the other strung out between the Moselle and the Nahe, was in apparent danger; yet little apprehension was felt on that score, because the country through which it moved was highly defensible—its right was covered by neutral Luxemburg, and part of the Second Army was sufficiently forward to protect the left.

A week earlier, there had been, indeed, a slight perturbation in Berlin, where the head-quarters still remained. By unceasing observation, a careful collation of reports, a diligent use of French newspapers, the King's Staff had arrived at a tolerably accurate estimate of the strength, positions, and internal state of the French Corps. They were cognizant of the prevailing disorder, and were well aware that not one Corps had received its full complement of reserve men. Arguing that the enemy would not have foregone the advantages of mobilization unless he had in view some considerable object, such as an irruption into the Palatinate, the Staff modified the original plan, as it affected the Second Army, and, on the 23rd of July, directed the Corps of which it was composed to quit the railway trains transporting them on, and not beyond, the Rhine. This was purely a measure of precaution, the contingency of which had been foreseen; yet one which was needless, as the French had already learned that they could not take the offensive in any direction. No other changes were made, and the only result of this modification was that the soldiers had to march further than they would have marched, and they probably benefited by the exercise. During this period, the bridge at Kehl had been broken, the boats and ferries removed from the Rhine from Lauterbourg to Basle, the railway pontoon bridge at Maxau protected, a measure suggested by the presence of river gunboats at Strasburg, and an unremitting watch had been kept on the land frontier by small

detachments of horse and foot.   Not the least surprising
fact is that no attempt was made by the French to
destroy the bridges over the Saar at Saarbrück, or
penetrate far beyond that river on its upper course.   On
the other hand, parties of German horse and foot made
several incursions between Sierck and Bitsche, and one
small party rode as far as into Alsace at Niederbronn.
It was not until the end of the month that large bodies
of cavalry were sent to the front to begin a career de-
monstrating afresh, if a demonstration is needed, the in-
estimable services which can be performed by that indispensable arm.   The German Army had been placed in the
field in little more than a fortnight, although the First
and Sixth Corps were still *en route* from the far North.
The Crown Prince reached Spires on the 30th, and the
next day, the King, with the Great Staff, left Berlin
for Mainz.   He had restored the " Order of the Iron
Cross," and had warmly expressed his gratitude for the
unexampled spirit manifested by the whole German
nation, " reconciled and united as it had never been
before."   Germany might find therein, he said, " a
guarantee that the war would bring her a durable peace,
and that the seed of blood would yield a blessed har-
vest of liberty and unity."

Here it may be stated that a French squadron had
appeared off the coast of Denmark on the 28th of July,
but only to disappear with greater promptitude, thereby
relieving the timid from any apprehension of a descent.
Large German forces were set free to face westward,
and in a brief space, not only the French marines and
sailors, but the ship guns were vehemently required to
fight in severe battles and defend the capital of France.

CHAPTER III.

STAGE THUNDER.

THE COMBAT AT SAARBRÜCK.

KING WILLIAM did not reach Mainz until the forenoon of the 2nd of August; and it is characteristically remarked in the official history of the War, that the journey from Berlin had been relatively slow, because it was necessary to fit the six supplementary trains bearing the great head-quarters into the series of military trains in such a way as would not retard the transport of troops. It is a small fact, but an apt illustration of the preference uniformly given to essentials in the Prussian arrangements for war. Soon after the Staff had arrived in the "Deutsche Haus," lent by the Grand Duke, whose son, Prince Louis, the husband of the British Princess Alice, commanded the Hessian Division, unexpected information greeted them. Telegrams reported first that a serious action was in progress at Saarbrück, and later that the Prussian troops had withdrawn from the town.

This was the famous combat, known at the time as the *Baptême de feu* of the unfortunate Prince Imperial. The Emperor Napoleon entered Metz on the 28th of July, and took the command of the "Army of the

Rhine." Until that moment, the seven *corps d'armée*
in the field were under the orders of Marshal Bazaine,
who received his instructions from Paris through
Marshal Lebœuf. They were to act strictly on the
defensive, advice which may be said to have been needless, since, as we have shown, not one of the corps was
in a condition to march and fight. When the Emperor
appeared on the scene, no great change for the better
had taken place, and there was still a dearth of real
information respecting the strength and position of the
enemy, while the reports brought in contained an
enormous percentage of error. Nevertheless, there
was a vague feeling at head-quarters that something
must be done to satisfy a public opinion which thought
that the French armies should have been already
beyond the Rhine; and on the 30th of July Marshal
Bazaine received orders to cross the Saar and occupy
Saarbrück. The task was to be entrusted to General
Frossard, supported by troops on the right and left,
drawn from the Corps of de Failly and Bazaine. Yet
this modest operation dwindled down, when discussed
in a sort of Council of War held the next day at
Forbach, into a simple cannonade, and the occupation of
the heights on the left bank! The Emperor was told
that his project could not be executed, and resigning
himself, as he always did, to the inevitable, he warned
MacMahon that no movement should be made on his
side before the lapse of eight days. The ostentatious
movement on Saarbrück was to be made on the 2nd of
August. Now, at that date, the place was occupied
by fractions of the Eighth German Corps, posted on
both banks of the river above and below the town.
They consisted of four battalions of foot, several
squadrons of horse, and one battery, and the nearest
immediate support was some miles to the rear, near

Lebach. Colonel von Pestel had held the position from the outset of the war, and was allowed to remain, at his own request, although a considerable army stood in his front at no great distance, that is, the three leading corps of the Army of the Rhine. But on the 2nd Count von Gneisenau was in command of the German outposts, and had orders, if pressed, to retire upon Lebach, but he stood fast, and even assumed the offensive, in order to ascertain exactly what the pressure might be, and test the intentions of the adversary. Against him, in the forenoon, advanced Frossard in the centre, Bazaine on the right, and de Failly, who had crossed the river at Saareguemines, on his left. It was a wonderful spectacle. The Emperor and the Prince Imperial were present on the hills to behold so vast an array moving out in parade order, to fight a sham battle with real shot and shell, against a dozen companies and six guns. It is not necessary to enter into a detail of this combat; it is sufficient to say that the Prussians held on to the left bank until they were obliged, after an hour's fighting, to retire before the development of several brigades. Finally, when a French battery on the Reppertsberg had opened fire on the bridges and the town, Count von Gneisenau withdrew his troops, first to a place near the town, and afterwards to a position further in the rear. At other points on the river the French had failed to pass, but in the evening they sent parties into Saarbrück, then unoccupied. The French in this skirmish lost 86, and the Prussians, 83 officers and men killed and wounded. It was the first occasion on which the soldiers of Napoleon III. had an opportunity of testing the qualities of the German Army, and they found that their secular adversaries, disciplined on a different model, and broken to new tactics, were as hardy, active, and formidable as those of Frederick the Great.

After this striking example of stage thunder, there was a pause—the French did not pursue the retreating companies of the Fortieth and Sixty-ninth, hold the town, or even destroy the bridges. Indeed, General Frossard, in his pamphlet, explains that although so few were visible, there must have been large numbers of the Eighth Prussian Corps near at hand, and insists that they were held back because the adversary did not wish to show his strength; so that the result actually had an unfavourable influence on the French—it inspired in them a feeling of apprehension. They dreaded the unknown. Without exact, and with what was worse, misleading information, the Marshals and Generals were bewildered by every adverse strong patrol, which boldly marched up and even looked into their camps; and out of these scouting parties they constructed full corps ready to pounce upon them. No master mind at head-quarters filled them with confidence, or gave a firm direction to their soldiers. At a very early period, even in the highest ranks, arose a querulous dread of " Prussian spies," and a belief that the hills and woods concealed countless foes. The apprehensions had no solid foundation, since the First Army was not nearer the Saar than Losheim and Wadern, and the only troops in the immediate front of General Frossard were those composing Gneisenau's weak detachment, which retired some miles on the road to Lebach. Yet the feeble operation of August the 2nd induced the Great Staff to concentrate the First Army at Tholey, that is nearer to the main line of march of the Second Army, and on the left flank of the probable French advance. None took place, and thenceforward the swift and measured development of the German movement southwards went steadily onwards.

PREPARING TO GO FORWARD.

After reviewing the general position of the opposing armies, the German head-quarters fixed on the 4th of August as the day on which offensive operations should be begun.   It was known in a sufficiently authentic way, that there were between Metz and the Saar, four French Corps and the Guard, the Left being at Bouzonville, south of Saarlouis, and the Right at Bitsche ; that the 1st Corps was south of Hagenau, in Alsace, and that the two remaining Corps were still incomplete, one being at Chalons, the other at Belfort. It was, therefore, determined that the Prussian Crown Prince should cross the Lauter on the 4th, while Prince Charles and General von Steinmetz, at a later date, should move upon Saarbrück, and grapple with the main Imperial Army as soon as they could bring the foe to battle.   Practically, the skirmish on the 2nd put everyone on the alert.   Acting, as was usual in the German Army, on their own discretion, yet still in the spirit of their instructions, the divisional and Corps commanders at once sprang forward to support Gneisenau; so that on the 3rd, the front lines of the First Army were nearer to the enemy than had been prescribed, and General von Steinmetz came up from Treves to Losheim.

During this period, the Second Army had continued its movement upon Kaiserslautern, and its cavalry had already established a connection with the First Army. It was not the intention of General von Moltke, who really spoke with the voice of His Majesty, that the Saar should be crossed until a later day.   He seems to have been under the impression that the French might still assume the offensive; he therefore held back the somewhat impetuous Steinmetz, and so ordered the movements that both armies should take up positions between Tholey and Kaiserslautern, which would enable them to act in concert. Thus, on the 3rd, the vast array between the Rhine and the Moselle, was in motion, left in front, in other words, the Prussian Crown Prince was the most forward, while the centre and right were drawn together, preparatory to an advance in a compact form. The French, it was noted with surprise, had not only refrained from breaking the substantial bridges over the Saar, but had left untouched the telegraph wires and stations on both banks of the stream, so that, says the official narrative, the Staff at Mainz were kept constantly informed by telegrams of the enemy's doings and bearing near Saarbrück. Such negligence would not be credited were it not thus authentically recorded by the General who found it so profitable.

By the 4th of August, the entire front of the Armies advancing towards the Saar was covered by several regiments of cavalry, actively engaged on and near the river, especially at Saarbrück, in closely watching the French, and sending information to the rear. There was not a point between Pirmasens and Saarlouis which escaped the notice of these vigilant and tireless horsemen. Behind them came the masses of the First and Second Armies, which latter, on the 4th, had passed " the wooded zone of Kaiserslautern," and had approached so closely to the First, that a species of controversy for precedence arose between Prince Charles and General von Steinmetz. Fearful of being thrust into the second line, the eager old soldier wanted to push forward on Saarbrück, and reap the laurels of the first battle, or, at all events, keep his place at the head of the advance. General von Moltke, who had

his own plans of ulterior action, which were not those
of Steinmetz, in order to settle the dispute, drew
what he supposed would be an effective line of demar-
cation between the two Armies. He also added the
First Corps, which had come up from Pommerania, to
the First Army; the Second, Tenth and Twelfth to
the Second, and the Sixth to the Third Army. While
directing the Crown Prince to cross the Lauter on the
4th, General von Moltke did not intend to pass the
Saar until the 9th, and then to act with the whole force
assembled on that side. In fact, rapidly as the
business of mobilization, the transit by railway, and the
collection of trains for so vast a body of men, horses,
and guns, had been performed, the work was not in all
respects quite complete, nor had the soldiers been able,
good marchers as they were, to cover the ground
between them and the adversary, before the date
assigned.

Yet von Moltke proposed, and von Steinmetz disposed, although he is acquitted by his chief of any
deliberate intention to act prematurely. The latter,
obliged to make room for Prince Charles, gave directions which brought his two leading Corps within reach
of the Saar and his advanced guards close to Völkingen
and Saarbrück in actual contact with the French outposts; and that disposition led to a considerable battle
on the 6th, a collision not anticipated at the head-
quarters in Mainz. It is, however, pointedly declared
that at the moment when he thrust himself forward
Steinmetz did not know what were the plans which had
been formed in that exalted region, to be carried out or
modified according to events, and therefore withheld
from him. The broad scheme was that the Third Army
should, after crossing the Vosges, march on Nancy, and
that the First should form the pivot on which the

Second Army would wheel in turning the French position on the line of the Moselle. Practically that was done in the end, and it was facilitated, perhaps, by the two battles fought on the 6th of August, which shattered the French, and obliged them to act, not as they might have wished, but as they were compelled.

POSITIONS ON AUGUST 4.

For the sake of clearness, the positions occupied by the rival Armies on the morning of the 4th may be succinctly described. The French stood thus: On the right, two divisions of the 5th Corps, one at Saareguemines, the other at Grossbliedersdorff; in what may be called the centre, three divisions of the 2nd Corps, on and over the frontier immediately south of Saarbrück; three divisions of the 3rd Corps echelonned on the highroad from Forbach to St. Avold, with one division at Boucheporn ; on the left, three divisions of the 4th Corps, one at Ham, a second at Teterchen, and a third at Bouzonville. The guard were in rear of the left at Les Etangs. The position of the cavalry it is difficult to determine, but they were not where they should have been—feeling for and watching the enemy. Nor is it easy to ascertain the numerical strength of the French Army at any given moment, because the reserves and battalions, as they could be spared from garrisons, were constantly arriving; but on the 4th there were about 150,000 men and 500 guns in front of Metz. That fortress, however, like all the other strong places on or near the frontier, such as Toul, Verdun, Thionville, and Belfort, had no garrison proper, or one quite inadequate to its requirements.

The German Armies on the 4th were posted in this order: The Crown Prince's was behind the Klingbach, south of Landau, assembled at dawn for the march

G

which carried it over the frontier; the Second, or Central Army, under Prince Charles, was in line of march through the Haardt Wald by Kaiserslautern, the advanced guard of the Fourth Corps being at Homburg, and that of the Third at Neunkirchen; while the Guard, the Tenth, Twelfth, and Ninth were still north or east of Kaiserslautern, which they passed the next day. The First Army, held back by orders from the Great Staff, was cantonned between Neunkirchen, Tholey, and Lebach. In front of the whole line, from Saarlouis to Saareguemines, were several brigades of cavalry, from which parties, both strong and weak, were sent out constantly to discover and report on the positions and doings of the enemy. The three Armies, as far as can be estimated from the official figures, brought into the field at the outset of the campaign, say the 4th of August, the First, 83,000 men and 270 guns; the Second, 200,000 men and 630 guns; and the Third, 170,000 men and 576 guns, an overwhelming array compared with that mustered by the adversary. These totals include only the active Army. The aggregate from which they were drawn amounted to the enormous sum of 1,183,389 men and 250,373 horses, which, of course, includes garrisons, depôts, and landwehr in course of formation. It has been laid down on indisputable authority that the number available for active operations, namely, that which can be put into the field, is, in all cases, as it was in this, less than half the nominal effective. The proportion of mobilized, to what may be called immobilized, troops in the French Army was for the moment, at all events, necessarily somewhat lower than in the German, because the Imperial military system, as we have already explained, was so clumsy, as well as so incomplete.

THE MORAL AND POLITICAL FORCES.

One other fact may be usefully noticed, because it had a considerable influence on the campaign. It is this—the moral force, represented by public opinion in politics, and in the Armies by what the French call the *moral*, which has nothing to do with morals, but means cheerfulness, good will, confidence—had passed almost wholly over to the German side. Public opinion, which ran in a strong and steady current, condemned the declaration of war, although a certain superstitious belief in the invincibility of French soldiers, at least when opposed to Germans, still prevailed, even among military men who ought to have been better informed and less under the sway of prejudice. While Germany was united and hearty, and willingly obeyed an executive which no one questioned, while Saxony and Hanover, Würtemberg and Bavaria vied in patriotic ardour with Pomerania and Brandenburg; there was no such complete and consentaneous feeling in France; and there was, on the one hand, a powerful, ambitious, and indignant group of Imperialists, who thirsted for the possession of office, which they strove to snatch from Emile Ollivier and his semi-Liberal colleagues, and on the other, outside all the Imperialist sections, the repressed, enraged, and sturdy republicans of Paris who, it is not too much to say, waited for the first decisive defeat of the Imperial Armies to overturn an arbitrary system of government which they detested on account of its treacherous origin, and dreaded, as well as despised, while they writhed beneath its power. Jerôme David and Clement Duvernois were resolved to expel the so-called constitutionalists; and Gambetta, Favre, and their friends were equally determined, if an opportunity occurred, to

destroy the Empire, root and branch. There were no
such elements of weakness beyond the Rhine.

Nor, as we shall see, did the conduct of the Empress
Eugénie, in her capacity as Regent, supply strength to
the Government or impart wisdom to its councils. She
had one dominant idea—the preservation of the dynasty
—and aided by a willing instrument, the Comte de
Palikao, she was the prime agent in the work of
depriving the French nation of the best and last chance
of saving Paris from investment and capitulation. If
the political conditions were adverse to the Imperialists
in respect of unity and moral force, they were not less
so when estimated from a military standpoint. The
French Army we will not say lost courage, but confidence, from the moment when it was brought to a stand-
still. The soldiers knew quite as well as the generals
why, on the 4th of August, the larger host, under an
Emperor Napoleon, was pottering to and fro, driven
hither and thither by orders and counter-orders, in the
country north of Metz, and why the smaller, commanded
by Marshal the Duke of Magenta, was still south of the
Lauter. They knew also, from daily experience, how
imperfect the Armies were, because the weakness of
the battalions, the scarcity of provisions, the defects of
equipment, the lack of camp utensils were things
which could not be hidden. They were also inactive
and unable to develop the power which springs up in
a French Army when engaged in successful offensive
operations; they deteriorated hourly in *moral*. The
Germans gained confidence at every step they took
towards the frontier, not only because they were
animated by a formidable patriotic spirit and were eager
for battle with their ancient foes, but because each
battery, squadron, and battalion had its full complement of men, because they put trust in their royal chief

and his illustrious assistant, and because they were intensely proud of an almost perfect war-apparatus, in which each officer and soldier was able, so solid yet elastic was the system of training, to harmonize obedience to orders with, when the need arose, discretionary, independent action.   So that as the huge but perfectly articulated masses of the German Armies moved swiftly and steadily to the frontier behind which the adversary awaited them, they bore along in their breasts that priceless belief in themselves and their cause which has so often carried troops to victory, even when they were few and their foes were many.   The contrast is painfully distressing; but it is also profoundly instructive, because when closely scrutinized it reveals the open secrets which show, not only how empires are lost and won, but what severe duties a great self-respecting people must perform to obtain securities for the right of cementing and preserving National Independence.

CHAPTER IV.

INVASION IN EARNEST.

THE first blow struck in the war—for the parade at
Saarbrück does not deserve the name of a blow—was
delivered on the Lauter by the Crown Prince. The
French Army in Alsace, commanded by Marshal Mac-
Mahon, had been collected at Strasburg from the garrisons in the Eastern region. At first it consisted of the
1st Corps, which included four infantry divisions, troops
of the Line, to which were added, before the end of
July, three regiments of Zouaves, and three of native
Algerians, which were distributed among the French
infantry brigades. There were three brigades of
cavalry, ninety-six guns, and twenty-four mitrailleuses,
the Emperor's pet arm. The Divisional Commanders
were Ducrot, Abel Douay, Raoult, and Lartigue; and
the horsemen were under the orders of Duhesme.
The 7th Corps, nominally at Belfort, under Felix Douay,
actually distributed in several places, one division being
at Lyons, another at Colmar, was also within the command of MacMahon; so that, on the 4th of August, he
was at the head of two Corps, one of which was many
miles distant from his head-quarters. He had, however,
m oved forward with Ducrot and Raoult to Reichshofen
and Lartigue to Hagenau, while Abel Douay was

pushed still further northward at Wissembourg, which he reached on the 3rd, but with a portion only of his troops. In fact, at that date, the army of MacMahon was strung out between the Lauter and Lyons, and even the portion which may be described as concentrated, consisted of fragments posted or on the march between Wissembourg and Hagenau. That very morning, the 1st Division of the 7th Corps started by railway from Colmar to join the Marshal. It was upon this scattered array that the Crown Prince was advancing. MacMahon, who had intended to assume the offensive himself on the 7th of August, did not know how near and how compact was the host of his foes. Abel Douay, established on the Lauter, was obliged to part with several battalions to keep up his communications, through Lembach, with the main body. He sent out a party on the evening of the 3rd, and early on the 4th, yet each returned bearing back the same report—they had seen and learned nothing of the enemy. Indeed, it would be difficult to find a single instance in which the researches of the French were thrust far enough to touch the Germans, all their reconnoitring excursions being carried on in a routine and perfunctory manner. Nevertheless, they had a strong force of cavalry in Alsace as well as Lorraine; but it was mostly in the rear, rarely much, never far in front. On the other hand, the Baden horsemen had looked, unseen themselves, into the French cavalry camp at Selz, and the scouts on the hills had signalled the successive arrival of battalions and artillery at Wissembourg. It must be stated, however, that the Germans did not know, precisely, until they came in contact with them, what forces were in, or were within reach of Wissembourg.

The object of the German forward movement was twofold—if MacMahon had crossed the Vosges to join

the Emperor, Strasburg was to be invested, and the
rest of the Third Army was to pass through the hills to
the Saar and effect a junction with the Second.   If the
Marshal were still east of the hills, then he was to be
assailed wherever found.   Consequently, the whole
Army was set in motion, but it was by a gift of fortune,
who, however, rarely favours the imprudent, that they
were enabled to defeat the division exposed to their
onset. At four and six in the morning, the Corps moved
out on a broad front stretching from the hills to the
Rhine.   Bothmer's Bavarians, on the right, marched
direct on Wissembourg, followed by the other divisions
of the Bavarian Army.   Next in order, to the left, came
the Fifth Corps, which was directed upon Altenstadt;
the Eleventh, which pushed through the Bien Wald;
and the Badeners, whose object was Lauterbourg; while
the remainder of the Army was still far to the rear.

THE COMBAT ON THE LAUTER.

Wissembourg, a picturesque old town, standing upon
the Lauter at a point where it enters the plain, is
defended by walls not armed with guns, and surrounded
by deep ditches filled from the stream, one arm of which
curves through the place.   There were three gates.
Under the archway of the northern, named after the
town of Hagenau, passed the great road from Strasburg, which, turning to the eastward, quitted the ramparts by the gate of Landau.   The western gate, a mere
entrance cut through the wall, having in advance a
small lunette, received the road from Pirmasens.   It
took its name from the fort of Bitsche, but the track
from that place came down the folded hills by the Col
du Pigeonnier, or Dove-cote Neck, and joined the Strasburg highway just outside the Hagenau gate.   Beyond

the walls were factories, pottery fields, and mills; above and below were the once famous Lines of the Lauter thrown up on, and following the right bank of the stream through the forest to Lauterbourg; while on the foot-hills were vines, which do not add to the beauty of any scene, and hop-gardens; and here and there the usual rows of stiff trees bordering, yet not shading, the roads. Distant about a mile or so to the eastward is a spur of the Vosges, the Geisberg thrust into the plain, falling steeply towards it, and crowned by a substantial château, seated above terraces difficult of access. From this elevation were visible, spread out like a map, the woodlands stretching towards the Rhine, the roads to the east and south, and the town, with its railway station, now silent, near the gate of Landau.

As Abel Douay had only available about eight thousand troops, he could not defend the approaches through the Bien Wald, or prevent a turning movement round his right flank. Still, had he not been under a delusion respecting the proximity of the enemy, he could and would have destroyed the few bridges over the Lauter, and so disposed his troops as not to be surprised. But his scouts had reported that the foe was not near, and thus, when the Bavarian advance appeared on the hills at eight o'clock and opened fire from a battery, the French soldiers were engaged in the ordinary routine of camp labours. Startled by the guns, they ran to their arms with alacrity; but an encounter begun under such conditions is always disadvantageous to the assailed. General Douay, an able soldier, came to a rapid decision. He placed two battalions in the town, another with a battery at the railway station, and posted the rest and twelve guns on the slopes of the Geisberg. The walls and ditches of the town, the railway buildings, and part of the Lauter

Lines, brought the Bavarians to a stand, and the combat of small arms and artillery on this point continued
amid the vineyards and hop-grounds, while the German
centre and Left were swinging round through the forest.
The operation occupied considerable time, as two hours
passed by, from the firing of the first gun, before the leading battalions of the Fifth Corps were brought into play.
At length, they came into action against the railway
station, and as the Eleventh Corps had also developed
an attack on the Geisberg from the east, it was evident
that the combat could not last long. The combined
efforts of the Bavarians and the Prussians, after severe
fighting and some loss, drove the French out of the
station, and captured the town, together with a battalion
of the French regiment of the Line, the 74th, which
was cut off, and forced to surrender. The assailants
had penetrated by the gates after they had been broken
in by artillery, and thus the town was won. It was
really the strong pivot of the defence, and its resistance
delayed the onset upon the Geisberg for some time. In
the meantime, General Abel Douay had been killed by
the explosion of the ammunition attached to a mitrailleuse battery; and the command had devolved upon
General Pellé.

The whole stress of the action now fell upon the
Geisberg and its castle. The height was steep, the
building pierced for musketry and strong enough to
resist anything but cannon-shot. The front was approached by successive terraces, and there was a hop-
garden near by on the Altenstadt road. The main
body of the French and all their artillery, except one
disabled gun which had been captured after a sharp
fight, were on the hills to the south, threatened every
moment on their right flank by the development of the
Eleventh Corps which had entered the area of battle.

The little garrison in the castle made a stout resistance, slew many of the assailants, who swarmed upon all sides, and compelled the more daring among them to seek shelter at the foot of the walls. Then the Germans with great labour brought up in succession four batteries, by whose fire alone they could hope to master the obstinate defenders who had manned even the tiled roof with riflemen. Surrounded, threatened with the weight of twenty-four guns, and seeing their comrades outside in full retreat, the garrison which had done its uttermost, surrendered as prisoners of war. They were two hundred, had killed and wounded enemies amounting to three-fourths of their own number, and had seriously injured General von Kirchbach, the commander of the Fifth Corps. When the castle had fallen the French retired altogether. Making only one show of resistance they disappeared among the hills, and what is remarkable were not pursued, for the Crown Prince riding up, halted all the troops and even the cavalry who were in full career on the track of the enemy. The Germans lost in killed and wounded no fewer than 1,550 officers and men; but the French loss is not exactly known. They left behind, however, nearly a thousand unwounded prisoners, their camp, and one gun.

It may fairly be said of this combat, especially considering they were surprised and greatly outnumbered, that the French sustained their old renown as fighting men and that the first defeat, although severe, reflected no discredit on the soldiers of the 1st Corps. By no chance could they have successfully withstood the well-combined and powerful onsets of their more numerous adversaries. Nevertheless, the death of Douay, the defeat, and the disorganization of the division had a profound moral effect, keenly felt at Metz and more

keenly in Hagenau and Reichshofen. Marshal MacMahon
called for instant aid from the 7th Corps; and the Emperor, moved by the news, decided to send him the 5th
Corps, which General de Failly was at once ordered to
assemble at Bitsche and then move up the great road to
Reichshofen. In the German head-quarters and camps,
on the contrary, there was rejoicing and that natural
accession of confidence in the breasts of the soldiers
now pressing towards the Saar which springs up in fuller
vigour than ever when they learn that their common
standard has floated victoriously over the first foughten
field. The Second and Third Armies were still distant
from the rocky steeps and thick woods where they also
were to gain the day; but the Third Army, which, by
the way, was a fair representative of South and North
Germany, had actually crossed the frontier, had penetrated into Alsace, through woods and field-works and
over streams renowned in story, and had inflicted a
sharp defeat upon the Gallic troops, whose rulers had
challenged the Teutons to wager of battle.

It is admitted that, on the evening of August 4th,
the Germans had lost touch of the adversary. The
reason was that the Fourth Cavalry Division, which
had been ordered up by the Crown Prince early in the
day, had found the roads blocked by an Infantry Corps,
and the vexatious delay prevented the horsemen from
reaching the front before nightfall. So difficult is it
to move dense masses of men, horses, and guns, in
accurate succession through a closed country, along
cross-roads and field-lanes. The few squadrons at
hand were not strong enongh to pursue on the several
roads which radiate from Wissembourg, and the defeat
could not be remedied until the next day. It was
known that the fugitives could not have followed the
southern roads, yet there were hostile troops in

that direction, and it was surmised that they must have retreated into the highlands by the western track, yet they might have traversed another way, lying under the foot of the hills. On the 5th of August, the cavalry, starting out at daylight, soon gathered up accurate information. General von Bernhardi, with a brigade of Uhlans, rode forward on the highway, into the Hagenau forest, where he was stopped by a broken bridge guarded by infantry; but he heard the noise of trains, the whistling of engines, and, of course, inferred the movement of troops; while on the east, nearer the Rhine, the squadrons sent in that direction were turned back both by infantry and barricaded roads. Towards the west, a squadron of Uhlans crossed the Sauer at Gunstett, a place we shall soon meet again; while Colonel Schauroth's Hussars found the bridge at Woerth broken, were fired on by guns and riflemen, and saw large bodies in motion, on the heights beyond the stream. Hence it was inferred that the army of MacMahon was in position about Reichshofen, an inference confirmed by the reports from the Bavarians who had marched on Lembach, from the Fifth Corps whose leading columns attained Preuschdorf, with outposts towards Woerth, and from the Badeners on the left, who found the enemy retiring westward. At night, the Crown Prince's Army had not wholly crossed the frontier. In front, were Hartmann's Bavarians at Lembach, the Fifth Corps before Woerth, the Eleventh, on the railway as far as Surburg; the Badeners on their left rear behind the Selz; Von der Tann's Bavarians at Ingolsheim, and the head-quarters and Fourth Cavalry Division at Soultz, otherwise Sulz. The Sixth Corps—having one division at Landau, formed a reserve. MacMahon's troops, except Conseil-Dumesnil's division of the 7th Corps, near Hagenau, were all in position between Morsbronn and Neewhiller behind the Sulz and the Sauer, a continuous line of water which separated the rival outposts. The Emperor had placed the 5th Corps at the disposal of MacMahon, yet he finally detained one-half of Lapasset's division at Saareguemines, and drew it to himself; while that of Guyot de Lespart was sent, on the 6th, towards Niederbronn, and Goze's, not wholly assembled at Bitsche on the 5th, remained with General de Failly, who, at no moment in the campaign—such was his ill-fortune—had his entire Corps under his orders.

FRENCH POSITION ON THE SAAR.

We may now revert to the positions occupied by the rivals on both banks of the Saar, in order to complete the survey of an extensive series of operations which stretched without a break, in a military sense, from the Rhine opposite Rastadt, towards the confluence of the Saar and Moselle. If the German Head-Quarter Staff at Mainz, considering how well it was served, and what pains were taken to acquire information, remained in some doubt as to the positions and projects of the Imperialists, at Metz, ill-served and hesitating, all was bewilderment and conjecture. Neither the Emperor Napoleon, nor his chief adviser Marshal Lebœuf, seemed capable of grasping the situation now rapidly becoming perilous to them; they had, indeed, fallen under an influence which tells so adversely on inferior minds—dread of the adversary's combinations; and, perplexed by the scraps of intelligence sent in from the front, they adopted no decisive resolution, but waited helplessly on events. No serious attempt was made to concentrate the Army in a good position where it could fight, or manœuvre, or retreat, although, as General Frossard and Marshal Bazaine both state such

a central defensive position had been actually studied
and marked out, in 1867. Whether the occupation of
the country between Saareguemines and Œtingen
would have produced a favourable effect on the
campaign or not, it would have prevented the Army
from being crushed in detail, and have given another
turn to the war. But there was no firmness nor insight
at Metz. The orders issued by the Emperor look like
the work of an amateur who had read much of war,
but who possessed neither the instincts of the born
soldier, nor the indefatigable industry and business-like
skill of a man who, thrust into an unwonted employment, compelling him to face hard realities, endeavours
to cope with them by a steady and intelligent application of the principles of common sense.

On the morning of the 4th, the Emperor did no
more than shift his left wing a little nearer to his
centre, by bringing General de Ladmirault into closer
contact with Marshal Bazaine, leaving Frossard in front
of Saarbrück, and directing de Failly to assemble two
divisions at Bitsche, and report to Marshal MacMahon.
The notion prevailing in the Imperial head-quarters was,
that the Germans designed to march upon Nancy, which
was not their plan at all, and that the Seventh Corps,
reported to be on the march from Treves, might make
an offensive movement to protect Saarlouis, forgetting,
as Frossard observes, that their rule was concentration
and not isolated operations; and that the railroad from
Saarbrück afforded the only serious inlet into Lorraine.
In the evening the news of Abel Douay's defeat and
" wound," not death, reached Metz, and created alarm,
but did not cause any serious modification of the
Imperial plans. The next day the Emperor, still
retaining the supreme direction of the Army, and
keeping the Guard to himself, formally handed over the

2nd, 3rd, and 4th Corps to Marshal Bazaine, "for military operations only;" and the 1st, 5th, partly at Bitsche,
and 7th, mainly at Belfort, to Marshal MacMahon.
The incomplete 6th Corps, under Marshal Canrobert,
had not yet moved out from the camp at Chalons.
Thus, there were practically two Corps remote from
the decisive points, and one in an intermediate position,
so handled by the Imperial Commander as to be
useless. Not only was the force called out for war
scattered over an extensive area, but—and the fact
should be borne in mind—the fortresses were without
proper and effective garrisons, and, what was equally
important, they had no adequate stores of provisions,
arms, and munitions; while the great works at Metz
itself, upon which such reliance had been placed, were
far from being in a defensive condition. Early on the
5th, in answer to a suggestion from Frossard, who was
always urging concentration, the Emperor directed
him, yet not until the 6th, to fix his head-quarters at
Forbach, and draw his divisions round about in such
a manner that, when ordered, he might remove his
head-quarters to St. Avold; instructions which left
him in doubt, and inspired him with anxiety. During
the evening, however, acting on his own discretion, he
thought it fit to place his troops in fresh positions,
somewhat to the rear on the uplands of Spicheren, with
one division, upon higher ground in the rear, yet that
step, though an improvement, did not remove his
apprehension respecting his left flank, which had been
weakened by the withdrawal of Montaudon's division
of the 3rd Corps to Saareguemines. General Frossard
has been much censured, but he was a man of real
ability, and almost the only general who, from first to
last, always took the precaution of covering his front
with field works.

GERMAN POSITION ON THE SAAR.

We have indicated, in the preceding chapter, the stages attained by the First and Second German Armies on the 4th; and have now only to repeat, for the sake of clearness, a summary of their array on the evening of the 5th. The several Corps of the Second were still moving up towards the Saar. The Fourth Corps was at Einöd and Homburg, the Guard near Landsthul; the Ninth about Kaiserslautern, and the Twelfth a march to the rear. Further westward, the Tenth halted at Cusel, and the Third was in its front, between St. Wendel and Neunkirchen. The First Army remained in the villages where it was located on the 4th, that is the Seventh and Eighth between Lebach and Steinweiler, with one division of the incomplete First Corps at Birkenfeld. On the evening of that day, however, General Steinmetz issued an order of movement for the next, which carried the leading columns of the Seventh and Eighth close to Saarbrück, and, as a consequence, brought on the battle of Spicheren, the narrative of which sanguinary and spirited fight will fall into its natural place later on. As the main current of the campaign flowed Metzward, it will be convenient to recount, first, the operations of the Crown Prince's Army, which though in a measure subsidiary, produced more telling and decisive effects upon the fortunes of the French, than the engagement which broke down their foremost line of battle on the Saar.

H

CHAPTER V.

Two Staggering Blows.

I.—WOERTH.

ALIKE in Alsace and Lorraine, the actions which made
the 6th of August a date so memorable in this swiftly
moving war were undesigned on the part of the assailant and unexpected on the part of the assailed. In
other words, as General von Moltke did not intend to
throw the force of his right and centre against the main
body of the Imperialists until all the Corps were closer
to the frontier and to each other, so the Crown Prince
proposed to employ the day in changing front from the
south to the west and then direct his serried lines upon
the front and flanks of MacMahon's Army, which he
confidently expected to find in position behind the Sulz
and the Sauer, covering the road to Bitsche. The
despatches of the French Marshal also show that he
counted on a day's respite, since his orders to de Failly
were that the two divisions commanded by that ill-used
officer were to march on the 6th to join the 1st Corps,
so that they might be in line to fight a battle on the
following day. But de Failly, harassed by fluctuating
orders from Metz, shifted hither and thither, now to
the right, now to the left, and never permitted to
keep his Corps in hand, was unable to do more than

start one division on the road to Reichshoffen, while he assembled the other at Bitsche, and left one-half the third on the Saar to share the misfortunes of Napoleon and Bazaine. No such hesitation and infirmity of purpose characterized the conduct of the German commanders. They had well-defined plans, indeed, and issued clear and precise orders, yet both the one and the other were so framed that they could be modified to deal with unexpected incidents, and adapted at once to the actually ascertained circumstances of the moment, which is the very essence of war. The spirit of the German training gives a large discretion to superior officers, who are taught to apply the rules issued for their guidance to the military situation which, in the field, is certain to vary from day to day, or even from hour to hour. Moreover, a German general who attacks is certain to receive the ready support of comrades who may be near, while those more remote, who hear the sound of battle or receive a request for help, at once hasten forward, reporting the fact to, without awaiting orders from, superior authority. Nothing testifies more effectively to the soundness of the higher education in the Prussian military system than the fact that it is possible not only to confer these large powers on subordinates, but to encourage the use of them. At the same time it must be acknowledged that, in any army where the officers do not make the study of war their daily and hourly business, and where the best of the best are not selected for command and staff duty, the latitude enjoyed by the Germans could not be granted, because its capricious and unintelligent use would lead to needless bloodshed, the frustration of great designs, and perhaps shameful defeat.

It has been already stated that both commanders had intended to assume the offensive and fight a battle on the 7th, the Crown Prince proposing to bring up the greater part of his Army and envelope the French, and Marshal MacMahon, who thought he was dealing with the heads of columns, having drawn up a plan to attack the Germans in front with the 1st and turn their right flank with the 5th Corps. Had he known how strong and how compact was the array of his opponent he never could have framed a scheme which would have transferred to the enemy all the advantages possessed by himself. The contingency of a forward movement on his part had been foreseen and guarded against, and the precautions adopted on the evening of the 5th would have become far more formidable had the next day passed by without a battle. But those very protective measures, as will be seen, tended to precipitate a conflict by bringing the troops into contact on the front and left flank of the French position. Marshal MacMahon had selected and occupied exceptionally strong ground. He posted his divisions on a high plateau west of the Sauer and the Sulz, between Neewhiller and Eberbach, having Froeschwiller as a kind of redoubt in the centre, and the wooded slopes of the hills running steeply down to the brooks in his front. The left wing, where General Ducrot commanded, was thrown back to guard the passages through the woodlands, which led down the right bank of the Sulz from Mattstal into the position. The centre fronted Woerth, which was not occupied, and the right, without leaning on any special protective obstacle, was in the woods and villages south-east of Elsasshausen, with reserves in the rear which, says the German official narrative, together with the open country, were a sufficient guard against a direct flank attack, an opinion not justified by the result. The Sauer was deep, the bridges had been broken, and the ascents on the French side were pro-

longed, except on one point, and swept by musketry
and cannon. Among the vines and copses, in the
villages and farmsteads, everywhere protected by open
ground, over which an assailant must pass, stood the
Frency Army—Ducrot on the left, facing north-west,
Raoult in the centre, Lartigue on the right, having
behind him Conseil-Dumesnil's division of the 7th
Corps. Pellé, who succeeded Abel Douay, was in
reserve; and the cavalry were partly in rear of the
right, and partly behind the centre. The official
German history speaks of the position as especially
strong, regards the mass of troops seated there, put
down at forty-five thousand men, as amply sufficient
for a vigorous defence, and contends that the defect of
numbers was balanced by a respectable artillery and
the superiority of the Chassepot over the far-famed
needle-gun. A Bavarian soldier-author, Captain Hugo
Helvig, however, says that the ground held by the
French had all the disadvantages of so-called " unassail-
able " positions—it had no issues to the front, consequently the defenders could not become the assailants;
its right was " in the air " and its left " rested on that
most doubtful of all supports to wings—a wood." Thus
the Bavarian captain differs from the General Staff.
The fact seems to be that the position was so formidable
that it could only be carried by onsets on both flanks,
which, of course, implies that the assailant must have
the control of superior numbers. Another point to be
noted is that the great road to Bitsche was a prolonga-
tion of the front and in rear of the left, and that, as
happened, in case of a severe defeat, the temptation
would be all powerful to retreat by cross roads on
Saverne, that is, away from instead of towards the main
body of the Imperial Army. Marshal MacMahon had
hoped to be the assailant, but he held that if the

German Army continued its march southward beyond
Hagenau, he would have to retreat, a movement the
Crown Prince was not likely to make, since the orders
from the King's head-quarters were to seek out and
fight the enemy wherever he might be found, a rule
which governed all the German operations up to the
fatal day of Sedan.

Early on the morning of the 6th, the German
columns were approaching, from the north and the
east, the strong position just described. Hartmann's
Bavarians, after marching westward through the Hochwald to Mattstal, had turned south down the Sulzbach.
The Fifth Corps, in position overnight at Preuschdorf,
had, of course, strong advanced posts between Goersdorf and Dieffenbach, while von der Tann's Bavarians
were on the march from Ingolsheim, also through the
lower Hochwald road, by Lampertsloch upon Goersdorf
and the Sauer.   Further to the left, the Eleventh
Corps and von Werder's combined divisions were
wheeling up to the right, so as to extend the line on
the outer flank of the Fifth Corps. The Hochwald
rose five or six hundred feet above the battlefield.
Like most uplands, it was intersected by vales and
country roads, and nearly every hollow had its beck
which flowed into the principal stream. This was the
Sauer. Rising in hills beyond Lembach, it ran in a
southerly direction along the whole German front,
receiving the Sulz at Woerth, and dividing into two
streams opposite Gunstett. These greater and lesser
brooks, though spanned by few bridges, were well
supplied with mills, which always facilitate the passage
of streams. Large villages, also, filled up the valley
bottoms here and there, and the country abounded in
cultivation. Through this peopled and industrious
region the main roads ran from north to south, gener-

ally speaking, the road and railway from Bitsche to Hagenau, and on to Strasburg, passing in rear of Mac-Mahon's position close to Niederbronn and Reichs-hoffen, and another highway to Hagenau, a common centre for roads in these parts, descended from Lembach, and, after crossing, followed the right bank of the Sauer. Thus there were plenty of communications in all directions, despite the elevated, wooded and broken character of a district, wherein all arms could move freely, except cavalry.

THE BATTLE BEGINS.

The action was brought on by the eagerness of each side to discover the strength and intentions of the other. In this way, General von Walther, at daybreak, riding towards the Sauer, hearing noises in the French camp, which he construed to mean preparations for a retreat, ordered out a battery and some infantry, to test the accuracy of his observations. The guns cannonaded Woerth, and the skirmishers, finding the town unoccupied, but the bridge broken, forded the stream, and advanced far enough to draw fire from the French foot and four batteries. The Prussian guns, though fewer, displayed that superiority over the French which they maintained throughout, and the observant officers above Woerth knew, by the arrival of the ambulance men on the opposite hills, that their shells had told upon the enemy. The skirmish ceased after an hour had passed, but it served to show that the French were still in position. Opposite Gunstett there stood a Bruch-Mühle, or mill in the marsh, and in this place the Germans had posted a company, supported by another in the vines. Their purpose was to protect the left flank of the Fifth Corps, and keep up a connection with the Eleventh, then on the march. The

French sent forward, twice, bodies of skirmishers against the mill, supporting them the second time by artillery, and setting the mill on fire; but on neither occasion did they press the attack, and the Germans retained a point of passage which proved useful later in the day.

These affairs at Woerth and Gunstett ceased about eight o'clock, but the cannonade at the former, echoing among the hills to the north, brought the Bavarians down the Sulz at a sharp pace, and thus into contact with Ducrot's division. For General Hartmann, on the highlands, could see the great camp about Froeschwiller, and, directing his Fourth Division on that place, and ordering up the reserve artillery from Mattstal, the General led his men quickly down the valley. An ineffective exchange of cannon-shots at long range ensued; but as the Bavarians emerged into the open, they came within reach of the French artillery. Nevertheless they persisted, until quitting the wood, they were overwhelmed by the Chassepot and fell back. A stiff conflict now arose on a front between Neewhiller and the Saw Mill on the Sulz, and even on the left bank of this stream, down which the leading columns of a Bavarian brigade had made their way. In short, Hartmann's zealous soldiers, working forward impetuously, had fairly fastened on to the French left wing, striking it on the flank which formed an angle to the main line of battle, and holding it firmly on the ground. The French, however, had no thought of retiring, and besides, at that moment, they had the vantage. When the combat had lasted two hours, General von Hartmann received an order directing him to break it off, and he began at once his preparations to withdraw. The task was not easy, and before it was far advanced a request arrived from the

Commander of the Fifth Corps for support, as he was about to assail the heights above Woerth. It was heartily complied with, all the more readily, as the roar of a fierce cannonade to the south swept up the valley; but as the Bavarians had begun to withdraw, some time elapsed before the engagement on this side could be strenuously renewed.

ATTACK ON WOERTH.

We have already said that the Crown Prince, not having all his Corps in compact order, did not intend to fight a battle until the next day. But what befell was this. The officer at the head of the staff of the Fifth Corps reached the front after the reconnaissance on Woerth was over. Just as he rode up, the smoke of Hartmann's guns was visible on one side, and the noise of the skirmishers at Gunstett on the other. In order to prevent the French from overwhelming either, it was agreed, there and then, to renew the contest, and shortly after nine o'clock the artillery of the Fifth Corps, ranged on the heights, opened fire. At the same time, a portion of the Eleventh Corps, hearing the guns, had moved up rapidly towards Gunstett, and three of their batteries were soon in line. Thus, the Bavarians rushed into battle in order to support the Fifth Corps, this body resumed the combat to sustain the Bavarians, and the advanced guard of the Eleventh fell on promptly, because the Fifth seemed in peril. The Prussian artillery soon quelled, not the ardour, but the fire of the French gunners; and then the infantry, both in the centre and on the left, went steadily into action, passing through Woerth, and beginning to creep up the opposite heights. They made no way, and many men fell, while further down the stream, opposite Spachbach and Gunstett, part of

the troops which had gone eagerly towards the woods,
were smitten severely, and driven back headlong over
the river. Still some clung to the hollow ways,
Woerth was always held fast, and when the foot
recoiled before the telling Chassepot, the eighty-four
pieces in battery lent their aid, averted serious
pursuit, and flung a shower of shells into the woods.
It was at this period that the defect of the French
position became apparent. If the hardy Gauls could
repel an onset, they could not, in turn, deliver a counter
stroke, because the advantages of the defensive would
pass, in that case, to the adversary. But the Germans
across the Sauer, who still held their ground, had much
to endure, and were only saved by the arrival of fresh
troops, and by seeking every available shelter from the
incessant rifle fire.   In the meantime, the Eleventh
Corps was marching to the sound of the guns. General
von Bose, its commander, had reached Gunstett in the
forenoon, and, seeing how matters stood, had called up
his nearest division, had ordered the other to advance
on the left, and had informed von Werder that an
action had begun, in consequence whereof the Badeners
and Wurtembergers were also directed on the Sauer.

It was about one o'clock when the Crown Prince
rode up to the front and took command. He had
ridden out from Soultz at noon, because he plainly
heard the sounds of conflict, and on his road had been
met by an officer from von Kirchbach, bearing a report
which informed the Commander-in-Chief that it was no
longer possible to stop the fray. At the time he
arrived, the advanced brigade of von der Tann's
Bavarians had thrust itself into the gap between
Preuschdorf and Goersdorf, and had brought three
batteries into action, but the remainder of the Corps
were still in the rear. The Crown Prince thus found

his front line engaged without any reserve close at hand, and that no progress had been made either on the centre or the wings; but he knew that the latter would be quickly reinforced, and that the former, sustained by two hundred guns, constituted an ample guarantee against an offensive movement. No better opportunity of grappling with a relatively weak enemy was likely to occur, and it was to be feared that if the chance were offered, he would escape from a dangerous situation by skilfully extricating his Army. The Crown Prince, therefore, determined to strike home, yet qualifying his boldness with caution, he still wished to delay the attack in front and flank until the troops on the march could reach the battlefield. No such postponement was practicable, even if desirable, because the fighting Commander of the Fifth Corps had already, before the advice came to hand, flung his foremost brigades over the Sauer. So the action was destined to be fought out, from beginning to end, on places extemporized by subordinate officers; but they were adapted to the actual facts, and in accordance with the main idea which was sketched by the Chief. It may be said, indeed, that the battle of Woerth was brought on, worked out, and completed by the Corps commanders; and the cheerful readiness with which they supported each other, furnished indisputable testimony to the soundness of their training, the excellence of the bodies they commanded, and the formidable character, as well as the suppleness of the military institutions, which, if not founded, had been carried so near to perfection by von Roon, von Moltke and the King.

Begun in the early morning by a series of skirmishes on the river front, the action had developed into a battle at mid-day. The resolute von Kirchbach, acting

on his own responsibility, had thrown the entire Fifth
Corps into the fight; yet so strong was the position
occupied by the defenders, that a successful issue
depended upon the rapidity and energy with which the
assaults on both flanks were conducted by brigades and
divisions only then entering one after the other upon
a fiercely contested field. At mid-day, the French line
of battle had been nowhere broken or imperilled.
Hartmann's Bavarians on one side had been checked; the
advance brigade of the Eleventh Corps, on the other, had
been driven back over the Sauer, and Lartigue's troops
were actually pressing upon the bridges near the mill in
the marsh, which, however, they could not pass. The
enormous line of German guns restrained and punished
the French infantry, when not engaged in silencing the
inferior artillery of the defender. But no impression
had been made upon the wooded heights filled with the
soldiers of Ducrot, upon Raoult's men in the centre
above Woerth, or on Lartigue's troops, who, backed by
Conseil-Dumesnil, stood fast about Morsbrunn, Eber-
back, and Elsasshausen. So it was at noon, when the
hardihood of von Kirchbach forced on a decisive issue.
Passing his men through, and on both sides of Woerth,
he began a series of sustained attacks upon Raoult, who
stiffly contested every foot of woodland, and even
repelled the assailants, who, nevertheless, fighting
with perseverance, and undismayed by the slaughter,
gradually gained a little ground on both sides of the
road to Froeschwiller. By comparatively slow degrees,
they crept up the slopes, and established a front of
battle; but the regiments, battalions, companies, were
all mixed together, and, as the officers fell fast, the men
had often to depend upon themselves. While these
alternately advancing, receding, and yet again advancing
troops were grappling with the centre, Hartmann re-

newed his onsets, part of von der Tann's Corps dashed
over the Sauer, filling up the gap in the line, and joining
his right to Hartmann's left; and the leading brigades
of a fresh division of the Eleventh Corps, moving steadily
and swiftly over the river below Gunstett, backed by all
the cannon which the nature of the ground permitted
the gunners to use, assailed the French right with
measured and sustained fury, and, indeed, decided the
battle.

ATTACK ON THE FRENCH RIGHT.

The French were posted in great force on their right
—where they had two divisions, one in rear of the other,
between the Sauer and the Eberbach, having in support
a powerful brigade of horsemen, Cuirassiers and
Lancers, under General Michel. The infantry, as a
rule, faced to the eastward; while the attacking columns
not only fronted to the westward, but also to the north-
west; in other words, they fastened on the front from
Spachbach, struck diagonally at the outer flank from
Morsbrunn, and even swept round towards the rear.
The area of the combat on this part of the field was
included on an oblong space bounded on the west by
the Eberbach, and on the east by the Sauer, having
Morsbrunn at the south-eastern angle and outside the
French lines; Albrechtshaüser, a large farmstead, a
little to the north of the former, and opposite Gunstett;
and beyond that point to the north-west the undulating
wooded uplands, called the Niederwald, whence the
ground slightly fell towards Elsasshausen, and rose
again to a greater height at Froeschwiller, the centre
and redoubt of the position. As the 22nd division of the
Eleventh Corps came up from Dürrenbach, they broke
obliquely into this oblong, the direction of their attack
mainly following the cross road through the forest from

Morsbrunn to Elsasshausen, while their comrades
pierced the woods to the north of the great farmstead.
No difficulty was encountered in expelling the handful
of French from the village, but at the farm the Germans
had a sharper combat, which they won by a converging
movement, yet the defenders had time to retire into the
forest.   Thus two useful supports were secured, almost
perpendicular to the French flank, and the pathways
leading towards Reichshoffen were uncovered.   General
Lartigue at once discerned the peril, and, in order that
he might obtain time to throw back his right, he directed
General Michel to charge the left flank of the Germans
before they could recover from the confusion consequent
on a rapid and irregular advance through the villages,
outbuildings, and hopfields, and array a less broken
front.

The French cavalry appear to have considered that
their main function was restricted to combats in great
battles.   The traditions handed down from the days of
Kellerman and Murat and Lasalle survived in all their
freshness, and the belief prevailed that a charge of
French horsemen, pushed home, would ride over any
infantry, even in serried formation. They had disdained
to reckon with the breechloader in the hands of cool,
well-disciplined opponents ;   and as their chance of
acting on their convictions had come, so they were ready
and willing to prove how strong and genuine was their
faith in the headlong valour of resolute cavaliers.
Instead of using one regiment, Michel employed both,
and a portion of the 6th Lancers as well.   He started
forth from his position near Eberbach, his horsemen
formed in echelon from the right, the 8th Cuirassiers
leading in column of squadrons, followed by the 9th and
the Lancers.   Unluckily for them, they had to traverse
ground unsuitable for cavalry.   Here groups of trees,

there stumps, and again deep drains, disjointed the close formations, and when they emerged into better galloping ground, indeed before they had quitted the obstructions, these gallant fellows were exposed to the deadly fire of the needle-gun. Nevertheless, with fiery courage, the Cuirassiers dashed upon the scattered German infantry, who, until the cavalry approached, had been under a hail of shot from the Chassepots in the Niederwald. Yet the Teutons did not quail, form square, or run into groups—they stood stolidly in line, hurled out a volley at three hundred yards, and then smote the oncoming horsemen with unintermitted fire. The field was soon strewn with dead and wounded men and horses; yet the survivors rushed on, and sought safety by riding round the German line or through the village, where they were brought to bay, and captured by the score. Each regiment, as it rode hardily into the fray, met with a similar fate, and even the fugitives who got into the rear were encountered by a Prussian Hussar regiment, and still further scattered, so that very few ever wandered back into the French lines. As a charge, Michel's valiant onset was fruitless; yet the sacrifice of so many brave horsemen secured a great object—it enabled General Lartigue to throw back his right, rearrange his defensive line in the woods, and renew the contest by a series of violent counter-attacks.

A furious outburst of the French infantry from the south-west angle of the Niederwald overpowered the German infantry, and drove them completely out of the farmstead so recently won. Yet the victors could not hold the place, because the batteries north of Gunstett at once struck and arrested them with a heavy fire, which gave time for fresh troops to move rapidly into line, restore the combat, and once more press back the dashing French infantry into the wood. On this point, the fighting was rough and sustained, for the French charged again and again, and did not give way until the Germans on their right, forcing their way through the wood, had crowned a summit which turned the line. The sturdy adversary, who yielded slowly, was now within the forest, and the German troops on the left had come up to Eberbach, capturing MacMahon's baggage, thus developing a connected front from stream to stream across the great woodland. In short, nearly all the Eleventh Corps was solidly arrayed, and in resistless motion upon the exposed flank of MacMahon's position, while part of the Würtembergers, with some horse, were stretching forward beyond the Eberbach, and heading for Reichshoffen itself. The Germans, indeed, had gained the north-western border of the woodland, and General von Bose had ordered the one-half of his guns and his reserve of foot to cross the Sauer, and push the battle home. His right was now in connection with the left of the Fifth Corps, which had continued its obstinate and sanguinary conflict with Raoult's division on both sides of the road from Woerth to Froeschwiller, without mastering much ground. As the Bavarians were equally held at bay by the French left, the issue of the battle plainly depended on the vigorous and unfaltering energies of the Eleventh Corps.

ATTACK ON ELSASSHAUSEN.

That fine body had been in action for two hours and a half, and, despite a long march on to the field, was still fresh, its too impetuous advanced brigade, alone, having been roughly handled, and thrust back earlier in the day. The task now before them was the capture of Elsasshausen, which would open the road to Froeschwiller, take off the pressure from the Fifth Corps, place Ducrot's steadfast infantry in peril, and enable the whole available mass of German troops to close in upon the outnumbered remnant of MacMahon's devoted Army. For these brave men, although obliged to give ground, were fighting in a manner worthy of their old renown, now dashing forward in vehement onslaughts, again striking heavy blows when overpowered and thrust back. Lartigue's and some of Raoult's troops stood on the right and left of Elsasshausen, supported by batteries on the higher ground, and two cavalry brigades in a hollow near the Eberbach. The foremost infantry occupied a copse which was separated from the main forest by a little glade, and this defensive wooded post had, so far, brought the extreme right of the Eleventh Corps to a stand. About half-past two, the centre and left had come up to the north-western edge of the Niederwald, and thus the French in the copse had fresh foes on their hands. They replied by a bold attack upon the adversary, whose front lines of skirmishers were immediately driven in. The gallant effort carried the assailants into the great wood, but not far; for behind the flying skirmishers, on both sides of the road, were troops which had more or less maintained a compact formation. Instead of yielding before the French advance, the German infantry, accepting the challenge, came steadily forward along the whole front, bore down the skirmishers, dispersed the supporting battalion, and, following the enemy with unfaltering steps, crossed the glade, and drove him into, and out of, the copsewood, which had hitherto been an impassable obstacle. As the entire line rushed forward, they arrived at the skirt of the wood, and, coming at once under the fire of the French guns on the heights, and the infantry in Elsasshausen, they suffered severe losses. Then their own artillery drove up and went into action, setting the village on fire, yet not dismaying its garrison. The

I

tension was so great, and the men fell so fast, that General von Bose resolved to risk a close attack upon an enemy whose position was critical, and whose endurance had been put to so exhausting a strain.

Thereupon, at the welcome signal, the bands of disordered foot soldiers—for nearly every atom of regular formation had long disappeared—dashed, with loud shouts, into the French position, carrying the village at a bound, and, pushing up the hillsides, took two guns and five mitrailleuses. The troops of the Eleventh had now crossed the deep road running south-westward from Woerth, had effected a junction with groups of several regiments belonging to the Fifth, which formed a sort of spray upon the inner flank; and had besides, as already noted, extended south-westward towards the road to Reichshoffen. Once more the French strove, if not to retrieve a lost battle, at least to ensure time for retreat. They fell upon the Germans along the whole line, making great gaps in its extent, and driving the adversary into the forest; but here, again, the artillery saved the foot, and, by its daring and effective fire, restored the battle, giving the much-tried infantry time to rally, and return upon their tracks. The Germans had barely time to recover from the confusion into which they had been thrown by a furious onset, than the four Cuirassier regiments, commanded by General Bonnemains, were seen preparing to charge. Unluckily for these stout horsemen, the tract over which they had to gallop was seamed with deep ditches, and barred by rows of low trees, so that not only could no compact formation be maintained, but the cavaliers were not, in some instances, able to reach their foes, who were well sheltered among the vine-stocks, and behind the walls of the hop-gardens. Moreover, the German infantry were assisted by batteries of guns, which were able to begin with shells, and end with grape-shot. The cavalry did all they could to close; but their efforts were fruitless, and the enormous loss they endured may be fairly regarded as a sacrifice willingly made to gain time for the now hardly bested army to retire.

MACMAHON ORDERS A RETREAT.

Indeed, the hour when a decision must be taken had struck, and MacMahon, who had cleverly fought his battle, did not hesitate. He determined to hold Froeschwiller as long as he could to cover the retreat, and then fly to Saverne. For, although neither Hartmann nor von der Tann, despite their desperate onsets, had been able to shake or dismay Ducrot, still, he was well aware that Raoult's and Lartigue's divisions had been driven back upon Froeschwiller, and he could see from the heights one fresh column of Bavarians moving towards Neehwiller, on his left, and another descending from the Hochwald to join the throng on the right bank of the Sulz. Moreover, two brigades of Würtembergers had come up to support the Eleventh Corps, and while one part of them, with horsemen and guns, threatened Reichshoffen, a Bavarian brigade, as we have said, was heading for Niederbronn. In addition, some of Ducrot's entrenchments were carried by a Prussian regiment on the right of the Fifth Corps, and it was evident that the fierce struggle for Froeschwiller would be the last and final act of the tragedy. Yet, so slowly did the French recede, that an hour or more was consumed in expelling them from their last stronghold; and except on that point, there does not seem to have been any serious fighting. The reason was that the place was held to facilitate the withdrawal of such troops as could gain the line of retreat, and although the disaster was great, it would have been greater had not Raoult, who was wounded and captured in the village, done his uttermost to withstand the concentric rush of his triumphant enemies.

THE CLOSE OF THE BATTLE.

No specific and detailed account, apparently, exists, of this last desperate stand. But it is plain that, as the French centre and right yielded before von Kirchbach and especially von Bose, as the impetuous infantry onsets were fruitless, as the cavalry had been destroyed and the French guns could not bear up against the accurate and constant fire of their opponents, so the Germans swept onwards and almost encircled their foes. When Ducrot began to retire, the Bavarians sprang forward up the steeps and through the woods, which had held them so long at bay; the stout and much-tried Fifth Corps pushed onward, and the Eleventh, already on the outskirts of Froeschwiller and extending beyond it, broke into its south-eastern and southern defences; so that portions of all the troops engaged in this sanguinary battle swarmed in, at last, upon the devoted band who hopelessly, yet nobly, clung to the final barrier. How bravely and steadfastly they fought may be inferred from the losses inflicted upon the Germans, whose officers, foremost among the confused crowd of mingled regiments and companies, were heavily punished, whose rank and file went down in scores. Even after the day had been decided, the French in Froeschwiller still resisted, and the combats there did not cease until five o'clock. But in the open the German flanking columns had done great execution on the line of retreat. A mixed body of Prussian and Würtemberg cavalry had ridden up on the extreme left, one Bavarian brigade had moved through Neehwiller upon Niederbronn, aud another had marched through Froeschwiller upon Reichshoffen. The horsemen kept the fugitives in motion and captured *matériel*; the first mentioned Bavarian brigade struck the division of General Guyot de Lespart, which had reached Niederbronn from Bitsche; and the second bore down on Reichshoffen.   The succouring division had arrived only in time to share the common calamity, for assailed by the Bavarians and embarrassed by the flocks of fugitives, one-half retreated with them upon Saverne, and the other hastily retraced its steps to Bitsche, marching through the summer night.   The battle had been so destructive and the pursuit so sharp that the wrecks of MacMahon's shattered host hardly halted by day or night until they had traversed the country roads leading upon Saverne, whence they could gain the western side of the Vosges.   Nor did all his wearied soldiers follow this path of safety.   Many fled through Hagenau to Strasburg, more retreated with the brigade of Abbatucci to Bitsche, and nine thousand two hundred officers and men remained behind as prisoners of war. The Marshal's Army was utterly ruined, Strasburg was uncovered, the defiles of the Vosges, except that of Phalsbourg, were open to the invader who, in addition to the mass of prisoners, seized on the field, in some cases after a brilliant combat, twenty-eight guns, five mitrailleuses, one eagle, four flags, and much *matériel* of war.   The actual French loss in killed and wounded during the fight did not exceed six thousand; while the victors, as assailants, had no fewer than 489 officers and 10,153 men killed and wounded.   It was a heavy penalty, and represents the cost of a decisive battle when forced on by the initiative of Corps commanders before the entire force available for such an engagement could be marched up within striking distance of a confident and expectant foe.

One other consequence of an unforeseen engagement

was that the Fifth Division of cavalry, which would have been so useful towards the close of the day, was unable to enter the field until nightfall. The Crown Prince and General Blumenthal, not having the exact information which might have been supplied by horsemen who rode at the heels of the fugitives, remained in doubt as to the line or lines of retreat which they followed. It was not until the next day that reports were sent in which suggested rather than described whither the French Army had gone. Prince Albrecht, who led the cavalry, had hastened forward to Ingweiler, on the road to Saverne, but he notified that, though a considerable body had fled by this route, the larger part had retired towards Bitsche. Later on the 7th he entered Steinburg, where he was in contact with the enemy, but, as infantry were seen, he was apprehensive of a night attack from Saverne, and judged it expedient to fall back upon Buchswiller. The division had ridden more than forty miles in a difficult country during the day. From the north-west came information that the patrols of the Sixth Corps had been met at Dambach, and that the French were not visible anywhere. The explanation of this fact is that one division of the Sixth, directed on Bitsche, had, in anticipation of orders, pushed troops into the hills, and had thus touched the right of the main body. The reason why neither MacMahon nor de Failly were discovered was that the Marshal had fallen back to Sarrebourg, and that the General had hurried to join him by Petite-Pierre; and thus contact with the enemy was lost by the Germans because the defiles of the Vosges were left without defenders.

2.—SPICHEREN.

As the critical hours drew nearer when the capacity of the Emperor Napoleon and Marshal Lebœuf, applied to the conduct of a great war, was to be put to the severest test, so their hesitation increased and their inherent unfitness for the heavy task became more and more apparent. Marshal Bazaine had been entrusted with the command of three corps "for military operations only," yet the supreme control was retained in Metz, and the Corps commanders looked more steadily in that direction than they did towards the Marshal's head-quarters at St. Avold. Along the whole front, at every point, an attack by the enemy was apprehended. General de Ladmirault was convinced that the Seventh Prussian Corps would strive to turn his left; Marshal Bazaine was disturbed by the fear that the same body of troops would come upon him from Saarlouis; General Frossard felt so uncomfortable in the angle or curve on the Saar, which he occupied, that he vehemently desired to see the Army concentrated in the position of Cadenbronn, a few miles to the rear of Spicheren; General Montaudon, wno had a division at Sarreguemines, was certain that the enemy intended to swoop down upon him; and General de Failly was in daily alarm lest the Prussians should advance upon the gap of Rohrbach. At Metz all these conflicting surmises weighed upon, we might almost say collectively governed the Emperor and the Marshal, who issued, recalled, qualified, and again issued perplexing orders. It is true that, owing to the supineness of the cavalry, and the indifference of the peasantry on the border, they were without any authentic information ; but if that had been supplied it is very doubtful whether they would have been able to profit by it; and they were evidently unable to reason out a sound plan which would give them the best chances of thwarting the adversary's designs or of facing them on the best terms. The sole idea which prevailed was

that every line should be protected; and thus, on the
5th, the Guard was at Courcelles; Bazaine's four
divisions, hitherto echeloned on the line from St. Avold
to Forbach, were strung out on a country road between
St. Avold and Sarreguemines; de Ladmirault, who
had been ordered to approach the Marshal, misled by
the apparition of Prussian patrols, gave only a partial
effect to the order; while Frossard, on the evening of
that day, instead of the next morning, made those
movements to the rear which attracted the notice of
his opponents and drew them upon him.   At dawn on
the 6th, "the Army of the Rhine" was posted over a
wide space in loosely-connected groups; yet, despite all
the errors committed, there were still three divisions
sufficiently near the 2nd Corps on the Spicheren heights
to have converted the coming defeat into a brilliant
victory.   That great opportunity was lost, because the
soldierly spirit and the warlike training, in which the
French were deficient, were displayed to such an
astonishing degree by the Germans whom they had so
unwisely despised.

The watchful cavalry on the right bank of the Saar
had noted at once the retrograde movement which
General Frossard effected on the evening of the 5th,
and the German leaders were led to infer from the
tenour of the reports sent in, that the whole French
line was being shifted to the rear, which was not a
correct inference at that moment.   Yet it was true and
obvious that Frossard had withdrawn from the hills in
close proximity to Saarbrück.   In order to ascertain, if
possible, how far and in what degree the French had
retired, small parties of horsemen crossed the river
soon after daylight, and rode, not only along the direct
route to Forbach, until they were stopped by cannon
fire, but swept round the left flank, and even looked

into the rear, observed the French camps, and alarmed both Marshal Bazaine and General de Ladmirault. Above Sarreguemines they tried to break up the railway, and did destroy the telegraph; and thus, by appearing on all sides, these enterprising mounted men filled the adversary with apprehensions, and supplied their own Generals with sound intelligence. Some information, less inaccurate than usual, must have reached the Imperial head-quarters at Metz, seeing that a telegram sent thence, between four and five in the morning, warned Frossard that he might be seriously attacked in the course of the day; but it does not appear that the same caution was transmitted to Bazaine, with or without instructions to support his comrade. It is a nice question whether the general conduct of the war suffered the greater damage from the active interference or the negligence of the Emperor and his staff.

While the cavalry were keeping the French well in view, the leading columns of the Seventh and Eighth Corps were moving up towards the Saar, and one division of the Third was equally on the alert. General von Rheinbaben had already ridden over the unbroken bridges, had posted some squadrons on the lower ground, and had drawn a sharp fire from the French guns. The German staff were astonished when they learned that the bridges had not been injured. The reason was soon apparent. The Emperor still cherished the illusion that he might be able to assume the offensive, a course he had prepared for by collecting large magazines at Forbach and Sarreguemines on the very edge of the frontier; and his dreams were now to be dispelled by the rude touch of the zealous and masterful armies whose active outposts were now over the Saar.

THE BATTLE-FIELD.

The ground occupied by the 2nd Corps was an undulating upland lying between the great road to Metz and the river, which, running in a northerly direction from the spurs of the Vosges, turns somewhat abruptly to the west a couple of miles above Saarbrück on its way to the Moselle. The heights of Spicheren, partly wooded and partly bare, fall sharply to the stream in the front and on the eastern flank, while on the west lies the hollow through which the highway and the railroad have been constructed. The foremost spur of the mass, separated by a valley from the Spicheren hills, is a narrow rocky eminence, which Frossard names the Spur, and the Germans call the Rotheberg, or Red Hill, because its cliffs were so bright in colour, and shone out conspicuously from afar. On the French right of this rugged cliff were dense woods, and on the left the vale, having beyond it more woods, and towards Forbach, farms, houses and factories. The upper or southern end was almost closed by the large village of Stiring-Wendel, inhabited by workers in iron, and having on the outskirts those unseemly mounds of slag with which this useful industry defaces the aspect of nature. The village stands between the road and railway, and as the heights rise abruptly on each side, all the approaches, except those through the woods on the west and north-west, were commanded by the guns and infantry on the slopes. It should be noted that west of the neck which connected the red horse-shoe shaped hill with the central heights in front of Spicheren village, there is a deep, irregular, transversal valley, which proved useful to the defence. General Frossard placed Laveaucoupet's division upon the Spicheren hills, in two lines, and occupied the Red Hill, which he had entrenched with a battalion of

Chasseurs. In rear of all stood Bataille's division at Œtingen. On the left front, Jolivet's brigade of Vergé's division occupied Stiring, and Valazé's was placed to the west of Forbach, looking down the road to Saarlouis. As Frossard dreaded an attack from that side, especially as the road up the valley from Rosseln turned the position, his engineer-general threw up a long entrenchment, barring the route. It was in this order that the 2nd Corps stood when some daring German horsemen trotted up the high road to feel for it, while others, on the west, pressed so far forward that they discerned the camps at St. Avold. Below the front of the position, and just outside Saarbrück, the foot-hills, Reppertsberg, Galgenberg, Winterberg, and so on, and the hollows among them were unoccupied by the French, and it was into and upon these that Rheinbaben pushed with his cavalry and guns, which, from the Parade ground, exchanged shots with the French pieces established on the Red Hill or Spur.

THE GERMANS BEGIN THE FIGHT.

On the German side, the determination to lay hands upon, and arrest what was supposed to be a retreating enemy, was identical and simultaneous; and it is the spontaneous activity of every officer and soldier within reach, to share in the conflict which is the characteristic of the day's operations. General Kameke, commanding the fourteenth division, Seventh Corps, when on the march, heard that Frossard had drawn back, and, asking whether he might cross the river, was told to act on his own judgment; so he pressed southward. General Goeben, chief of the Eighth Corps, had ridden out to judge for himself, and finding his comrades of the Seventh ready to advance, offered his support. General von Alvensleben, commanding the Third

Corps, a singularly alert and ready officer, ordered up his fifth division, commanded by General von Stülpnagel, but before the order arrived, General Doering, who had been early to the outposts, had anticipated the command, because he thought that Kameke might be overweighted. General von Schwerin, later in the day, collected his brigade at St. Ingbert, and sent a part of them forward by rail. In like manner General von Barnekoff, commanding the Sixteenth Division, Eighth Corps, hearing the sound of artillery, had anticipated the desire of Goeben, and by mid-day his advanced guard, under Colonel von Rex, was close upon the scene of action. General von Zastrow, who had permitted Kameke to do what he thought fit, applied to von Steinmetz for leave to push forward the whole Seventh Corps, and the fiery veteran at once complied, saying, "The enemy ought to be punished for his negligence," a characteristic yet not necessarily a wise speech, as the business of a General is not to chastise even the negligent, unless it serves the main purpose of the operations in hand. Thus we see that the mere noise of battle attracted the Germans from all quarters; and hence it happened that the fronts of the two armies, then in line of march, hastened into a fight by degrees—in detachments, so to speak— which would have produced a heavy reverse had all the French brigade and divisional commanders who were within hail, been as prompt, persistent and zealous as their impetuous opponents.

Until near noontide, there had been merely a bickering of outposts, chiefly on the north-western side; and it was only when the Fourteenth Division crossed the river and moved up the foot-hills, that the action really began. At this time it was still supposed that the battalions, batteries, and sections of horsemen visible were a rear-guard, covering what is now called the " entrainment " of troops at Forbach; for the greater part of Laveau-coupet's soldiers were below the crests, and in the forest-land, while Jolivet's brigade made no great show in and about the village of Stiring. Kameke's young soldiers went eagerly and joyously into their first battle. They consisted of six battalions, led by General von François, and were soon extended from the Metz road on the German right, to the wooded ascents east of the Red Hill, which, in reality, became the main object of attack. The plan followed was the favourite tactical movement, so often practised with success—a direct onset on the enemy's front, and an advance on both flanks. These operations were supported by the fire of three batteries, which soon obliged the French gunners on the Red Spur to recede. An extraordinary and almost indescribable infantry combat now began over a wide space, sustained by the battalions of the fourteenth division fighting by companies. On one side they endeavoured to approach Stiring; in the centre they were a long time huddled together under the craigs of the Rotheberg; further to the left they dashed into the Giffert Wald, and emerged into comparatively open ground, only to find themselves shattered by a heavy fire, and obliged to seek cover. For the battalions engaged soon discovered that, instead of a rear-guard, they had to encounter half a *corps d'armée;* and, although reinforcements were rapidly approaching, yet, as the afternoon wore on, it became evident that the assailants could only maintain their footing by displaying great obstinacy, and enduring bitter losses. After two hours' hard fighting five fresh battalions, belonging to von Woyna's brigade of Kameke's division came into action on the right, and sought to operate on the French left flank, some following the railway, others pressing into the thick woods on the west. The density of the copses threw the lines into confusion, so that the companies were blended, and, as guidance was almost impossible, trust had to be reposed in the soldierly instincts and training alike of officers and men, and on the genuine comradeship so conspicuous throughout all ranks of the Prussian Army. Practically, at this moment, the French, although beset on all sides by their enterprising foes, had a distinct advantage, for they smote the venturesome columns as they emerged here and there, and it may be said that, between three and four o'clock, the German artillery on the Galgenberg and Folster Hohë, held the French in check, and averted an irresistible offensive movement. Yet the German infantry were tenacious ; when pressed back they collected afresh in groups, and went on again; and General Frossard was so impressed by the audacity of his foes, that he brought up Bataille's division from Œtingen, and directed Valazé to quit the hill above Forbach, and reinforce the defenders of Stiring. Indeed, threatened on both flanks, the whole of the 2nd Corps was gradually drawn into the fray, and its commander, though somewhat late, appealed for aid to Marshal Bazaine, who himself did not feel secure at St. Avold.

THE RED HILL STORMED.

Shortly after three o'clock, General von François, obeying the orders of his chief, von Kameke, resolved to storm the Red Hill. The German leader was under the impression that the French were yielding on all sides, which was not strictly correct, for the fresh troops were just coming into action, and the Germans were superior, alone, in the range and accuracy of their superb artillery. The gallant François, sword in hand, leading the Fusilier battalion of the 74th Regiment, climbed the steep, springing from ledge to ledge, and dashed over the crest, and drove the surprised French chasseurs out of the foremost entrenchment, and fastened themselves firmly on the hill. The chasseurs, who had retired into a second line of defences, poured in a murderous fire; General von François, heading a fresh onset, fell pierced by five bullets, yet lived long enough to feel that his Fusiliers and a company of the 39th, which had clambered up on the left, had gained a foothold they were certain to maintain. There were many brilliant acts of heroism on that day, but the storming of the Red Hill stands out as the finest example of soldiership and daring. Nor less so the stubbornness with which the stormers stood fast; especially as the French, at that moment, had thrown a body of troops against the German left, so strong and aggressive, that the valiant companies in the Giffert Wald were swept clean out of the wood.

Fortunately, at the same time, the advanced guards of the Fifth and Sixteenth Divisions, already referred to, had crossed the Saar. General von Goeben, who had also arrived, took command, and formed a strong resolution. He decided that, as the battle had reached a critical stage, it would be unwise to keep reserves; so he flung everything to hand into the fight, on the ground that the essential thing was to impart new life to a combat which had become indecisive, if not adverse to the assailant. Accordingly, the artillery was brought up to a strength of six batteries, and one part of the fresh troops was sent to reinforce the left, and another towards the Red Hill. Shortly afterwards, von Goeben had to relinquish the command to his senior, von

Zastrow, the commander of the Seventh Corps; but the chief business of the principal leaders consisted in pushing up reinforcements as they arrived; the forward fighting being directed by the Generals and Colonels in actual contact with the enemy.

PROGRESS OF THE ACTION.

For two hours, that is, between four and six o'clock, the front of battle swagged to and fro, for the French fought valiantly, and, by repeated forward rushes, compelled their pertinacious assailants to give, or repelled their energetic attempts to gain, ground. A German company would dash out from cover, and thrust the defenders to the rear; then, smitten in front and flank, it would recede, followed by the French, who, taken in flank by the opportune advent of a hostile group, would retreat to the woods, or the friendly shelter of a depression in the soil. Nevertheless, in the centre, and on their own left, the Germans made some progress. A battalion of the Fifth Division mastered the defence in the Paffen Wald on the French right; a group of companies crowned the highest point in the Giffert Wald; and the new arrivals, drawn alike from the Eighth and the Third Corps, pushed up the ravine on the East, and the slopes on the West of the Red Hill, until their combined fire and frequent rushes forced the French out of their second line of entrenchments on the neck of high land which connected the Red Hill with the heights of Spicheren. The French strove fiercely, again and again, to recover the vantage ground, yet could not prevail; but their comrades below, in the south-west corner of the Giffert Wald, stoutly held on, so that the fight in this quarter became stationary, as neither side could make any progress.

On the German right, during the same interval of

time, there had been sharper alternations of fortune. Here the French held strong positions, not only in the village of Stiring-Wendel, but on the hill-sides above it, and especially on the tongue of upland called the Forbacher Berg. The assailant had succeeded in taking and keeping the farmsteads on the railway, the "Breme d'or" and the "Baraque Mouton;" but the efforts of General von Woyna to operate on the French left had been so roughly encountered that he drew back his troops to a point far down the valley. In fact, General Frossard had strengthened Vergé, who held fast to Stiring, by Valazé's brigade, and General Bataille had also sent half his division to support his comrade. The consequence was that the German projects were frustrated; while, on the other hand, their heavy batteries on the Folster Hohë had such an ascendency that the French could not secure any advantage by moving down the vale.

Yet they were not, as yet, worsted in the combat at any point, save on the salient of the Red Hill. Upon that eminence the German commanders now determined to send both cavalry and guns. The horsemen, however, could gain no footing, either by riding up the hill-sides, or following the zigzags of the Spicheren road, which ascends the eastern face of the promontory. The artillery had better fortune. First one gun, and then another, was welcomed by the shouts of the much-tried and steadfast defenders; eight pieces first succeeded in overcoming all obstacles; finally, four other guns, completing the two batteries, came into action, and their fire was efficacious in restraining the ardour of the French, and rendering the position absolutely secure from assault. But they suffered great losses, which were inflicted not only by the powerful batteries on the opposite height, but by the Chassepot fire from the front and the Giffert Wald. The German commanders had discovered by a harsh experience that the battle could not be won either by an offensive movement from the centre, or flanking operations on the left, because the neck of highland south of the Red Hill was too strongly held, while the deep valley interposed between the forests and the Spicheren Downs brought the flanking battalions to a halt, under cover. It was then determined to employ the latest arrivals, the troops of the Fifth Division, in an effort to storm the Forbacher Berg from the Metz road valley, and at the same time to renew a front and flank attack upon Stiring-Wendel.

Here we may note two facts which are apt illustrations of that efficiency, the fruit of wise forethought, which prevailed in the German host. One is that a battery, attached to the First Corps, arrived on the Saar, by railway, direct from Königsberg, on the confines of East Prussia, and, driving up, actually went into position, and opened fire from the Folster Hohë. It was the first light battery commanded by Captain Schmidt, whose exploit was, then, at least, without parallel. The other is that the 2nd battalion of the 53rd Regiment, starting at six in the morning from Wadern, actually marched, part of the time as artillery escort, nearly twenty-eight miles in thirteen hours, and, towards sunset, stood in array on the field of battle. The like goodwill and energy were displayed by all the troops; but this example of zeal and endurance deserves special record.

FROSSARD RETIRES.

The final and decisive encounters on this sanguinary field were delivered on the western fronts. Four battalions were directed along or near the Metz road upon the heights above Stiring, while the troops on the extreme German right, which, it will be remembered, had suffered a reverse, resumed their march upon the village. These simultaneous onsets were all the more effective, because the French commander was alarmed by the advance guard of the Thirteenth Division, which, having moved up from Rosseln, was now near to Forbach itself. He had become apprehensive of being turned on both flanks, for Laveaucoupet was, at that moment, engaged in a desperate, although a partially successful strife against the Germans in the Giffert Wald. The flank attack on the Forbacher Berg, skilfully conducted, drove back the adversary, yet could not be carried far, because he was still strong and it was growing dusk. In like manner, Stiring itself was only captured in part. On the other hand, so vehement a rush was made upon the Giffert Wald that the French once more penetrated its coverts. Practically, however, the battle had been decided. General Frossard, receiving no support from Bazaine's divisions, greatly disturbed by the news that the head of a hostile column was close to Forbach, unable to oust the Germans from the Red Hill or effectively repel their onsets on the Metz road had, half an hour before a footing on the Forbacher Berg was won, given orders for a retreat upon Sarreguemines, so that the furious outburst of French valour in the Giffert Wald was only the expiring flash of a finely-sustained engagement, and the forerunner of a retrograde night march.

Indeed, General Frossard is entitled to any credit which may accrue from the stoutness with which he held his main position until nightfall. He himself assigns the march of von Golz from Rosseln upon Forbach as the reason for his retreat. Having been obliged to leave the heights north-west of Forbach practically undefended, in order to support Vergé in Stiring-Wendel, he lost, or thought he had lost, control over the high road and railway to Metz, and felt bound to retire eccentrically upon Sarreguemines, a movement which it is not easy to comprehend. It is true that the guns of von Golz, firing from the hills above Forbach, drove back a train bringing reinforcements from St. Avold, but a couple of miles to the rear was Metman's entire division; and it was from and not towards this succour that the main body of the French took their way. The most astonishing fact connected with this battle is that during the whole day three of Bazaine's divisions were each within about nine miles of the battlefield. It was not the Marshal's fault that not one assisted the commander of the 2nd Corps. Each had been directed to do so, but none succeeded. General Montaudon did, indeed, move out from Sarreguemines, but halted after covering a few miles. General de Castagny, as soon as he heard the guns, and without waiting for orders, marched his division from Puttelange; but, unluckily for him, the sound led him into the hills, where the dense woods and vales obstructed the passage of the sound. Hearing nothing he returned to Puttelange, but no sooner had he got there than the roar of artillery, more intense than ever, smote his ear. The ready veteran at once set out afresh, this time following the route which would have brought him into the heart of the Spicheren position. He was too late; night came on apace, the distant tumult died down, he endeavoured to communicate with Frossard, but his messenger only found Metman, who, coming on from Marienthal, had halted at Bening, and did not move upon Forbach until nearly dark. Thus were three strong divisions wasted, and a force which would have given the French victory, spent the day in wandering to and fro or in weak hesitation. General de Castagny was the only officer who really did his utmost to support the 2nd Corps; for Metman awaited orders, and they came too late. During the night, or early in the morning, they all, except de Castagny, who was called up to St. Avold, assembled near Puttelange, wearied and disgusted with their fruitless exertions; and there they were joined by the 2nd Corps.

The Germans bivouacked on the field. They had had in action twenty-seven battalions and ten batteries, and the day's irregular and confused fighting had cost them in killed and wounded a loss of no fewer than 223 officers and 4,648 men; while the French lost 249 officers and 3,829 men, including more than two thousand prisoners. The great disproportion is due to the fact that the Germans were the assailants and that throughout the day and on all points they fought the battle with relatively small groups, parts of the Seventh, Eighth, and Third Corps, which arrived in succession on the scene. That the victory was not more complete must be ascribed to the improvised character of the conflict. Both Woerth and Spicheren were accidental combats due to the initiative of subordinate officers, a practice which has its dangers; but the success attained in each case is a striking proof that the discipline and training of all ranks in the German Army had created a living organism which could be trusted to work by itself.

CHAPTER VI.

VACILLATION IN METZ.

Two such staggering and unexpected blows filled the civil population with terror, the aspiring soldiers at head-quarters with anger, and the Imperial Commander-in-Chief with dismay. Disorder, consternation, and amazement reigned in Metz. And no wonder. From Alsace came the appalling news that the 1st Corps had been hopelessly shattered and that the Marshal was already fleeing for safety, by day and night, through the passes of the Vosges. Strasburg reported the arrival of fugitives and the absence of a garrison. "We have scarcely any troops," wrote the Prefect; "at most from fifteen hundred to two thousand men." The chief official at Epinal asked for power to organize the defence of the Vosges at the moment when the passes were thronged with MacMahon's hurrying troops. It was known that General Frossard had been defeated and that he was in full retreat, but during twenty-four hours no direct intelligence came to hand from him. That de Failly, left unsupported at Bitsche, would retire at once was assumed, but the orders directing his movements did not reach him until, after a severe night march, he had halted a moment at Lutzelstein, or, as the French call the fort, La Petite Pierre. From Verdun and Thionville arrived vehement demands for arms and provisions; and from the front towards the Saar no report that was not alarming. Turning to the south-east, the Imperial head-quarters did not know exactly where Douay's 7th Corps was; and in an agony of apprehension ordered the General, if he could, to throw a division into Strasburg, and "with the two others" cover Belfort. When the telegram was sent one of these had been heavily engaged at Woerth, and the other was at Lyons not yet formed! The anxiety of the Emperor and his assistants was embittered by the knowledge that not one strong place on the Rhine had a sufficient garrison; and that the rout of MacMahon had not only flung wide open the portals of Lorraine, but had made the reduction of ill-provided Strasburg a question of weeks or days. So heedlessly had the Ollivier Ministry, the Emperor and Empress rushed into war, at a time when even the fortifications of Metz were glaringly incomplete, when the storehouses of the frontier fortresses were ill-supplied, when arms and uniforms were not or could not be furnished to the Mobiles; when, in short, nothing could be put between the Germans and Paris except the troops hastily collected in Alsace and Lorraine—now a host in part shattered, in part disordered, and the whole without resolute and clearsighted direction.

Prince Louis Napoleon, sitting passively on his horse in the barrack-yard of Strasburg, in 1836, was defined by a caustic historian as a "literary man" whose characteristic was a "faltering boldness." The phrases apply to the Emperor in Metz. It may be said that he could use the language employed by soldiers, that he had some military judgment, but that, when called on, he could not deal at all with the things which are the essence of the profession he loved to adopt. After a lapse of more than thirty years, he found himself, not alone in a barrack-yard facing an "indignant Colonel," but at the head of a great, yet scattered and roughly handled Army, with formidable enemies pressing upon his front, and equally formidable enemies pouring through the rugged hill paths upon his vulnerable flank, and threatening the sole railway which led direct through Chalons to Paris. He was now a man, old for his years, and a painful disease made a seat on horseback almost intolerable. He could not, like his uncle in his prime, ride sixty miles a day, sleep an hour or two, and mount again if needful. He was an invalid and a dreamer, who had, against his fluctuating will, undertaken a task much too vast for his powers. The contemptuous words applied to him by Mr. Kinglake seem harsh, still, in very truth, they exactly describe Louis Napoleon as he was at Strasburg in 1836, and as he sat meditatively at Metz in 1870. Yet, be it understood, he never at any period of his career, was wanting in coolness and physical courage, though what Napier has finely called "springing valour" had no place in his temperament. He was scared by the suddenness of the shock and the rapidity of events, and he was bewildered because he was incapable of grasping, co-ordinating, or understanding the thick-coming realities presented by war on a grand scale; and stood always too much in awe of the unknown. He could not "make up his mind," and in the higher ranks of the French Army there was not one man who could force him to make it up and stand fast by his resolution. But, inferior as they were when measured by a high standard, it is probable that any one of the Corps Commanders, clothed with Imperial power, would have conducted the campaign far better than the Emperor. Another disadvantage which beset

him was a moral consequence inseparable from his
adventurous career. He could not add a cubit to his
military stature; but he need not have "waded
through slaughter to a throne." In Paris before he
started for the frontier, in Metz on the morning of
August 7th, he must have felt, as the Empress also felt,
that his was a dynasty which could not stand before
the shock of defeat in battle. He had, therefore, to
consider every hour, not so much what was the best
course of action from the soldier's standpoint, as how
any course, advance, retreat or inaction, would affect
the political situation in Paris. Count von Bismarck's
haughty message through M. Benedetti in 1866, if
Benedetti faithfully delivered it, must have come back
to the Emperor's memory in 1870. Remind the
Emperor, said Bismarck, that a war might bring on a
revolutionary crisis; and add, that "in such a case,
the German dynasties are likely to prove more solid
than that of the Emperor Napoleon." It was a consciousness of the weak foundations of his power, breed-
ing an ever-present dread alike in the capital and the
camp, which, making him ponder when he should act,
falter when he should be bold, imparted to his resolutions the instability of the wind.

It is on record that the first impulse of the Emperor
and his intimate advisers was to retreat forthwith over
the Moselle and the Meuse. General de Ladmirault
was ordered to fall back on Metz; the Guard had to
take the same direction; Bazaine, who had responsibility without power, was requested to protect the
retirement of Frossard, who, driven off the direct, was
marching along the more easterly road to Metz,
through Gros Tenquin and Faulquemont, which the
Germans call Falconberg; de Failly was required, if he
could, to move on Nancy. MacMahon, it was hoped,

would gather up his fragments, and transport them to Chalons, where Canrobert was to stand fast, and draw back to that place one of his divisions which had reached Nancy. Paris was placarded with the Emperor's famous despatch; and the Parisians read aloud the ominous sentences which heralded the fall of an Empire. " Marshal MacMahon," said the Emperor, " has lost a battle on the Sauer. General Frossard has been obliged to retire. The retreat is conducted in good order." And then followed the tell-tale phrase, used by Napoleon I. himself on a similar occasion— " *Tout peut se rétablir,*" all, perhaps, may come right again. But so inconstant was the Imperial will, that the hasty resolve to fly into Champagne faded out almost as soon as it was formed; for the next day the dominant opinion was that it would be better to remain on the right bank of the Moselle. MacMahon and de Failly accordingly got counter orders, indicating Nancy as a point of concentration, and based on a feeble notion that they could both be drawn to Metz; while once again Canrobert was told to bring the infantry of the 6th Corps up to the same place by rail. Orders and counter orders then showered down on de Failly—thus, he was and he was not to move on Toul—but the enemy's movements dictated the future course of a General rendered as powerless as his superiors were vacillating; and finally both the Marshal and his luckless subordinate, as well as Douay's 7th Corps, made their way deviously to the camp of Chalons.

THE EMPEROR RESIGNS HIS COMMAND.

When the Emperor suddenly revoked the order to retire upon Chalons, he was influenced partly by military, but chiefly by political considerations. Remonstrances were heard in the camps, remonstrances arrived

from Paris, and the combined effect of these open
manifestations produced an order to establish the Army
in position behind the French Nied, a stream which,
rising to the southward, flows parallel to the Moselle,
and, after receiving the German Nied, runs into the
Saar below Saarlouis.   The weather had been wet and
tempestuous; the retiring troops, exhausted by night
marches and want of food, struggled onward, yet showed
signs of " demoralization;" in other words, were out of
heart, and insubordinate.   Frossard's men, who had
passed the prescribed line before receiving the new
instructions, had to retrace their steps ; and Decaen,
now in command of the 3rd Corps, begged for rest on
behalf of his divisions.   Yet the three Corps and the
Guard occupied, on the 10th, the new position which,
selected by Marshal Lebœuf, extended from Pange to
Les Etangs.   It was intended to fight a battle on that
ground, and the men were set to work on entrenchments, some of which were completed before another
change occurred in the directing mind.   The position
was found to be defective; and, on the 11th, the entire
Army, abandoning its wasted labours, moved back upon
the outworks of Metz itself, almost within range of its
guns.   Thus had three precious days been spent in
wandering to and fro at a time when the military
situation required that the Army should be transferred
to the left bank of the Moselle, and placed in full command of the route to Chalons, even if it were not compelled to fall back further than the left bank of the
Meuse.   One explanation, drawn by the official writers
of the German Staff history, from French admissions, is
that, instead of Metz protecting the Army, the Army
was required to protect Metz, seeing that the forts were
not in a state to hold out against a siege of fifteen days!
The Imperial Commander had not even yet quite made

up his mind; but, late on the 12th, finding the burden too severe, and the clamour of public opinion too great, he appointed Marshal Bazaine Commander-in-Chief of "the Army of the Rhine." It was a *damnosa hœreditas;* for the campaign was virtually lost during ten days of weakness and vacillation, and especially by the want of a prompt decision between the 7th and the 10th of August, while there was yet time.

As we have said, the main reason was political. The eager aspirants for power, and the friends of the Empress in Paris, ousted the Ollivier Ministry on the 9th, and the new combination, with the Comte de Palikao at its head, felt that they could not retain office, that the "dynasty" even could not survive unless the Emperor and the Army fought and won. Everything must be risked to give the dynasty a chance. The Regency and the Camp fell under the influence of hostile public opinion, which had already begun to associate the name of Napoleon, not only with the reverses endured, but the utter want of preparation for war, now painfully evident to the multitude as well as to the initiated. Yet so menacing and terrible did the actual facts become that even the Emperor could not resist them, and, in handing over the command to Bazaine on the 13th, he ordered that unfortunate, if ambitious, officer to transfer the Army with the utmost speed to the left bank of the Moselle, place Laveaucoupet's Division in Metz, and gain Verdun as quickly as possible. It was too late, as we shall see; for the Prussians were ready to grasp at the skirts of a retreating Army, and once more thwart the plans of its leaders. In order to track the course of events to this point, the narrative must revert to the morrow of Spicheren.

THE GERMAN ADVANCE.

On the morning of the 7th of August, some French troops were still in Forbach, and Montaudon's Division had not departed from Sarreguemines. The fronts of the two invading armies were hardly over the frontier, and the chiefs had not yet learned the full extent of the double shock inflicted on the adversary. A thick fog enveloped the Spicheren battlefield, and clung to the adjacent hills and woods, and through the mist the patrols had to feel their way. No serious resistance could be offered by the French detachments at any point; Forbach, together with its immense stores, was occupied at an early hour; while, so soon as the vigilant cavalry saw the rear-guard of Montaudon quit the place, they rode into Sarreguemines. Patrols were pushed out along the roads towards Metz, but no advance was made, partly because the respective Corps composing both the German Armies were still on the march, and partly because the Staff, mistaken respecting the route followed by MacMahon, had ordered several movements with the object of intercepting and destroying his broken divisions. The consequence was that the leading columns stood fast while the Corps to the rear and left were brought up to and beyond the Saar. MacMahon and de Failly, as we have seen, were hurrying southward, and thus von Moltke's precautions proved needless. During the 8th, the cavalry, despatched far and wide, between St. Avold and the Upper Saar, found foes near the former, who at once retired, but none on the course of the river. The next day, the horsemen, still more active, sent in reports which satisfied the cautious Chief of the Staff that the French had really fallen back on Metz, yet inspired him with some doubts respecting their intentions. He thought it possible that they might assume the offen-

sive in the hope of surprising and routing part of the
German Armies—a project actually discussed by the
Emperor and Bazaine, but soon thrown aside. Von
Moltke, however, determined to guard against that
design, kept his several Corps within supporting distance; and, on the 10th, began a great movement forward. The First Army, in the post of danger, was to
serve as the pivot upon which the Second, effecting a
wheel to the right, swung inwards towards the Moselle
above Metz. Von Steinmetz, much to his disgust, had
to halt about Carling, with his supports towards
Teterchen and Boulay, and the Ninth Corps in support at
Forbach. On his left, the Second Army was advancing
in echelon on roads between Harskirchen, near Saar
Union, where the Fourth Corps touched the outposts of
the Crown Prince's Army, and Faulquemont, where the
Third Corps stood on the railway, having on its left the
Tenth about Hellimer, and the Guard at Gueblange.
The Twelfth was still on the Saar, and the Second, awaiting its last battalions, in Rhenish Prussia. Thus the two
Armies stood on the 11th, covered by brigades of
cavalry, whose operations, better than anything else,
illustrate the audacious, yet elastic and painstaking,
methods employed by the Germans in war.

THE GERMAN CAVALRY AT WORK.

Never before had the principle that cavalry are the
eyes and the ears of an army been more extensively
applied. We have already seen these well-trained horsemen watching the line of the Saar, and even looking into
the rear of the French camps; we shall now see them
literally infesting the country between the Saar and
the Moselle without let or hindrance from the French
cavaliers. After Spicheren, the German cavalry divisions were distributed along the front of the Corps in

motion; and the hardy reiters were soon many miles
ahead of the infantry, some penetrating up the easy
western slopes of the Vosges, where they found no
enemies, others riding towards Nancy and the points
of passage over the river below that town; and others
again hovering pertinaciously on the rear of the backward moving French Corps, picking up stragglers,
capturing prisoners, interrogating officials, and inspect-
ing, from coigns of vantage, the camps and positions of
the enemy.   In this way they learned that the Emperor
had visited Bazaine at Faulquemont; that the greater
part of the French were Metzward, and that on the
left towards the hills there were none to be seen.   The
cavalry divisions rode out long distances, detaching
flanking parties and pushing patrols to the front, so
that the whole range of country between the right and
left of the Infantry Corps was thoroughly searched
by these indefatigable and daring explorers.   Thus, a
troop of Uhlans, starting from Faulquemont, rode as
far as the woods near Berlize, and keeping well under
cover, yet quite close to the enemy, took note of his
positions at and beyond Pange, saw large bodies
moving from Metz to take ground behind the Nied, and
learned that reinforcements, the leading brigades of
the Canrobert's Corps, in fact, had arrived at Metz.
Another patrol of Lancers, moving on the St. Avold
road, confirmed the report that the French had occupied the Nied line; while, on the opposite flank, a
Hussar patrol found no enemy about Chateau Salins,
but laid hands on the bearer of important despatches.
On the 11th, the screen of inquisitive horsemen became
thicker and more venturesome, trotting up to the river
Seille itself at Nomény, on the road to Pont à Mousson.
The mounted men of the First Army had hitherto been
held back, but now the two divisions, passing forth on

the flanks, approached and examined the left of the
French line.   One troop arrived near Les Etangs just
in time to see de Ladmirault's Corps folding up their
tents, and soon beheld the French march off towards
Metz; indeed the deep columns were moving in that
direction from the left bank of the Nied.   The Uhlans
followed de Ladmirault through Les Etangs until
they saw him go into position at Bellecroix close to the
place. In like manner, other Uhlans, operating further
up the stream, found the camps and entrenchments
abandoned, so that it became certain, on the evening of
the 11th, that the French Army had been drawn back
under the guns of Metz.   The next day the activity of
the cavaliers increased, and they pressed forward until
they were in contact with the French outposts, and
were able to observe the whole new position between
Queleu and Bellecroix, working up on the left to a
point within three miles of Metz, and proving that as
far as the right bank above the town, the country was
unoccupied.   On the 12th, Uhlans had ridden into
Nancy, on one side, and, on the other, a body of
Cuirassiers actually found the gates of Thionville open,
captured a *garde mobile* belonging to the garrison, and
brought off a Prussian reserve man who had been
detained in the town.   At Dieulouard a patrol crossed
the Moselle on a bridge just constructed by the French,
and were only driven from the railway, which they had
begun to destroy, by infantry—the last detachments of
Canrobert's Corps allowed to get through by train from
Chalons.   A daring attempt was made upon Pont à
Mousson by some Hussars; but here General Margueritte, sent with his Chasseurs d'Afrique from Metz,
drove back the invaders, killing a great number.   These
examples will suffice to give some idea of the admirable
use which the Germans made of their cavalry, to

conceal their movements, harass the enemy, and, above all, gain priceless information, while the adversary, whose horse were idle, could obtain none. The dash made by Margueritte to relieve Pont à Mousson is the one solitary instance of alertness shown by the French, and even he and his troopers were withdrawn, leaving the river line above Metz wholly unprotected, and the bridges unbroken!

THE GERMANS MARCH ON THE MOSELLE.

From these wide-ranging enterprises, conducted by keen and resolute soldiers, the Great Staff obtained nearly as minute a knowledge of the French proceedings as they possessed themselves, and were enabled to direct the march of the German Armies with firmness and precision. Their great object was to secure the unguarded line of the Moselle by seizing, as rapidly as possible, all the points of passage above Metz, and the only doubt entertained at head-quarters was suggested by the apprehension that the energy displayed by the cavalry might attract attention to these undefended spots. Accordingly, while the First Army, again, was ordered to protect the right of the Second, by advancing on the Nied, taking up ground between Pange and Les Etangs, the Second was to move upon the Seille, and endeavour to secure the bridges at Pont à Mousson, Dieulouard and other places, sending the cavalry once more in force over the stream. Von Moltke's calculation was that if the French attacked von Steinmetz, Prince Charles could form up and threaten their flank; if they tried to operate against the Second Army by ascending the Moselle, von Steinmetz could then assail them in line of march, as they must cross his front; while if passing through Metz they moved up the left bank, Prince Charles could effect a junction with the

Crown Prince, and von Steinmetz could cross the Moselle and attack the French rear. The combination was strong, but the Emperor, as we have stated, had then no idea of assuming the offensive in any direction, his only anxiety being to seek a temporary shelter behind the Meuse.

Throughout the 13th, the German Corps, horse and foot, sprang forward, displaying that alacrity and hardihood which had marked their conduct from the outset of the war. The Dragoon brigade of the Guard swooped down upon Dieulouard, and finally sundered the direct railway communication between Chalons and Metz. Two other cavalry brigades, forming the Fifth Division, entered Pont à Mousson early in the morning, and were followed by half the Tenth Corps from Delme. In order to hide, as far as possible, the movements of the Second Army, an entire division of cavalry, the Sixth, was employed; one brigade extending from Courcelles sur Nied, to Corny on the Moselle, and the other posted at Verny supported the front line, and linked itself by patrols to the Fifth at Pont à Mousson. The First Division of Cavalry, during the forenoon, crossed the Nied at Pange, and occupied the villages to the right and left, so that a continuous line of mounted men stretched from the Nied to the Moselle. Behind this barrier, the several Corps toiled forward in full security. At the close of the day, however, only one-half the Tenth Corps was over the Moselle, the other moiety being one march to the rear; the head of the Third Corps stood at Buchy; the Ninth at Herny; the Twelfth at Chemery; the Second, now complete, at St. Avold; the Guard at Lémoncourt, and the Fourth at Chateau Salins.

By this time, the Third Army, except the Sixth Corps, and the Baden Division which had been directed upon Strasburg, had made its way through the defiles of the Vosges, had emerged into the valley of the Upper Saar, and was, therefore, in direct communication with the Second Army; so that the German host occupied a wide region extending from Sarrebourg to villages in front of Metz; yet at the vital points the Corps stood near enough to support each other should it be necessary to assemble on a field of battle.   The passage of the Vosges had been obstructed only by nature and the forts of Bitsche and Phalsbourg.   These were turned, and the hardships of cross roads and restricted supplies had been overcome.   The divisions trickled through the valleys on a broad front, gathering up as they touched the Saar and the country of lakes about Fenestrange.   As Phalsbourg did not command the railway, that important highway fell into the hands of the Germans.   The tunnels in the Zorn valley west of Saverne had not been destroyed, and the whole line was complete, yet it could not be used for the transport of troops and stores until a later period.   On the 13th, when the First Army was closing in on the French outside Metz, and the Second heading for the Moselle, the Third quitted the Upper Saar, and, once more expanding, approached on a broad front the valley of the Meurthe.   During the next day, when their comrades were hotly engaged with the enemy, they reached the banks of that stream, and their forward cavalry rode into the streets of Lunéville and Nancy, the old capital of Lorraine.   At this critical moment, Marshal Mac-Mahon was hastening to Chalons; de Failly, after having been ordered hither and thither from hour to hour, had received final orders—he was to join the Marshal; but Douay's 7th Corps, although Dumont's Division had arrived, increasing the total to about 20,000 men and 90 guns, had not yet been, and was not for three days, directed from Belfort upon the great camp in the plans of Champagne.

CHAPTER VII.

VON MOLTKE KEEPS THE WHIP HAND.

WEARY of his task, weakened in body by a painful malady, depressed in mind by a series of disasters, and worried by advice from Paris, the Emperor Napoleon, on the evening of the 12th of August, transferred to Marshal Bazaine the burden which he could no longer bear. Whatever may have been his other aptitudes, he was not born to command Armies in the field; nor had he that power of selection which may enable an inferior to choose and clothe with his authority a superior man. Had a Radetzky, instead of an Emperor, commanded the Austrian Army in 1859 it is probable that the stability of the "dynasty" would have been tried by defeat and the unity of Italy deferred until a later day. Whether the Emperor Napoleon recognized his incompetence, or whether, as he often did, he yielded to pressure, matters little except to the students of character. He nominally gave up the command, yet retained a certain indefinite control, and he placed at the head of his Army a Marshal who, although the senior in rank to the recently promoted Marshall Lebœuf, the late chief of the Staff, was still the junior of Marshal Canrobert; both, fortunately, were loyal men and the latter ready to serve under his junior. Yet it is doubtful whether Bazaine ever exercised that moral ascendency which is essential at all times, and never more so than at a crisis when the fate of Armies depends not only on wise direction but prompt and willing obedience. The Marshal, appointed on the 12th, did not take up his command until the next day, and then he was required to remedy in less than twenty-four hours the deep-seated mischief produced by a fortnight of terrible blundering. His special task was to transport the Army over the Moselle. Four days earlier that might have been done without a shot being fired, because even if the German horse had come up to look on they must have been idle spectators as their infantry comrades were far in the rear. The fatal error was committed when the Emperor did not overrule all opposition, and, adhering with unswerving firmness to his first thought, neither halt, ponder, nor rest until the Moselle flowed between him and his foes. The military position on the morning of the 7th dictated that step; his adversaries believed or surmised that he would take it, because it was the right step to take. Nor can we doubt that, as Commander-in Chief, Louis Napoleon, who had a little of " le flair militaire," saw at once the proper course, but that, as Emperor, he dared not, on reflection, run the risk. It was a false calculation, even from a political standpoint, because, so long as he was in the field with, or at the head of an Army, his republican and monarchical enemies would not have moved, and time would have been gained. By retiring promptly over the Moselle, and leaving Metz to defend itself, he might have been defeated in battle or manœuvred back upon Paris; but there would have been no Sedan and no Metz, and even the Parisians would have hesitated to plunge headlong into civil war when a French Army was still afoot, and a formidable host of invaders, pressing on its weaker array, was

" trampling the sacred soil." The fate of the campaign
about Metz was, then, really decided when the Emperor
did not avail himself of the days of grace, beat down all
opposition, and compel his Marshals and Generals to
march their troops over the Moselle. Neither Bazaine
nor any one officer present with the Army is entitled
to be called a great captain; but whatever he was the
blame of failure does not rest on him alone; it must be
shared, in a far greater degree, by those who preceded
him in command. It is necessary to insist on this fact,
because one of the most valuable lessons taught by the
campaign would be lost were the capital error committed by the Imperial Staff, when the order for retreat
was countermanded and five days were wasted in abortive operations, not described with the emphasis it
deserves. Campaigns have been lost as much by postponed retreats as by rash advances; and it was the
ill-fortune of the French Generals in August, 1870, to
present egregious examples of both forms of fatal error.

THE FRENCH PROPOSE TO MOVE.

When Marshal Bazaine took over the command, on
the morning of the 13th, he was required to do in haste
what his superiors might have done at leisure. The
prolonged indecision of the Imperial mind, held in suspense down to the last moment and against its better
judgment, between the alternative of attack or retreat,
was disastrous; no margin was allowed for error of
design, error in execution, and—the unforeseen. The
Emperor had ordered Coffinières, the Governor of Metz,
to build as many bridges as he could above and below
the place, and the General declares, what no one
disputes, that he did construct from twelve to fifteen
bridges, which provided seven lines of march over the
stream. He also mined the permanent bridges above

the fortress, so that on the 12th facilities for crossing
abounded, and the means of destruction were prepared.
Then came in the unforeseen. Rain had fallen heavily,
and consequently the Moselle rose, flowed over the
tressle bridges, damaged the rafts, disconnected the
pontoons with the banks, and spread far and wide over
the approaches. In short, the increase in the volume
of water was so great and unusual, if not unparalleled,
that the calamity was attributed to the Germans—they
must, it was said, have destroyed the sluices near
Marsal and have allowed the lake water of that region
free access to the Moselle—as if they did not wish to
cross the river themselves! Be the cause what it might,
there was the obstruction; so that the first information
received by the Marshal was that the retreat, which he
had been ordered to execute, could not begin until the
next day, except by Canrobert's 6th Corps, which was
near permanent bridges. Consequently, the Army
remained another day on the right bank. The Corps
were in position between forts Queleu and St. Julien,
Frossard on the right, Decaen in the centre, and
de Ladmirault on the left, the Guard being in rear of
the centre behind Borny, where Marshal Bazaine had
set up his head-quarters. Practically the line was a
curve extending from the Seille to the banks of the
Moselle below Metz; and the defensive obstacles were
a watercourse with steep banks, patches of dense woods,
two châteaus, or country houses, which were readily
made defensible, and of course the villages and farms
scattered over the pleasant fields. The main body of
the Army was covered throughout its front by outposts
thrown forwards towards the Metz-Saarbrück railway
on the right, beyond the brook in the centre, and about
Vremy, Nouilly, and Servigny on the left. So they
stood all day, some of them aware that the Germans

were dangerously near; more who were anxious to get over the river; and yet others who would have staked everything upon the risk of a battle, so intolerable is suspense to men of ardent and exciteable temperaments. The night passed over quickly, and on the 14th, yet not until a late hour in the forenoon, the Corps began to file off to the rear. Canrobert was already across; Frossard sent his guns and horsemen over the town bridges, while his infantry splashed through the meadows and over the partially submerged temporary constructions; and leaving Grenier's division to cover his retreat, de Ladmirault set out for the left bank over the Isle Chambière. The Marshal at Borny, with his old Corps, now under Decaen, and having the Guard in support, remained to protect the extensive and perilous movement to the rear in the face of a watchful and intrepid enemy.

Released on the evening of the 12th from the imperative orders which held him fast, and directed to move forward upon the French Nied, General von Steinmetz advanced the next day with characteristic alacrity. Two Corps, the Seventh and the First, were posted on a short line between Pange and Les Etangs, the Eighth being held back at Varize on the German Nied, and the two cavalry divisions being thrown round the flanks General von Golz, who commanded the twenty-sixth brigade, took the bold step of transferring it to the left, or French, bank of the stream, and he thus came into contact with the outposts of Decaen's 3rd Corps. Nevertheless, along the whole line, on the evening of the 13th and morning of the 14th, each side maintained a strictly observant attitude, and held aloof from hostile action; the French because they wished to glide off unassailed, the Germans because their Commander-in-Chief desired to secure a solid footing for the

Second Army on the left bank of the Moselle before the French retired. Watched as these were by keen-sighted horsemen, they could not stir without being seen; and so soon as the state of the Moselle permitted a movement to the rear, the fact was reported to the German chiefs. A Hussar party notified, about eleven, that Frossard's outposts were falling back; a little later that the tents were down; and then that columns of all arms were retiring. So it was in the centre and on the left; Decaen's Corps remained, but two divisions of de Ladmirault's Corps, it was noted, were no longer on the ground they had held in the morning. General von Manteuffel, inferring that de Ladmirault might have gone to join in an attack upon the Seventh Corps, at once put two divisions under arms, a fortunate precaution, though suggested by an erroneous inference. In front of the Seventh Corps, the facts admitted of no misinter-pretation. The enemy was plainly in retreat, and General von Golz felt that it was his duty to inter-rupt the process. Therefore, about half-past three, notifying his intention to the Divisional Commanders of his Corps, and requesting support from the First, a request promptly granted, von Golz sprang forward to attack the French, in full reliance upon the readiness and energy with which his superiors and comrades would follow him into the fray. His bold resolve did stop the retreat, and his onset brought on, late in the afternoon,

THE BATTLE OF COLOMBEY-NOUILLY.

The scene of this sharp but severe conflict was the gentle uplands immediately to the eastward of Metz, and a little more than cannon-shot beyond the forts which forbid access to that side of the place. The village of Borny, indeed, is nearly on a line with the Fort des Bordes, and no point of the area within which the action raged is more than three miles from the fortifications. The ground slopes upward from the Moselle, rising into undulating hills, the summits of which are two or three hundred feet above the bed of the stream. Near to Metz these elevations are clothed with copses devoid of underwood, the great patches of verdure extending on a curve from Grimont close to the Moselle, as far as the right bank of the Seille. To the northward are more woods just outside the battle-field, the area of which was, from north to south, included between them and the railway to Saarbrück. A little to the north of this line, near Ars-Laquenexy, a village on the road from Sarreguemines, were the sources of a rivulet which flowed northward along the whole front of the French position, receiving on its way brooks which trickle down the hollows in the hills to the eastward. The heights east of the stream were bare of wood, and the most prominent objects were the village and church tower of St. Barbe on the crown of a rounded hill to the north-east. From this elevated hamlet another brook rose, and found its way along the bed of a gully to Lauvalliers, where all the water-courses united, and, under the name of la Vallières, ran thence to the Moselle. The French troops, four divi-sions of Decaen's Corps, were posted in the woods, and on the heights above the first-mentioned rivulet from the neighbourhood of Ars-Laquenexy to the point where all the streamlets joined. The outposts were in Mercy le Haut, sometimes called Mercy les Metz, in the woods facing Ars-Laquenexy, in the Chateau D'Aubigny and Montoy, beyond the brook, in Colombey, a village on the south bank, and in Nouilly, a large village in the St. Barbe ravine. Beyond the confluence of the hill streams stood a division of de Ladmirault's Corps upon the high ground east of Mey, and it was this body

which had its outguards in Nouilly. Although it was
divided by the brook Vallières on the left, the French
position was strong, chiefly because the approaches were
through defiles, over open ground, or up steep banks,
but also because the woods afforded shelter to the
infantry of the defenders. Three great roads intersected
the field—one from Pange, through Colombey, to
Borny, a second from Saarbrück, which, after passing La
Planchette, ran, at Bellecroix, into the third, which
came from Saarlouis, and passed through Lauvalliers,
entering Metz near the fort called les Bordes. The
Germans, early in the morning, were on the hills to the
eastward, the First Corps being beyond St. Barbe, and
the Seventh near, and west of, Pange, with outposts well
forward, and both cavalry and infantry in practical contact with the enemy, into whose position they looked
from all sides.

VON GOLZ DASHES IN.

It was the spectacle of a departing and decreasing
host which made the eager von Golz, without awaiting
permission, dash impetuously forward with his brigade.
So energetic was the onset that the French were at
once driven out of the Chateau d'Aubigny, Montoy,
and La Planchette. The usual tactics were applied,
the companies working together, turning a flank where
the front was too strong, and following up a success
until the weight of fire brought them to a halt, or even
thrust them back. The batteries attached to the
brigade came at once into action and persisted, though
they were hard hit by the French. But the advance
of von Golz was not to be arrested, and the impetus
of his first movement forward carried part of the
brigade over the ravine and watercourse, and into the
village and enclosures of Colombey. That point, how-

ever, was the limit of his progress, for the French developed strong lines of skirmishers in the woods, and although they were unable to expel the audacious intruders, these were obliged to expend all their energy upon holding what they had won. On the right, that is to the north of Colombey, the assailants were brought to a stand on the eastern edge of the ravine, and at this early stage the farms, gardens and houses of Colombey formed a salient offensive angle exposed to the brunt of the French fire from the side of Borny.

At the first indication of a combat, General von Manteuffel, two of whose divisions were already under arms, sent their advance guards down the hills and through the hollow ways from St. Barbe; joined his line of battle on to the right of von Golz and fell smartly on the outpost of Grenier's division which de Ladmirault had left about Mey to cover his retrograde march upon the Moselle. The noise of combat, also, and the appeals sent in from the daring brigadier, put the rest of the Seventh Corps in motion, so that the fourteenth as well as the thirteenth division sprang to arms and approached the fight. General von Zastrow, however, did not quite approve of the temerity of his subordinate; but seeing that the Corps was committed to an engagement, he permitted General von Glümer to use the twenty-sixth brigade on the right and General von Woyna to employ the twenty-eighth on the left while he held the twenty-seventh in reserve. In like manner, the French turned fiercely on their adversaries. Canrobert and Frossard were over the Moselle, but Decaen's four divisions were speedily arrayed; the Guard behind them fell in and marched Brincourt's brigade towards the Seille to protect Montaudon's right; and de Ladmirault instantly counter-marched his two divisions, moving de Lorencez towards the north-east, hoping to turn the right of Manteuffel, and ordering de Cissey, who had partially crossed the Moselle, to rein- force Grenier at Mey. About five o'clock, then, in consequence of the hardihood of a brigadier, a furious action raged along the whole French front, towards which comrades were hurriedly retracing their steps, and upon which adversaries were hastening forward with equal ardour.

The rapid development of an attack, which had in it some elements of a surprise, alike unwelcome and un- expected, and the tenacity with which a few battalions clung steadfastly to the advantage gained, astonished but did not disconcert the French, who frankly answered the challenge of their foes. Nevertheless, the opening movements of the First Corps were as successful as those of von Golz. The artillery, always foremost in this campaign, going straight and swiftly to the front, soon had batteries in position, protected by cavalry, while behind them on the roads from Saarlouis and Saar- brück the infantry were quickly moving up. The leading battalions of the first division poured through and round Noisseville and Nouilly, pressing back the French skirmishers and, following them fast, actually stormed the barricaded village of Mey, directly under Grenier's main position in the wooded hill above. The second division directed upon Montoy, Lauvalliers and the mills at the confluence of the streams, fell on with alacrity; but the resistance was so keen that although they soon wrested the eastern, they suffered great loss and were once promptly repulsed by the defenders when attempting to master the western bank. Yet aided by the fire of batteries concentrated south of the St. Barbe ravine, these persistent troops ultimately crowned the ascent, and established the front of battle on the French side of the brook throughout its length. From one point, however, the French could not be dislodged. There was a cross road, leading from Colombey to Bellecroix. It was a hollow way, bordered by trees two or three deep, and having in front, by way of salient, a little fir wood. This position effectually frustrated every effort of the Germans either to debouch from Colombey or push forward towards Bellecroix. Naturally strong and valiantly held it was not carried until nearly seven o'clock, and then only by the repeated onsets of the twenty-fifth brigade which von Zastrow, about half-past five, had permitted to take a share in an engagement which he did not like, but which he was bound to sustain. Thus was von Golz succoured and partially relieved from the heavy pressure put on him; a pressure further mitigated by the advance of the twenty-eighth brigade, Seventh Corps, on his left, and the capture of the wood of Borny. Still further the left the eighteenth division of the Ninth Corps, which had marched up from Buchy on hearing the cannonade, and some cavalry appeared on the field towards dark and thus added to the disquietude of Montaudon on the French right who, however, held fast to his main position above Grigy.

The action on the French right and centre may fairly be regarded as an indecisive combat, although the front occupied in the morning had been driven inwards, and the daring assailant had won some ground. On the French left the combat had been equally fierce, but less favourable to the defenders. General de Ladmirault, indeed, when obliged to turn and succour his comrade and subordinate, Grenier, had at once resolved to assume the offensive. It was a timely determination, for Grenier's troops had been pushed back and shaken, and, if left without aid, they would have been driven under the guns of St. Julien. But the approach of de

Cissey, and the threatening direction imparted to de Lorencez, at once altered the aspect of affairs; for de Cissey struck in with vigour, and the German troops which had entered Mey retreated fast upon Nouilly; then General von Manteuffel, hastening the march of his brigades which were still on the way to the field, formed his line to the north-west, between Servigny, Nouilly, and the mills at the confluence of the brooks, with a reserve at Servigny. As the guns, like the troops, arrived successively, they were arrayed on the new line, and, before de Ladmirault could develop his flank attack effectively, the First Corps had ninety guns in positions between Lauvalliers and Poix, which enabled them to bar any infantry advance upon St. Barbe. The effect of this disposition was to frustrate the aggressive designs of de Ladmirault, but he is entitled to the credit of having saved his exposed division, and also of having made the only movement during the day which had the semblance of a real endeavour to strike for victory against a foe whose troops and artillery were plainly coming up in detachments along the whole line. Nor can it be denied that his vehement onset drove back the Germans, and recovered a large extent of ground up to the skirts of Nouilly and the water mills. Moreover, it gave great assistance to Aymard's Division of Decaen's Corps, and enabled it, at one moment, to scatter the companies operating in the angle formed by the streams, and drive them headlong over the ravine upon Lauvalliers. But the advent of German battalions, and the. action of the guns, finally restored the combat, and as the twilight deepened into darkness the German right once more gained the ascendency, and the French divisions retired to their bivouacs nearer to Metz.

Long after the sun had set, portions of the First Corps

still arrived on the scene ; but then the battle was
over.   General de Ladmirault, three years afterwards,
naturally proud of his conduct, insisted that the French
had won the day.   The German accounts, however,
place the fact beyond dispute, since they show that the
leading troops of the First Corps did reach Vautoux,
Mey, and Villers l'Orme, which proves that the
adversary must have retired towards Bellecroix and the
banks of the Moselle.   No doubt the Germans were
wisely drawn back, at a late hour, and on that ground
the French put in a claim to the victory.   For General
Steinmetz had ridden on to the field just as the contest
was coming to an end.   He was angry because a battle
had been fought, and apprehensive lest a counter-attack
in force should be made at dawn ; so he ordered the First
and Seventh Corps to retire upon the positions they occupied on the 13th.   Nevertheless, von Zastrow, who did
not receive the order, insisted that his Corps should
bivouac under arms on the battlefield, so that the
wounded might be collected, and the honour of the Army
vindicated.

THE END OF THE BATTLE.

In this action the French lost not quite four thousand, and the Germans nearly five thousand men; on
both sides more than two hundred officers had been
killed or wounded, General Decaen, commanding the
3rd Corps, mortally, while Bazaine and Castagny were
slightly hurt.   The French had actually on the field,
including the Guard in reserve, with one brigade in the
front line, three Corps d'Armée; for, though Lorencez
did not press far forward, still the whole force under de
Ladmirault was present, and in action.   The Germans
brought up successively two Corps and one division,
but a large portion of the First could not reach the scene

of actual fighting until dark. It is impossible to ascertain exactly, and difficult to estimate the numbers engaged; but one fact is manifest—that the German assailants were numerically inferior, especially during the first two hours; that the disproportion was only lessened between six and seven; and that, at no time, were the French fewer in number. Marshal Bazaine emphatically states, in his report to the Emperor, that he held his position without employing the Guard, which is true, but it is not less true that the whole front of his line was driven in; and that he stood at the close within the range of the heavy guns in the forts. The French fought well, but they fought a defensive battle, and that is why they exacted from the assailant a much heavier penalty than he inflicted on them. The retreat of the Imperialists was delayed; but in the Great Head-quarter Staff serious misgivings began to spring up, and a fear lest the habit of bringing on improvised battles might not become a real source of danger. An able and enterprising General in command of the French at Spicheren and Borny would have read a severe lesson to German advance-guards, and would have made them pay for their temerity.

Not until a late hour did the news of the battle reach the King, who had established his head-quarters at Herny, on the railway. Prince Frederick Charles, at Pont à Mousson, was only informed of the event the next morning. His Army, the Second, had been engaged in marching up to and towards the Moselle and at eventide the several Corps halted at these points. The Fourth Corps was over the Seille, and not far from Custines and Marbache, places just below the confluence of the Meurthe and Moselle; the Guard had one division a little lower down at Dieulouard; the Tenth Corps, entire, was at Pont à Mousson, with a brigade to the

M

westward; the Third, the Ninth, and the Twelfth, were
facing the Moselle between Pont à Mousson and the Left
of the First Army, prepared either to frustrate a French
advance up the right bank—a possible movement always
present to the mind of von Moltke—or cross the river.
The Second Corps had come up to Falquemont; and a
Reserve Landwher Division, under General Kummer,
was being organized at Sarrlouis.   To complete the
survey, it should be added that Gneisenau's Brigade,
sent to surprise Thionville, an enterprise which failed,
was returning to rejoin the First Army; and that on the
evening of the 14th, the foremost troops of the Crown
Prince's Army were some squadrons of cavalry in
Nancy, and an infantry brigade in Lunéville.

THE FRENCH RETREAT.

Throughout the night the wearied French divisions,
which had been either engaged in combat or standing
under arms, filed over the Moselle, and the Emperor
took up his quarters at Longeville, outside the town.
Marshal Bazaine's order, dated the 13th, directed the
whole Army on the road to Gravelotte, whence one portion was to continue by Mars la Tour, and the other
turn off to the right and march on Conflans.   The
rigorous construction of the Marshal's order yields that
interpretation, but he contended, at his trial, that he
merely indicated the general lines of retreat upon
Verdun, and that the Staff and Corps Commanders
should have used any and every road or track which
would have served the main purpose.   There are, or
at least were, in 1870, only two roads out of Metz
available for the march of heavy columns of troops of
all arms and large trains—the excellent highway to
Gravelotte, which is a long defile, and the road through
Woippy, turning the uplands on the north.   All the

intermediate lanes or cross-roads are rugged and narrow, and only one, that passing by Lessy, has or had any pretension to the character of an inferior village road. Guns and carts can move along and up them in Indian file, but not easily if numerous, and nowhere at a good pace. Thus, even, on the 14th, the Corps of Frossard and Canrobert, who both started late, found the Gravelotte road so encumbered by trains that they could only make their way slowly, and did not arrive at Rozérieulles until after dark. The Emperor was still at Longeville, anxiously awaiting the issue of the fight which revived all his apprehensions. Metz was excited and alarmed, and the streets were crowded during the afternoon and evening, with passing soldiers, guns, baggage waggons and provision carts. Night brought no rest, for the Guard and the 3rd Corps came hastily over the river, and were densely packed inside the town and outside the ramparts in the space between the walls and Mount St. Quentin; while General de Ladmirault was engaged until morning in passing his divisions across the Isle Chambière, and Metman had also strayed from Bellecroix to that side of the town.

Marshal Bazaine had quitted Borny at dusk. He rode through Metz " with difficulty," and made his way to the Imperial head-quarters. Here Napoleon, who was in bed, welcomed him with his usual kindness, and when the Marshal explained his fears lest the Germans should cut in on his line of retreat, and referring to his wound, begged to be superseded, the Emperor, he writes, " touching my bruised shoulder and the fractured epaulette, gracefully said, ' It will be nothing, an affair of a few days, and you have just broken the charm.' " Apparently, Napoleon still clung to the belief that the allies he had sought would come to his

aid. " I await an answer from the Emperor of Austria
and the King of Italy," he said; "compromise nothing
by too much precipitation, and, above all things, avoid
fresh reverses." He counted on one sovereign whom he
had defeated in battle, and another whom he had helped
to enlarge his kingdom, and he counted in vain, partly
because he was unsuccessful, but chiefly because the
national political interests of both countries prevailed
over the gratitude felt by Victor Emmanuel, and the
desire to turn the tables on the House of Hohenzollern
which was still strong in the House of Hapsburg-
Lorraine.

" You will drag us out of this hornet's nest, Marshal,
won't you ? " exclaimed an officer, as Bazaine quitted
the Imperial quarters. It was a task beyond his
strength. When day dawned a thick fog shrouded the
valley of the Moselle, and before the camp at Longeville was astir, a shell from the opposite bank burst
near a tent, "cut a Colonel in two," to use the
soldatesque language of Marshal Canrobert, "carried
off the leg of a battalion commander, and wounded two
officers standing near a drummer." The lucky shot
came from a patrol of German cavalry, which had
ridden forward as far as the railway station, unopposed,
and its commander, observing a camp at Longeville,
had brought his guns into action, and proved, once
again, that the hornets were abroad and making a bold
use of their offensive weapons. A battery hastily ran
out, and the heavy metal of St. Quentin drove off the
intruders; but they had learned that the foe was over
the river before they retired. Soon afterwards, by
Bazaine's order, a mine was fired, and one section of
the railway bridge was destroyed.

Then the retreat was continued. Finding the road
obstructed by an endless stream of carts and waggons,

Marshal Lebœuf turned aside, and struggling on, amid transport vehicles, threaded his way by Lessy and Chatel St. Germain to Vernéville, where about seven in the evening he had assembled the tired infantry Divisions of Castagny and Montaudon; but his cavalry and reserve artillery did not reach the bivouac until night; while Aymard's Division was forced to halt in the defile, and Metman was at Sansonnet in the Moselle valley. Frossard, followed by Canrobert, had marched during the day as far as Rézonville, where both halted; and the Guard with the Emperor and Prince Imperial attained Gravelotte. General de Ladmirault did not stir at all on the 15th, he put a strict construction on Bazaine's orders, and affected also to be uncertain whether he was to continue his retreat or not. But he had allowed Lorencez to press through the town and thrust himself into the Lessy defile, where his troops, unable to get on, had to pass the night. These disjointed and irregular movements testify to the confusion of a hurried retreat, to the flurry which had got the upper hand, and to the absence of anything like a firm control over troops and generals. How could it be otherwise ? The Emperor still commanded, or was believed to command, and it is plain that, at no time, did the Marshal secure prompt and cheerful obedience, or inspire confidence, always essential to success, and never more so than when an Army has to be extricated from what the Imperial Guardsman graphically called a " hornet's nest."

THE GERMANS CROSS THE MOSELLE.

Far otherwise had the hours been employed by the German host. Early in the morning King William had ridden from Herny to the heights above the battlefield, and there the Head-quarter Staff, from actual observation, were able to form a correct judgment on the actual state of affairs. At first they took precautionary measures against a possible counter attack, and it was not until eleven o'clock that, evidence sufficient to convince von Moltke having come in, decisive steps were taken. All the Corps of the Second Army were directed upon or over the Moselle, the First Corps was moved to Courcelles-Chaussy; and the Seventh was posted at Courcelles sur Nied to guard the railway line and the depôts; and the Eighth was on its left, echeloned on the Lunéville road. At nightfall the Third Corps had crossed the Moselle between Pagny and Novéant, where they found the bridge intact; the Tenth had one division at Pont à Mousson and one westward at Thiaucourt; the Guard was at Dieulouard, and the Fourth Corps astride the river at Marbache-Custines. The Second Corps had come up to Han sur Nied. The Crown Prince's advanced troops were at Nancy, St. Nicholas on the Meurthe, and Bayon on the Upper Moselle.

THE CAVALRY BEYOND THE MOSELLE.

But the most interesting and effective operations were those carried out by the Fifth Cavalry Division, commanded by General von Rheinbaben. They had traversed the Moselle on the 14th, and were directed to gain the Verdun road in order to ascertain the exact whereabouts of the French. At the same time the Third Cavalry Division attached to the First Army was instructed to pass the river below Metz and push out towards Briey; but the French had removed all the boats, no crossing could be effected, and the division was employed elsewhere. No such obstacles arrested the Fifth Division. It consisted of three strong brigades under von Redern, von Barby, and von

Bredow, in all thirty-six squadrons, and was accompanied by two batteries of horse artillery. Leaving Barby at Thiaucourt to await the arrival of Bredow coming up from the Moselle, Redern marched through the fog at four in the morning to La Chausée, whence he detached two squadrons towards the Verdun road. During their absence von Redern, riding on towards Xonville, discovered and was fired on by a body of French cavalry on the hills about Puxieux. These were French dragoons detached from de Forton's division, then *en route* for Mars la Tour, and they were reinforced from the main body as soon as the vedettes had opened fire. The French, led by Prince Murat, ascended the hill, but soon after the Germans had brought a battery to bear Murat withdrew his men, followed by von Redern. On crowning the ridge de Forton's division was plainly seen moving in the valley, or halting near Mars la Tour, supported by twelve guns. Von Redern, who did not think it prudent to attack, retired until a fold of the hills gave him protection. Here he was joined by two squadrons of hussars, which had approached Rezonville, captured nine prisoners, and when pursued had got deftly away. The sound of the cannon had attracted the rest of the brigade, and von Redern again moved towards Mars la Tour, and again drew off without a fight. But by this time the cannonade had called up both Barby and Bredow, so that there were soon thirty-four squadrons and two batteries on the ground. The French General, de Forton, who believed erroneously that German infantry occupied Puxieux, was of opinion that he had fought a successful skirmish; yet instead of closing with enemies who were actually close to the line of retreat upon Verdun, he fell back as far as Vionville, and went into camp. Three French divisions of horse in the van of the retiring Army allowed a German division to sit down within a short distance of the Verdun road and many miles from all infantry support. On the other hand, a squadron of Uhlans pushed almost to Conflans, and stumbling on Du Barail's division, was smartly punished; but a captain of hussars, during the evening, rode towards Rézonville and halted close enough to see Frossard's fantassins cooking their suppers. Meantime, the Prussian Guard Cavalry, moving north-west from Dieulouard, had placed its advanced brigade at Thiaucourt; and a squadron of Guard Uhlans had audaciously summoned the Governor of Toul to surrender. No such memorable examples of activity can be found in the record of the French cavalry, which had forgotten the traditions of Napoleon the Great.

ORDERS FOR THE FLANK MARCH.

That evening General von Moltke issued a set of memorable instructions to General von Steinmetz and Prince Frederick Charles. The First Army was to leave a corps at Courcelles sur Nied, and place the others at Arry and Pommérieux, between the Seille and the Moselle. "It is only by a vigorous offensive movement of the Second Army," wrote von Moltke, "upon the routes from Metz to Verdun by Fresne and Etain that we can reap the fruits of the victory obtained yesterday. The commander of the Second Army is entrusted with this operation which he will conduct according to his own judgment and with the means at his disposal, that is, all the Corps of his Army." It was further announced that the King would transfer his head-quarters to Pont à Mousson in the afternoon of the 16th. Preparations were thus made to place the whole force on the left bank of the Moselle, except the First Corps, the Third Division of

Cavalry, and the Second which was still two marches from the river. In this way von Moltke hoped to keep the whip hand of his opponents, and cut them off from the shelter they sought beyond the Meuse.

THE EMPEROR QUITS THE ARMY.

Before narrating the battle which the French style Rezonville and the Germans Vionville-Mars la Tour, we may turn to the Imperial head-quarters at Gravelotte at dawn on the 16th, because the scene presents so vivid a contrast to that in the German camp. When Marshal Bazaine saw the Emperor on the preceding evening walking meditatively up and down before his quarters, he was surprised by the question, "Must I go?" The Marshal frankly admitted that he had not been informed respecting the situation in front, and asked him to wait. "The answer," writes Bazaine, appeared to please him, and turning to his suite he said, loud enough to be heard by all, "Gentlemen, we will remain, but keep the baggage packed." The troops, sad and depressed, continued to defile before the inn; no shout, no vivat was evoked by the sight of the sovereign and his son. Yet that night the Emperor had made up his mind. In the morning he summoned Bazaine, who found him in his carriage with the Prince Imperial and Prince Napoleon. The baggage had already gone on in the night, and the lancers and dragoons of the Guard, commanded by General de France, were in the saddle ready to serve as an escort. Bazaine rode to the side of the carriage, and the Emperor said, "I have resolved to leave for Verdun and Chalons. Put yourself on the route for Verdun as soon as you can. The gendarmerie have already quitted Briey in consequence of the arrival of the Prussians"—a singularly erroneous statement, but one showing how ill-informed the head-quarters were from first to last. The Emperor then drove off from Gravelotte by the road to Conflans, through the wooded ways which were so soon to be the scene of a sanguinary encounter. Three hours after he started von Redern's guns opened suddenly on the French cavalry camp near Vionville, and began, by a stroke of surprise, the most remarkable and best-fought battle of the campaign.

CHAPTER VIII.

The French Retreat Thwarted.

VIONVILLE—MARS LA TOUR.

THAT feebleness and hesitation which had been so conspicuous on the side of the French from the outset of the campaign were not likely to cease when dangers and difficulties increased with every passing hour. The Emperor, while he commanded, had been incapable of taking, not merely a bold, but any resolution, and the mental qualities of Marshal Bazaine were not sufficiently far above the average to enable him to remedy the mischievous effects of the long course of erroneous conduct to the heritage of which he succeeded. Moreover, neither Bazaine nor any other French commander, despite recent experiences, had formed a correct estimate of German energy and enterprise. Least of all could they believe that a single Corps and two divisions of cavalry would venture to plant themselves across the road to Verdun. The evil consequences were increased by the inactivity of the cavalry, and the bad, unsoldier-like habit of making perfunctory reconnaissances carried only a mile or so to the front and on the flanks. Marshal Bazaine's phrase—"les reconnaissances doivent se faire *comme d'habitude*"—reveals the whole secret. At Wissembourg, on the 4th of August, General Abel

Douay's horsemen returned from a short excursion and reported that no enemy was near; and at eight in the morning of the 16th, General Frossard was informed by the patrols which had come in that there was no adversary in force on his front. The German horse were near at hand, yet de Forton's cavaliers had not felt out as far as their bivouac. Marshal Bazaine's original intention was that the two corps ordered to follow the Mars la Tour road should start at four o'clock; and Frossard had his men out in readiness to move at that hour when a fresh order postponed the march until the afternoon. During the night Marshal Lebœuf, alarmed at the absence of two divisions and at the continued sojourn of de Ladmirault in the Moselle valley, had suggested that it would be better to stand fast until the several Corps had been once more brought within supporting distance; and Marshal Bazaine had readily yielded to the suggestion. Still no measures were taken to ascertain whether foes were approaching or not, and the soldiers, horse and foot, took up their ordinary camp duties as they would have done had they been at Chalons in time of peace. The actual situation, if they had known it, required that every horse, man and gun should have been in motion at dawn, yet they all lingered; and it may be said that neither superiors nor subordinates were alive to the peril in which they stood—not of defeat, still less rout, the odds available against German enterprise were too great,—but of a blow which would make them reel and, perhaps, turn them aside from the paths to the Meuse.

THE VIONVILLE BATTLEFIELD.

The road from Gravelotte to Verdun passes by the villages of Rezonville, Vionville and Mars la Tour through a generally open and undulating country. The ground slopes irregularly and gently upward on all sides from the highway; the villages on the route are in the hollows or shallow valleys.   North and south of Rezonville a ridge separated two ravines, the larger, on the east, formed by the Jurée brook, had its origin north of Gravelotte, the smaller on the west, came down also from the northern uplands and parallel to its bed ran the principal road from Gorze to Rezonville. At the southern declivity of the ridge, and extending eastward as far as the Moselle, were a series of forests— the Bois de Vionville, Bois St. Arnould, the Bois des Ognons, the Bois des Chevaux.   To the west and south-west of Rezonville the country was generally open; but there was a clump of trees shading a pool near Vionville, and, north of the high road, were larger patches of woods, named after the village of Tronville. North also of the highway, and within the French lines, woodlands covered the hill sides towards St. Marcel, the hamlet of Villers aux Bois being seated on the highest ground.   Along this upper plateau are traces of a Roman road, running due west, the ancient route from Verdun to Metz; traces visible also in the fields nearer to the fortress.   The French occupied the higher stretches on the eastern and north-eastern edge of this irregularly undulating and wooded region. General Frossard was posted on the left of the line in front of Rezonville; Canrobert on the heights towards St. Marcel; Leboeuf had his troops about Vernéville, the Guard stood at, and in rear of Gravelotte, and the careless cavalry brigades under de Forton and Vala-brègues had set up their camps west of Vionville, and thence kept a listless watch towards the heights and hollows, west and south-west, just in their immediate front.

THE FRENCH ARE SURPRIZED.

Suddenly, about nine o'clock, they were struck by shells fired from a battery which seemed to have sprung out of a rounded hill a few hundred yards to the west of Vionville. The missiles fell among the tents and burst about a squadron filing up in watering order to the tree-shaded pool. In quick succession three additional batteries appeared on the crest and opening fire added to the confusion below. Murat's dragoons broke and fled and, accompanied by the baggage train, horses, carts, men, galloped and ran off towards Rezonville; and de Gramont's troopers, further to the rear, mounted and retired in good order up the northern slopes, halting on the right of the 6th Corps. The batteries, six in number, then moved up to a height closer in to Vionville and smote the infantry camps. They were promptly answered by the guns of Frossard's Corps, while his brigades stood to their arms, formed up and sprang forward with alacrity. About the same time, a solitary German battery, visible to the south, fired a few rounds into the French left and then withdrew over the crest unable to bear the storm of Chassepot bullets which were poured from the aroused and irritated infantry.

The collision, so unwelcome to the French, had been brought about in this wise. Prince Frederick Charles had ordered the Third and Tenth Corps and the Sixth Division of Cavalry to start early in the morning and strike the Verdun road west of Rezonville. As General von Voights-Rhetz, commanding the Tenth, intended to move upon St. Hilaire, beyond Mars la Tour, he instructed von Rheinbaben to reconnoitre in the direction of Rezonville, increased his horse artillery, and sup-

ported him with an infantry detachment from Thiaucourt.   About the same time that the Tenth Corps
advanced its foremost brigades from Thiaucourt, and
the rest from Pont à Mousson, the Third Corps and the
Sixth Division of Cavalry also made for the hills west
and south of Vionville, the right division proceeding by
Gorze, and the left, by Buxières, towards Tronville.
Thus these two Corps were moving on two parallel curves,
the Third being next to the enemy, and the Tenth
on the outer and larger arc.   The Prince and his
Generals did not anticipate a battle, but they all hoped
to fall in with and punish a rear-guard, or, by striking
far to the westward, intercept and compel the French
Army to halt and fight before it reached the Meuse.
It was Rheinbaben's abrupt and thorough home-thrust
which revealed the fact that the French had not passed
Rezonville, or, at least, that a large part of the Army
was near that village.   His advance-guard, three
squadrons and a battery, had moved within musket-
shot of de Forton's camp " without encountering a
single patrol;" and, taking advantage of such supineness, his artillery, hastening forward, created the panic
near Vionville, which has already been described.
Frossard's Corps, which always behaved well, speedily
took up defensive positions.   Bataille occupied Vionville and Flavigny, and the high ground above the
villages ; Vergé prolonged the line to the left, and
placed one brigade facing south to front the Bois de
Vionville, and connect the array with Lapasset's
brigade on the ridge which, from the north, overlooked
the Bois St. Arnould and the ravine leading to Gorze.
The 6th Corps, encamped north of the main road, continued the line on that side, and rapidly developed a
front facing south-west between the highway and the
Roman road.   The sound of the cannonade was heard

as far off as Jarny and Conflans, startled Lebœuf at
Vernéville, and aroused the Marshal, busy in his
quarters at Gravelotte.

THE THIRD CORPS STRIKES IN.

Rheinbaben's bold horsemen and gunners had done
their work; they had gained for the oncoming infantry
that species of moral advantage which always accrues
from a surprise. As they fell back to more sheltered
positions behind the swelling hills, the right wing of the
Third Corps, under Stülpnagel, entered the field from the
south; the left wing, directed by the fiery Alvensleben
himself, came down into the arena from the south-west,
and several batteries, urged on by von Bulow, dashed
up and formed the centre of the assailants. Indeed,
the guns were in action before the infantry could march
over the distance between their starting points and the
outward spray of the French line of battle; so that for
an appreciable interval the groups of batteries had to
depend upon themselves. Yet not for long. Stülpnagel's
battalions plunged into the dense woods on the right,
and waged a close combat with the skirmishers of
Jolivet's brigade, who were slow to give ground.
Beyond the thickets, the left wing of the division drove
Valazé's skirmishers from an eminence, the highest in
those parts, and a battery was speedily in action on its
bare summit. By degrees, as they came up, the
battalions of the Tenth Brigade went forward on the
left, or western, flank of the height, where the contest,
conducted with vigour on both sides, eddied to and fro,
until the German onset, repeated and sustained, gained
the mastery, and cleared the slopes so effectually that
five other batteries, driving up the hill as fast as they
could clear the defile, took ground on its top, and gave
support to the companies in the wood and on the open

down. About an hour was consumed in this desperate work, made all the more arduous because the German infantry pushed eagerly into the fight, not in compact masses, but one battalion after another as each struggled up to the front. Major-General Doering was killed, and many officers went down in this sanguinary strife; one battalion which dashed forward to resist a French attack at a critical moment lost every officer. But as it retired, broken and wasted, the French were smitten in turn by its comrades, forced to give way, and the position was, at this heavy cost, secured. For the troops engaged in the forest had now attained the northern edge of the Bois de Vionville, the batteries on the lofty hill were safe, and Stülpnagel's Division was solidly established upon the most commanding uplands in that part of the field.

To their left rear was the Sixth Cavalry Division; but between them and the fields west of Vionville were no infantry, only lines of guns, protected by a few squadrons of horse. For the Sixth Infantry Division, coming on from Buxières, had gradually wheeled to the right until they faced to the east, the 11th brigade crossing the high road, north of Tronville, the 12th moving upon Vionville; so that they formed a line of attack directed upon Bataille's division which held Vionville and Flavigny, having on its right, beyond the Verdun road, the division of Lafont de Villiers belonging to Canrobert's Corps. While Stülpnagel was striving to obtain a grip of the woods and heights on the French left, Buddenbrock, the other divisional commander, acting under the eyes of his chief, threw the weight of his division upon the two villages which covered what was then the French centre. Vionville was first carried by the usual turning movement, and its capture was followed by the outburst of a still more

N

murderous conflict.   The French had brought up more
and heavier pieces, and these poured a crushing fire
into the village.   The Germans answered by continuing
the attack on the French infantry.   Yet so confused
was the engagement on the bare hill side, so completely
was it a "soldiers' battle," such was the swaying to
and fro of the mingled companies which, crushed and
mangled, yet welded themselves together and pressed
on, that, once more, the official German historian re-
nounces the task of minute description.   But the effect
of the hurly-burly was soon manifest—Bataille's entire
division, unable to endure the torment, and seeing its
General fall wounded, went about and retired; Valazé's
brigade, "taken in flank," says Frossard, by a German
battery, and losing its gallant commander, also marched
off through Rezonville; and the nearest brigade of
Canrobert's Corps likewise receded, either under pressure or weakened in purpose by example.   The Germans paid a great price for the immense advantage
secured; but as Flavigny fell into their hands, as the
left of Stülpnagel's Division joined in its capture, and
as the front of battle was now no longer an arc but its
chord, the prize was well worth its cost.   The sole
reinforcements which had arrived to aid the Third
Corps, were two detachments, parts of the same brigade,
and pertaining to the Tenth which, on their way to
join that Corps then moving westward, had turned aside,
attracted by the magnetism of the cannonade.   How
much of the success obtained was due to the valour,
devotion, and endurance of the artillery may be
gathered from the French narratives.   No troops
could have fought with greater hardihood and dash—
not fleeting, but sustained—than the infantry of the
Third Corps, all Prussians from the Mark of Brandenburg.   But they had their equals among the dauntless

gunners, deserving to be called "*tirailleurs d'artillerie,*"
who literally used their batteries as battalions, dragging
them up to the very outward edges of the fight, often
within rifle-shot, and when pressed, retiring some
scores of paces, then halting and opening at short range
upon their pursuers.   The line, composed of groups of
batteries, especially in the forenoon, was the backbone
of the battle.

ARRIVAL OF BAZAINE.

Just as Frossard's infantry, yielding to the vehement
pressure, retreated behind Rezonville, Marshal Bazaine
appeared on the scene, and rode into the thick of the
contest.   At Frossard's request he directed a Lancer
regiment, supported by the cuirassiers of the Guard,
to charge and check the pursuers.   The Lancers went
forth with great spirit, but soon swerved aside, broken
by the infantry fire.   The Guard horsemen, however,
led by General du Preuil, rode home upon the eager
and disordered companies who were marching to the
east of the flaming village of Flavigny.   But these foot
soldiers, reserving their fire until the mailed cavaliers
were within two hundred and fifty yards, plied them
with shot so steadily that the squadrons swerved to the
right and left, only to fall under the bullets from the
rear ranks which had faced about.   " The cuirassiers,"
says General du Preuil, " were broken by the enemy's
infantry, which received them with a murderous fire.
After the charge, the wreck of the regiment rallied at
Rezonville, having left behind on the field 22 officers, 24
sous officiers, about 200 men and 250 horses.   When the
regiment was re-organized, instead of 115 mounted men
per squadron, there were only 62 ! " Colonel von Rauch
had close to Flavigny two Hussar regiments; with
one he pressed on the flying cuirassiers, and with the

other charged the French infantry struggling rearward. Bazaine had just brought up, and was posting a battery of the Imperial Guard, when the Hussars charged down upon him, taking the battery in front and flank. It was here that the Marshal was surrounded, separated for a moment from his staff, and obliged, as he himself says, to "draw his sword." Two squadrons of his escort came to his relief, and a rifle battalion opened upon the Prussian horse, who had to retreat, leaving behind the battery which they had temporarily seized. General Alvensleben had ordered up the Sixth Division of Cavalry, but when they arrived, Bazaine had brought forward the Grenadier Division of the Guard to replace the 2nd Corps in the front line, for Jolivet's brigade, on the French left, had also retired to the high ground in its rear. The Sixth formed up to the south of Flavigny and advanced, but they could not make any impression upon the reinvigorated enemy, and they drew back, having lost many officers and men. "This demonstration, apparently without any result," says the official German account, "was still useful, since it provided the artillery with an opportunity so vehemently desired of pressing up nearer to the front." In fact, the lines of the artillery were now between the edge of the wood of Vionville and Flavigny, and to the right, left, and front of Vionville itself—a distinct approximation towards the French infantry and guns; so that there were changes on both sides, with the difference that the French brought up fresh troops, while the same German guns, horsemen and infantry continued the struggle.

The crisis of the battle had now arrived; for General von Alvensleben, in order to diminish the violent pressure on his left, which was beyond the Verdun road, had been obliged to thrust his sole reserve of infantry

into the deadly encounter. Colonel Lehmann, commanding a detachment of the Tenth Corps, consisting
of three battalions and a half, had come up to the outskirts of the field in the forenoon, and he was directed
to take post near Tronville. When, in consequence of
the reverse inflicted on Frossard, Bazaine arrayed the
Guard in front of Rezonville and Canrobert put his
reserve brigades into line on their right, and both
established their reserve artillery on the heights to the
north and east, Alvensleben sent forward Lehmann's
battalions, which, with great difficulty, managed to
keep their ground in the Copses of Tronville beyond
the Verdun road. It was about two o'clock in the
afternoon and the German leader had no reserves, every
foot soldier and gun was engaged, while the greater
part of the Tenth Corps was still remote from the field.
Luckily for him, the reports of the fugitive peasantry
and the steady advance of the German right through
the southern woods, aroused in the mind of Bazaine a
fear that he might be turned on his left, a fear shared
by at least one of his subordinates. He, therefore,
caused the Guard Voltigeurs to form front to the south
in the Bois des Ognons, so as to watch the ravines,
down one of which the Mance flowed to Ars, and in the
bed of the other the Jurée ran to Novéant. Lapasset,
who barred the road from Gorze, was reinforced by a
regiment of Grenadiers, and Montaudon's division of
the 3rd Corps was taken from Lebœuf and placed near
Malmaison, a little to the north of Gravelotte. Thus
the French line, instead of standing north and south,
faced generally to the south-west, between the Bois des
Ognons and the high ground north of the Copses of
Tronville. At this time Lebœuf, with one division
and a half—for Metman had not yet joined him—
was moving south-west from Vernéville, and de

Ladmirault's divisions—for he had quitted the Moselle valley in the morning—were only just showing their leading troops towards Doncourt. Nevertheless, Canrobert, who had developed a strong line of guns as well as infantry on the right of Picard's Grenadiers, both on the face and flank of the German left, determined to attempt the recapture of Vionville and Flavigny. He was led to do so by a belief that the partial cessation of the German fire indicated exhaustion, and, aided by the whole of his artillery, he certainly delivered a formidable onset carried up to the very outskirts of the two villages. It was then that Alvensleben called upon the cavalry to charge, solely with the object of gaining time and relieving the wearied foot, and hardly-treated gunners.

BREDOW'S BRILLIANT CHARGE.

Bredow's heavy brigade, the 7th Cuirassiers of Magdeburg, and the 16th Uhlans of Altmark, eight squadrons, from which two were withdrawn on the march to watch the Tronville Copses, was selected to assail Canrobert's destructive batteries and stinging infantry. Von Bredow drew out his two regiments, led them into the shallow but protecting hollow on the north of Vionville, and, without pausing, wheeled into line on the move, so that the array of sabres and lances fronted nearly eastward. Then breaking into a headlong gallop the troopers rushed like a torrent over and through the infantry on their broad track and into the batteries, near the Roman Road, which for the moment they disorganized. But now the French horse swarmed forward on all sides, and the survivors of von Bredow's heroic men, having cheerfully made the heavy sacrifice demanded from them, turned about to retreat through the French infantry, punished as they rode back by de

Forton, Gramont, Murat and Valabrègue who brought
up three thousand dragoons, chasseurs and cuirassiers
against the remains of the devoted brigade.   Von
Bredow sought safety behind Flavigny, whither von
Redern had ridden up with a regiment of hussars, but
he did not attack because the hostile cavalry halted in
their pursuit.   The charge had cost the Magdeburgers
and Altmarkers 14 officers and 363 men, nearly one-
half the strength with which they started on their
astonishing ride; but the glorious remnant had the
proud satisfaction of knowing that the two regiments
had put an end to offensive attacks from the side of
Rezonville, that their infantry comrades of the Brandenburg Corps had received effectual succour in time
of need, and that the steadfast artillery had gained
precious moments which they used to prepare for fresh
exertions.

THE FIGHT BECOMES STATIONARY.

During the next three hours, and, indeed, to the end
of the day, the combat on the German right and centre
remained stationary, varied by desperate attempts to
win ground from the Imperial Grenadiers which cost
many lives and achieved no marked success.   Seven
fresh batteries, however, came successively into action,
so that about four o'clock, the German line of guns,
between the wood of Vionville and Flavigny had been
increased to more than a hundred pieces and their fire
effectually stayed the French from advancing.   Some
portions of the Seventh, Eighth and Ninth Corps, which
had struggled up from the Moselle valley during the
sultry afternoon, entered the woods, were pushed up
the ravine road from Gorze or were thrown forward in
front of the big battery which was the mainstay of the left
wing.   Prince Frederick Charles himself arrived about

four o'clock. He had ridden straight from Pont à
Mousson on learning that a serious engagement was
afoot, and as he cantered up to the front he was heartily
welcomed by the men of the Third Corps which he had
commanded for ten years.

ARRIVAL OF THE TENTH CORPS.

Surveying the scene from the lofty upland above the
wood for a time, he rode off to another eminence near
Flavigny, because the stress of battle was then on the
left wing, where the rest of the Tenth Corps, so long
absent from the field, had appeared just in time to encounter the fresh troops which had been led forward by
Marshal Lebœuf and General de Ladmirault. When
von Bredow's Brigade rode against Canrobert's Corps,
von Barby's horse were sent to guard the extreme left
against a surprise from the masses of French troops
gathering on the Doncourt hills. They pushed far
northward, and sustained a cannonade from the enemy,
who soon forced them to' retreat ; for Lebœuf, with
Aymard's Division — Bazaine had now called for
Nayral's as well as Montaudon's—moved down towards
the Tronville thickets, and Ladmirault, whose infantry
had at length reached him from the Moselle valley, sent
Grenier forward in line with Aymard. These two divisions, driving the horsemen back towards Tronville, at
once assailed the woodlands, so often named, and com-
bining their attack with that of Tixier, whose division
formed the right of Canrobert's Corps, they expelled the
German infantry from the northern section of the wood.
Lehmann's Hanoverians and the wreck of the Branden-
burgers gave ground slowly, but, after an hour's severe
bush-fighting, the left of the Third Corps was obliged to
yield, and nothing restrained the advancing French
infantry save the terribly effective fire of the German

gunners, upon whom the brunt of the battle fell. As the most forward German guns were retired south of the highway, Grenier sent three batteries over the ravine, and fortune seemed, for the first time, to favour the Imperial soldiers. But, at this trying moment, the Twentieth Division of the Tenth Corps—the men had already marched that day twenty-seven miles—appeared on the heights of Tronville. General von Kraatz, its commander, brought with him eight battalions, four squadrons, and four batteries, an opportune reinforcement, which had been led thither because the summons, given by faint reverberations of a heavy cannonade, heard at Thiaucourt, had been clenched by the arrival of a note written on the field of battle.

The artillery, as usual, took the lead, hastening to the field across country, and, before the infantry could advance twenty-four guns in action north of Tronville, checked the French skirmishers, and obliged Grenier's batteries to recross the ravine. Then the foot went into the wood, and soon chased the French from all the copses except a patch on the north. At this time, General de Ladmirault, who had been joined by heavy masses of cavalry, had on the heights, near the farm of Greyère, abundance of artillery and de Cissey's Division. On his right ran a deep and steep ravine towards Mars la Tour; he was about to cross this obstacle, and had, in fact, entered the hollow, intending to sweep down upon the German left, when he became aware that a strong hostile body was approaching from the west. It was General von Schwarzkoppen, commanding a division of the Tenth Corps. He brought on to the field the thirty-eighth brigade, diminished, however, by detachments to five battalions, two companies of pioneers, twelve guns, and six squadrons of Dragoons of the Guard. General de Ladmirault's proceedings had been closely watched by some German horse, and his advance-guard of Chasseurs d'Afrique had been driven out of Mars la Tour by the Dragoons of the Guard.   Seeing the oncoming enemy, he hastily re-crossed the ravine, and placed de Cissey and his artillery in position to resist any attack.   The intelligence that an enemy had shown himself on the West had run along the French line, and had induced Grenier and Lebœuf to suspend their apparently prosperous onset, thus diminishing the pressure upon von Kraatz in the Tron-ville wood, and also on the artillery, which had been so long engaged near Vionville.   General Schwarzkoppen had, during the day, marched to St. Hilaire on his way to the fords of the Meuse; but, hearing the cannonade, he halted, sent out patrols, and finally moved off towards the battle, guided by columns of dust, clouds of smoke, and the deep-toned muttering of the rival guns.   When he reached Mars la Tour, Voights Rhetz, the Corps Commander, rode up.   Both he and Prince Frederick Charles, who watched the fight from a hill above Flavigny, were under the delusion that the French right could be taken in flank by an attack from Mars la Tour; and von Wedell, who commanded the newly-arrived brigade, was ordered to fall on.   But, for once, the German Staff did not show their far-famed skill; for they did not reconnoitre the ground, nor had they observed the formidable array of de Cissey's brigades. Von Wedell's men dashed forward with alacrity, but found in their path a deep hollow, which covered the French front, as well as flank, on that side.   Never-theless, the battalions, in two lines, hurried down one bank and up the other, and then met an entire French Division.   A brief and bloody fight at close quarters— the opposing lines were separated in some places by only fifty yards—ensued; but so continuous and deadly

was the French fire that the sturdy Westphalians had
to yield. Their dead and dying covered the summit,
and filled the hollow way; two-thirds of the 16th
Regiment were left on the field, and the whole brigade,
shattered into a shapeless crowd of fugitives, hurried to
the rear. Then forward to their succour came bound-
ing the 2nd Dragoons of the Guard, Colonel von
Auerswald at their head, spurring headlong to the front
through the disordered crowd, taking the hedges and
ditches in their stride, and galloping furiously into
the midst of the pursuing French, who had leaped forward from the right of Grenier's Division. It was a
hopeless charge—a ride to certain death—but the readiness of the Dragoons saved the right of the brigade; yet
at great cost, for they left dead on the field their brave
Colonel, a Major, and three Captains. Nine officers in
all, and seventeen men were killed; four officers and
sixty men were wounded; while one officer and five
men were captured. Two of Count Bismarck's sons,
privates in this regiment, rode in the charge; the eldest,
Herbert, was shot in the thigh, the youngest, Wilhelm,
a stout trooper, lifted a wounded comrade on to his
horse, and carried him off the field. The charge of the
Dragoons enabled the broken battalions to draw off
towards Tronville, but the guns in position still held on
near Mars le Tour, west of which, towards Ville sur
Yron, a horse battery and a squadron of the 2nd
Dragoons of the Guard were engaged in a smart
skirmish with a body of Chasseurs d'Afrique. This encounter was followed shortly afterwards by

THE GREAT CAVALRY COMBAT.

Ladmirault had sent six regiments of horse over the
gully on his right—Legrand's Hussars and Dragoons,
du Barail's solitary regiment of Chasseurs d'Afrique,

and the superb brigade of Lancers and Dragoons of the
Guard commanded by General de France. On the
other side von Barby's brigade had approached Mars la
Tour during the fatal attack upon de Ladmirault's
infantry, and soon after it was joined by two squadrons
of the 4th Cuirassiers, the 10th Hussars, and the 16th
Dragoons. Sweeping round to the north of the village,
Barby formed up his troopers in the narrow space
between the Yron and the Greyère ravine, while
Legrand and his comrades showed their compact
masses to the north. The French regiments were
placed in echelon, Legrand's Hussars, led by General
Montaigu, on the left, Gondrecourt's Dragoons on his
right rear, and next the Guard Lancers and Dragoons.
The Chasseurs d'Afrique were behind all. The first
shock fell upon the 13th Dragoons which, having taken
ground to the right, had only time to wheel partially
into line before Montaigu's Hussars rode through the
squadron's intervals, and it would have fared ill with the
Prussians had not Colonel von Weise plunged in with
the 10th Hussars and overset the French. Von Barby
on the left, at the head of the 16th Uhlans and 19th
Dragoons, met the French Guard Cavalry in full shock,
and then ensued a furious confused fight upon the whole
line. Each side endeavoured to fall upon a flank, and
the squadrons swayed to and fro amid a huge cloud of
dust. Suddenly, a squadron of Prussian Guard Dragoons, returning from a patrol, came riding across
country from the west and struck the flank of the
French Guards. Du Barail's Chasseurs d'Afrique and
Gondrecourt's Dragoons dashed into the *melée*, but the
Westphalian Cuirassiers drove like a wedge into the
opposing ranks, and the 16th Dragoons fell upon and
smote them in flank and rear. Legrand was killed,
Montaigu wounded and a prisoner, and the· French

cavalry, wheeling about, rode out of the fight, throwing into disorder a brigade of Chasseurs, which had been sent by General de Clérambault to cover the retreat. The Gallic horse had brilliantly sustained their reputation, yet they were overmatched by the Teutons, who also lost three commanding officers. But von Barby was able to reform his victorious squadrons on the plateau and withdraw them at leisure, watched, but not pursued, by a squadron of Dragoons belonging to de Clérambault's division. General Ladmirault surveyed the field from the heights of Bruville, and came to the conclusion that no more could be accomplished by the French right wing. He had only two divisions, his cavalry had been defeated, and he "discovered" between Tronville and Vionville "an entire Corps d'Armée." So he rested and bivouacked on the hills about the Greyère farm. The forces of his next neighbour on the left, Lebœuf, had been reduced to Aymard's division, for Marshal Bazaine had called away Nayral to support Montaudon near Rezonville; indeed, at one moment he had abstracted one of Aymard's brigades, but, yielding to Lebœuf's remonstrances, he sent it back.

END OF THE BATTLE.

It was now past seven o'clock, and both sides were exhausted by the tremendous strain which they had borne so long; yet the battle continued until darkness had settled over the woods and villages and fields. For Barnekow's division and a Hessian brigade had entered the woodlands and pressed forward on the Gorze road, creating new alarm in the mind of Bazaine, who throughout the day was governed by his belief that the Germans intended to turn his left and cut him off from Metz. So that when Colonel von Rex pushed boldly up the ravine against Lapasset and his flankers opened fire from the edge of the Bois des Ognons, the French Commander drew still more troops to that flank. Between Rezonville and the ridges near Gravelotte he had, by eventide, placed the whole of the Guard, Frossard's Corps, Lapasset's brigade, and one-half of Lebœuf's Corps. Fearing the storming columns which ever and anon surged outward from the woods towards the commanding heights south of Rezonville, Bourbaki brought up fifty-four guns and arrayed them in one long battery. The closing hours of the day witnessed a stupendous artillery contest, which was carried on even when the flashes of flame alone revealed the positions of the opposing pieces. The thick smoke increased the obscurity, and yet within the gloom bodies of German infantry, and even of horse, sallied from the woods or vales and vainly strove to reach the coveted crests or storm in upon Rezonville itself. At the very last moment a violent cannonade burst forth on both sides, yet to this day neither knows why it arose, where it began, or what it was to effect. At length the tired hosts were quiet; the strife of twelve hours ended. The German line of outposts that night ran from the Bois des Ognons along the Bois St. Arnould, then to the east of Flavigny and Vionville through the Tronville copses; and after the moon rose upon the ghastly field the cavalry rode forth and placed strong guards as far westward as Mars la Tour and the Yron. The French slept on the ground they held, the heights south of Rezonville, that village itself, and the ridges which overlook the highway to Verdun as far as Bruville and Greyère. It had been a day of awful carnage, for the French had lost, in killed and wounded, nearly 17,000, and the Germans 16,000 men.

It is impossible to state exactly the numbers present on the field—probably, 125,000 French to 77,000 Germans. The latter brought up two complete Corps, the Third and Tenth, two divisions of cavalry, the 5th and 6th—these sustained the shock and bore the chief loss—a brigade of the Eighth Corps, the 11th Regiment from the Ninth, and four Hessian regiments of that corps under Prince Louis, the husband of the British Princess Alice. They also had, in action or reserve, 246 guns. The French mustered the Imperial Guard, the 2nd Corps, three divisions and one regiment of the 6th Corps, three divisions of the 3rd, and two of the 4th Corps, five divisions of cavalry, and 390 guns; so that on the 16th they were, at all times, numerically superior in every arm. When Alvensleben came into action a little after ten o'clock with the Third Corps and two divisions of cavalry—perhaps 33,000 men—they had in their front the 2nd and 6th Corps, the Guard, and the Reserve Cavalry—not less than 72,000, the guns on the French side being always superior in number. The 3rd Corps, less one division, was at ten o'clock only three miles from the field; these and half the 4th Corps arrived in the afternoon, adding more than 50,000 men to the total, while the Germans could only bring up the Tenth, and parts of the Eighth and Ninth, fewer than 40,000, some of them marching into line late in the evening. The French Marshal, who fought a defensive battle, did not use his great strength during the forenoon, or in the afternoon when his right wing had wheeled up to the front. The result was an "indecisive action"—the phrase is used by the official German historian—and that it was indecisive must be attributed, at least in part, to the fact that Marshal Bazaine, nor he alone, stood in constant dread of an overwhelming inroad of "Prussians" on his left, with intent to cut him off from Metz and thrust him, unprovided with munitions of all kinds, on to the Briey-Longuyon road. But it may be inferred from the mode in which the battle was fought by the

French commanders, from the first shot to the last, that the Germans had obtained a moral ascendency over the leaders and the led, and that such an ascendency had a great influence upon the tactics, as well as the strategy, of Marshal Bazaine and his subordinates in command. Nothing supports the correctness of this inference more strongly than the fact that an Army of 120,000 men considered a great success had been achieved when it had resisted the onsets of less than two-thirds of its numbers, and had been driven from its line of retreat!

CHAPTER IX.

Pressed Back on Metz.

Darkness had set in, and the last shot had been fired, when Marshal Bazaine rode back to his head-quarters at Gravelotte. There he became impressed with the scarcity—" penury"—of munitions and provisions; there he acknowledged to the Emperor that the direct road to Verdun had been closed, and that he might be obliged to retreat by the north; and there he wrote the order which was to move his entire Army the next day nearer to Metz. The troops began their retrograde march as early as four o'clock, by which hour Prince Frederick Charles was up on the hill above Flavigny, intently watching his antagonists. Rezonville was still occupied by infantry, a cavalry division was drawn up between that village and Vernéville until late in the forenoon, and the marches of troops to and fro kept the cautious German Commanders, for some time, in a state of uncertainty.

It has now to be shown how they had employed the 16th outside the area of the conflict, where the several Corps stood in the evening, and by what means the Great Staff, on the 17th, acquired the knowledge that the " Army of the Rhine " had retired upon the line of hills immediately to the westward of Metz.

o

The movement of troops comes first under notice. On the extreme left the Fourth Corps having crossed the Moselle at Marbache, had pushed forward in a south-westerly direction, part of the Corps making a dashing but fruitless attempt to intimidate the garrison of Toul, so important because it barred the railway to Chalons, and at the end of the day was still under orders to march upon the Meuse. The Guard, preceded by its cavalry, advanced from Dieulouard to several points half-way between the Moselle and the Meuse, the right being at Bernecourt and the left about Beaumont. The Twelfth Corps, Saxons, crossed the Moselle at Pont à Mousson, and had one division there and one about Regnièville en Haye. The Second Corps, still approaching the Moselle by forced marches, had attained villages east of the Seille. It will be readily understood that, as the Fourth and Second Corps were so far distant from the centre of action west of Metz, they could hardly be moved up in time to share in the impending struggle; and they, therefore, for the present may be omitted from the narrative. It was otherwise with the remaining Corps, and it was the aim of the Great Staff to bring them all up to the Verdun road.

From the very earliest moment, General von Moltke held the opinion that the full consequences of the action on the 14th could only be secured by vigorous operations on the left bank of the Moselle; and as the reports came in from the front on the 16th, that sound judgment was more than confirmed. The Royal head-quarters were transferred in the forenoon to Pont à Mousson, whither King William repaired; and von Moltke, who had preceded the King, found information which led the general to the conclusion that a new chapter in the campaign had been opened. Accordingly, he desired to push up to the front the largest possible

number of troops, so that he might, if such a design
were feasible, have ample means wherewith to shoulder
off the French to the northward, and sever their communications with Chalons. At this stage, the idea of
shutting them up in Metz had not yet been conceived.
The Seventh, Eighth and Ninth were ordered to hasten
forward on the road towards Vionville, and some part
of them, as we have seen, were engaged on the 16th.
Extra bridges were erected on the Moselle, the roads
were cleared of all impediments, and the results
rewarded the foresight, energy and goodwill displayed
by officers and men. The Twelfth Corps was eighteen,
and the Guard twenty-two miles from the battlefield,
but so keen and intelligent were their commanders,
that, inferring from the information they received what
would be required of them, they stood prepared to
execute any order as soon as it arrived. The former
body, indeed, marched off northward in the night, and
sent word of the fact to the Guard, which led the commander to assemble the divisions on the instant and
stand ready to step forth. So that when the formal
orders were brought, the Guard started at five in the
morning, when the Saxons were already on the road.
The Eighth Corps, or rather its remaining division,
were on the way at dawn, preceded by the Ninth, and
followed by the Seventh from its cantonments on the
left bank of the Seille. Thus the whole available portions of the Second and First Armies were in motion, to
sustain the Third and Tenth, if they were attacked
on the 17th; to act, as circumstances required, if the
French abandoned the battlefield.

Prince Frederick Charles, who had slept at Gorze,
took horse at dawn, and reached his watch-tower on the
hill south-west of Flavigny at half-past four o'clock,
early enough to distinguish by the increasing light the

French line of outposts between Bruville and Rezonville. About six o'clock the King joined the Prince,
and at the same time the Ninth Corps took post near
the right wing of the Third. What the staff had now
to determine was whether the French intended to retire
or ·attack, and if they retired whither they went.
Patrols, busy on all sides, gave in contradictory or
rather discordant reports, which for some time left it
doubtful whether the retreat was not actually being
carried out by the Conflans on the Briey road; but by
degrees the head-quarters arrived at the conclusion that
the French would not attack, that they had not withdrawn far, and that the task of grappling with them
must be deferred until the next day. Soon after noon,
when General Metman, acting as rear guard, quitted
Rezonville, there were on or near the field no fewer
than seven German Corps and three divisions of cavalry;
so that had the French renewed the battle for the
Verdun road, even early in the morning, they would
have found it a severe task to make their way at least
along the southern or Mars la Tour high road. About
eight in the morning General von Moltke had dictated
an order on the height near Flavigny, in obedience to
which the Seventh Corps marched by Corny and Ars
upon Gravelotte,following the Mance brook, and occupying the woods on the right and left; while the Eighth,
already in part on the field, ascended the watercourse
and ravine which gives access to Rezonville. The
object of the double movement was to accelerate the
retreat of the French from these places. It was not
accomplished without some wood-fighting, but about
half-past three General Metman withdrew his flankers,
and glided out of sight beyond the ridge near Point du
Jour. But the firing had alarmed von Moltke, who,
dreading lest the fiery Steinmetz should bring on a

general or even partial engagement, sent him positive orders to stop the combat. The veteran, however, pressed forward himself with von Zastrow, von Kameke and their staff officers. Emerging from the woods into the open, they beheld across the deep ravine the French camps on the opposite plateau, and even discerned the works thrown up by the careful Frossard to cover his guns and infantry. A mitrailleuse at once opened fire on the group of horsemen, and drove them away, but not before they had seen enough to prove, when combined with the cavalry reports from the north-west flank, that the French Army was encamped on the heights to the west of Metz, and had not attempted to withdraw by any of the still open roads towards Mézières or Chalons. Therefore, the German armies halted, and the Generals had a little leisure to frame a plan of operations for the 18th.

MARSHAL BAZAINE.

Human ingenuity has imputed various motives to the French Marshal, some of them being discreditable to his loyalty, all based on a low estimate of his character as a man, and capacity as a soldier. His own account is that he did not persevere in trying to effect his retreat, either by force or skill, partly because the Army was not well supplied with food and munitions, and partly, as is apparent from his evidence and books, because he had formed a military theory which he proposed to work out near Metz to the disadvantage of the enemy. He held that he had a strong post on the flank of the German communications, and that, if he could make his adversaries waste their troops in repeated attacks upon " inexpugnable " positions, he might be able to resume the offensive when the Army at Chalons should take the field. Secretly, we suspect, he had become imbued

with a belief or apprehension that what the French call
the *moral* of the Army had been seriously impaired;
that their staying power in action was not what it should
have been, and that they could not be trusted to perform so delicate an operation as a long flank march
within reach of a foe exalted by victory, aided by a
powerful and audacious cavalry, and an infantry capable
of marching twenty miles a day, and enjoying the
advantage of greatly superior numbers.   As usual, the
motives of Bazaine were " mixed," but there does not
seem any good reason to believe that he was selfishly
disloyal to the Emperor, faithless to France, or insensible
to the charms of " glory."   His chief defect was that
he did not possess sufficient military competence to
command a large army—a defect he shared with his
comrades of high rank; and his misfortune was that he
succeeded to an inheritance of accumulated error en-
tailing severe penalties, from the infliction of which only
a rare genius, like that of the First Napoleon, could
have saved himself and his Army.

Active warfare had now continued for a fortnight,
and at sundown on the 17th of August the " Army of
the Rhine " found itself obliged to form front facing,
not Berlin, but Paris; while the formidable Armies of
King William, with their backs to the French capital,
turned their eyes towards the Rhine.

THE BATTLEFIELD OF GRAVELOTTE.

Whatever may have been his motives, Marshal
Bazaine directed his Army to retire upon a position of
exceptional strength on the heights to the westward of
Metz, which look towards the wooded ravine of the
Mance brook throughout its course, and beyond its
source over the undulating plain in the direction of the
river Orne.   This ridge of upland abuts on the Moselle

near Ars, is covered at its broad southern end by the
Bois de Vaux, is intersected by the great highway from
Metz to Verdun, which is carried along a depression
where the wood terminates, and over the shoulder
above Gravelotte. North of the road the high ground,
with a westerly bias, runs as far as Amanvillers, and
thus trending slightly eastward, ascends to St. Privat la
Montagne and Roncourt, and back to the Moselle bottom
lands below Metz. The left of the position, opposite the
Bois de Vaux, is curved outwards, its shape being
indicated by the high road, which, after bending round
and creeping up the hill as far as Point du Jour, turns
abruptly to the west, and crosses the Mance upon a
causeway east of Gravelotte. This bulwark, occupied
by Frossard's Corps, from near Point du Jour to St.
Ruffine in the lowlands, was made more formidable by
shelter-trenches, field works, and gunpits. The two
houses at Point du Jour were pierced for musketry, and
the immense quarries in the hill-side, at the elbow of the
ridge facing the Mance, were filled with troops. The
only mode of reaching the front was either up the
narrow causeway by St. Hubert, or across the deep
ravine. Behind this strong front the ground sloped inwards, so that the troops and reserves could be, and
were, screened from view as well as from fire. In the
bottom stood the village of Rozérieulles ; and above,
the eminences on which the engineers had planted the
forts of St. Quentin and Plappeville. The hollow
through which the highway ran was bordered with
vineyards, and near to Metz villages and houses
clustered thickly astride of the road. On the right of
Frossard were the four divisions forming the Corps of
Lebœuf, extending as far as the farm of La Folie,
opposite Verneville. Here the ground was high and
open, yet also sloping to the rear as well as the front,

and its chief strength lay in the strongly-built farmsteads of St. Hubert, seated on the roadside just above
Gravelotte, in those of Moscow and Leipzig, standing
on the bare hill-side; and in the Bois de Genivaux, a
thick wood, which filled the upper part of the Mance
ravine.   Beyond the 3rd Corps lay the 4th, under de
Ladmirault, having its left in the farm and château of
Montigny le Grange, and its right at, and a little north
of, Amanvillers, a considerable village, planted in a
depression at a point where one of the roads from Metz
quits the deep defile of Chatel St. Germain, and bends
suddenly westward to join, at Habonville, the road to
Briey.   The track of the railway, then unfinished,
ascends this wooded gully, and winds on to the open
ground at Amanvillers.   The country in front of the
ridge, from that place to Roncourt, is an extensive open
descent, which has been compared to the glacis of a
fortress, at the foot of which stand the villages of
Habonville, St. Ail, and St. Marie aux Chênes.   On the
southern edge of this succession of bare fields is the
Bois de la Cusse, which was not, strictly speaking, a
continuous wood, but a sort of common irregularly
strewed with copses; and on the north were the valley
of the Orne and the woods bordering its meandering
course.   The 6th Corps, Canrobert's, occupied and
guarded the right flank, having an outpost in St. Marie,
and detachments in the villages beyond Roncourt; but
placing its main reliance on St. Privat, which, looked at
from the west, stood on the sky line, and, being nearly
surrounded by garden walls, had the aspect of a little
fortress.   The Imperial Guard, considered as a reserve,
was drawn up in front of the fort of Plappeville, on the
east side of the deep ravine of St. Germain.   The fort
of St. Quentin looked well over, and protected the whole
of the French left, and served especially as a support to

Lapasset's Brigade at St. Ruffine, which faced south. Here the edge of the position touched the suburbs of Metz, and was within cannon-shot of the right bank of the Moselle, opposite Jussy.

It will be seen that the battlefield may be divided into two portions, differing from each other in their external aspects. The bold curved ridge held by Frossard rose between two and three hundred feet above the bed of the Mance, having in rear ground still higher, and was backed by the mass upon which stands Fort St. Quentin. It was, indeed, a natural redoubt open to the rear, covered along its front by the steep sides of a deep ravine, and accessible only by the viaduct built over the brook, a solid embankment, except where a vaulted opening allowed the stream to pass. On the French side of the bridge was the strong farmstead of St. Hubert, well walled towards the assailant ; and further north the thick woods of Genivaux, which ran near to and beyond the farm of Leipzig; so that while a deep gully protected Frossard, Lebœuf had defensive outposts in the wood, which he entrenched in a series of recessed field works, and in the stout farm buildings, which stormers could only reach by passing up gentle acclivities, every yard whereof could be swept by fire. The right half of the line was different in every respect from the left—for there was no wood, and the whole front, from Amanvillers to Roncourt was, for practical purposes, though not so steep, as free from obstacles as the slope of the South Downs. The left and centre were supplied with artificial defences, but the right, which did not rest on any natural support, and might be turned, was not fortified by field works, because Marshal Canrobert's entrenching tools had been, perforce, left behind at Chalons. The great defects of this " inexpugnable " position were that

it had bad lateral communications, no good lines of
retreat, and a weak right flank.   Marshal Bazaine, who
misjudged the formidable strength of his left wing, and
gave his opponent the credit of contemplating an
attack on that side, had taken post in Fort Plappeville,
where he placed the reserves, and whence he could not
see the right, which it does not appear that he had ever
examined.   The penalty for so grave an error was the
loss of the battle.

THE GERMAN PLANS.

Before starting from the hill over Flavigny for Pont
à Mousson on the afternoon of the 17th, General von
Moltke had issued an order to Prince Frederick Charles
and von Steinmetz, indicating the operations which
were to begin the next morning.   Their purport was
that while the Seventh Corps stood fast, and the Eighth
leant towards the right of the Second Army, the Corps
composing it should move forward, left in front, facing
north.   It was a general direction, intended to place
the troops in such an array as would enable them to
strike and stop the French, if they still sought to reach
Chalons by the northern roads, or by a right wheel
bring the whole German force to bear upon the enemy
if he were found in position before Metz.   By six
o'clock on the morning of the 18th, King William and
his staff were once more on the height near Flavigny,
soon after which time the whole Army was in movement,
and a sputter of musketry had begun on the extreme right
between Frossard's foreposts and those of the Seventh
Corps in the woods.   The Eighth had come up near to
Rezonville; the Ninth was moving between that village
and St. Marcel; the Guard was passing Mars la Tour;
and the Twelfth was on the road to Jarny.   Behind, in
second line, were the Tenth and Third, the Fifth and

Sixth divisions of cavalry being attached to the latter
Corps respectively; while the Second Corps, which had
bivouacked at Pont à Mousson, had started on another
forced march, in order, should there be a battle, to
enter the field before dark.   The morning wore away,
and, except on the right where his left was visible and
his skirmishers active, no evidence of the enemy's
presence could be found.   The Saxon cavalry division,
scouting northward and westward, lighted only on
stragglers and patrols; the horsemen and staff officers
out in front of the other Corps watching as well as they
could the movements of the French, sent in divergent
statements, leaving it doubtful where their main body
was, and what it was doing or intended to do.   Great
uncertainty, in short, prevailed until after ten o'clock,
and even then General von Moltke and the staff were
under the impression that the French right was near
Montigny la Grange; but, believing that the adversary
would fight, an order went forth at 10.30 a.m., which
finally brought the German Armies into line facing eastward.   Meantime Prince Frederick Charles had, by
degrees, also arrived at the conclusion that the French
would accept battle, and, at half-past ten, he likewise
instructed General von Manstein to move towards La
Folie and begin an attack with his artillery, provided
the enemy's right was not beyond Amanvillers.
Immediately afterwards, while von Moltke still believed
that the flank he wished to turn was at the last-named
village, the Prince acquired certain information, from a
Hessian cavalry patrol, that the French right rested on
St. Privat la Montagne.   By such slow degrees was the
long-sought flank discovered.   Orders were then given
directing the Twelfth and the Guard to wheel to the
right and move on St. Marie aux Chênes and Habonville; but before they could come into line, Manstein's

guns were heard, and von Moltke became apprehensive lest the exciting sounds of conflict would carry away the impetuous Steinmetz, lest the First Army, always so eager for battle, might strike in prematurely and injure a combination which depended so much upon a simultaneous onset. Accordingly, the rein upon that General was tightened, and he was told that he might use artillery, yet not do more with his infantry than attract the notice of the enemy and keep his attention on the strain. But so thoroughly were the chiefs of the German Corps imbued with the same principles of conduct, that the Prince Royal of Saxony and Prince Augustus of Würtemberg had already, in anticipation, prepared to play the part which was to be assigned them. Having learned, from their own scouting parties, where the French right stood, and having heard the guns at Vernéville, they had both wheeled their divisions to the eastward, and pushed out their advance Guards. Thus they were ready to march at the moment when the order arrived; in fact, the order was in course of execution before it reached the officers to whom it had been addressed. Meantime, acting on the first instructions from the Prince, drawn up when he believed the right rested on Amanvillers, General von Manstein, a little before noon, had begun

THE BATTLE OF GRAVELOTTE.

At this moment, it should be noted, the French camps on the right centre and right did not know that an enemy was within a long mile of their bivouacs. The usual patrols had been sent out and had returned—even scouts selected by the local officials for their knowledge of the country—to report that they had not seen anybody. Marshal Canrobert, in his evidence on the Bazaine court-martial, expressly testifies to the fact, and adds that the first intimation he received came from the boom of hostile guns on his left front. The troops of Ladmirault's Corps, encamped on both sides of Amanvillers, were peacefully engaged in cooking their noontide meal, when General von Manstein, who seems to have been endowed with some of the impetuosity of his namesake, who figured in the wars of Frederick II., riding ahead of his corps, caught sight of the quiescent camp. The temptation could not be withstood. From the hills near Vernéville he could not see the troops at St. Privat, but he had been informed by the Hessian Cavalry that the French were there. He had been formally enjoined to attack if the enemy's right was near La Folie; it was much to the north of that farm; yet Manstein, unable to neglect the opportunity of startling a negligent camp by an outburst of fire, sent the solitary battery which had accompanied him into instant action from a rising ground east of Vernéville. The first shot was fired at a quarter to twelve, and its successors roused the French line from St. Privat to the centre, for Frossard and Lebœuf seemed to have been on the alert. General von Blumenthal, with the leading infantry battalions, was at that time moving on the farm of Chantrenne, and he was stopped by the lively musketry salute which greeted his men. Manstein, seeing that his guns were too distant from their living targets, now ordered the battery forward, and it was soon joined, first by the divisional then by the corps artillery; the whole finally forming a long line of fifty-four pieces, each battery having, as it dashed up, wheeled to the right and opened fire. The movement was a grave error, for the long rounded hill on which the batteries stood faced southeast, offered no shelter except on its low right shoulder, and the guns were exposed to a fire from the front, the

flank, and even from the left rear.   Two batteries were
slewed round to the left, but that did not remedy the
original mistake.   There were no infantry at hand to
keep down the fire of the French foot, which, lurking
in the hollows, sent a hail of bullets among the guns.
Committed to this false position, the superb German
artillerymen did their utmost to make it good; but no
heroism could avail against its cruel disadvantages.
General Blumenthal, indeed, had carried the Chantrenne
farm, but the enemy, at the first shot, had thrown a
garrison into another homestead named Champenois,
whence the Chassepots smote the front of the batteries.
The Hessians, also, had developed a powerful attack
through the Bois de la Cusse towards the railway
embankment and Amanvillers, thus taking off some of
the severe pressure from the devoted gunners.   But the
French infantry crept nigher and nigher; under the
rush of shells, shrapnel, and bullets, officers, men, and
horses fell fast and faster.   By concentrating their aim
the Germans crushed one or silenced another battery;
by using shell they sometimes scattered oncoming
infantry; still the penalty of haste and a wrong direction had to be paid.   The left battery, disabled, was
caught in the tempest and borne down by a rush of
French foot.   Two pieces were dragged away by hardy
men and wounded horses; two were left on the field;
and two were captured.   Yet this astonishing artillery,
though horribly shattered, continued to hold its ground.
It was saved, at a later moment, from a persevering
attack on its vulnerable flank by the steady onset of an
infantry battalion, which lost nearly half its strength in
succouring the guns.   Then, for the position was really
untenable, all the batteries, except three on the right,
where there was a little shelter, at length drew reluc-
tantly, in succession, out of the shambles and went

rearward to refit. It was half-past two; they had been more than two hours in the jaws of death, and had lost no fewer than 210 officers and men and 370 horses. So audaciously, if sometimes unwisely, was this grand arm employed in battle that no one need be astonished to learn how Canrobert, who loved a picturesque phrase, called his dreaded and admired opponents, "*tirailleurs d'artillerie*."

PRINCE FREDERICK CHARLES AT THE FRONT.

Manstein, who was to have attacked the French right, had dashed somewhat impetuously against the right centre, and for some two hours his Corps sustained the brunt of the engagement, for the Guards and the Saxons were still on the march, the first heading for Vernéville and Habonville, the second on St. Marie aux Chênes, into which Canrobert had hurried three battalions. North of the artillery, whose bloody adventure has been described, the Hessian division, under Prince Louis, posted astride of the railway embankment, which, running from Amanvillers to Habonville, cut the line of troops at right angles, held the copses of the Bois de la Cusse, and, supported by thirty guns, formed the backbone of the German attack in that exposed quarter. Further south, the other half of the Ninth Corps, the 18th Division, had its reserves near Vernéville, with troops established in Chantrenne and L'Envie; but they could make no way, because the French were solidly planted in Champenois, in the Bois de Genivaux, in a spinney projecting to the westward of La Folie, in that farm and on the higher ground above. About half-past two the contest in the centre had become defensive on the part of the Ninth Corps, and the energies of the leaders and the troops alike were taxed to retain the ground already occupied and extricate the artillery. Prince Frederick Charles, on

learning just before noon, from the cavalry reports,
where the French right actually stood, became anxious
when he heard at St. Marcel the uproar of a hot artillery
engagement, and he rode off at once towards the sound
and smoke which rose in clouds above the woods. On
reaching Habonville he was able to survey the conflict,
and also discern, in outline, the enemy's position at
St Privat. The great head-quarters were still imperfectly informed, yet they wished to restrain precipitate
action and prevent a home-thrusting central attack until
strong bodies could be launched against the French
right. The Prince, however, saw that the combat could
not be broken off, and he set himself to make all secure
by placing a brigade of the Guard, as a reserve, to assist
the Ninth Corps, which was all that Manstein requested,
and by ordering up four batteries from the Third Corps,
the infantry masses of which were not far from Vernéville. Prince Augustus of Würtemberg had preceded
the Guard Corps, and as soon as General Pape, commanding the first infantry division, arrived with the
advanced guard it was arranged that his four batteries
should go into action to the south-west of Habonville,
that is on the left of the much-tried Hessians, and cover
the march of the Guard towards St. Marie. The spot
first selected for the guns was found defective, and the
batteries, at a gallop, took up new ground further to the
left, to the south-west of St. Ail. Thereupon, that
village was occupied by the Guard ; Prince Augustus sent
for the corps artillery, and soon nine batteries were
arrayed between the two villages, on a diagonal line
pointing to the north-west, that is, so disposed as to
bring to bear a heavy fire on St. Privat, a succour which
gave further relief to the gunners of the Ninth Corps.
For not only Canrobert's cannon, but his infantry,
lurking in the shallow valleys along the front, now

directed their shells and bullets upon the Guard batteries.
Although the French did not attempt any heavy stroke,
they were active and enterprizing, and kept their
swarms of skirmishers within a thousand yards of the
guns, but, as the official historian remarks, over and
over again, beyond the range of the needle-gun.   Before three o'clock the Guard Corps was up, and the
Twelfth, or rather half of it, had approached near
St. Marie.   Such was the condition of the battle on
that side ; and it is now necessary to describe the
daring operations of the First Army, on the German
right wing.

STEINMETZ ATTACKS THE FRENCH LEFT.

It will be remembered that the Seventh and Eighth
Corps, commanded by von Steinmetz, upon whom it
was necessary to keep a tight hand, had been brought
up to the south and west of Gravelotte, the left of the
Eighth touching Manstein's right.   The Seventh provided the outposts which lined the fringe and salient of
the Bois de Vaux, and these troops were engaged in
an intermittent and bickering contest with the French
infantry thrown out upon that flank.   The first division
of cavalry, from the right bank, crossing the Moselle at
Corny, rode up about noon as a support, and General
von Fransecky, preceding the Second Corps, assured
the King, whom he found near Flavigny, that one division would arrive in time to form a reserve for the
First Army.   Von Steinmetz, on a height near Gravelotte, nervously observed the French, sent in repeated
information that they were moving off, and evidently
desired to adopt the tactics which he had applied on
two previous occasions.   He was ordered to be still,
and when the guns spoke at Vernéville, von Moltke,
knowing their effect upon the veteran warrior, intimated

afresh that he must stand expectant yet awhile. Permission was given, as already mentioned, to use his
guns ; but when the despatch was handed to Steinmetz
he had already opened fire with the batteries of the
Seventh Corps, arrayed to the south, and of the Eighth
to the north of Gravelotte ; and the infantry had been
moved eastward to the edge of the region just clear of
the French fire. The troops in the Bois de Vaux were
reinforced, the mill of the Mance and the gully itself
were occupied, and an ample force was posted above
the ravine to protect the line of guns.

The expectant attitude, always distasteful to von
Steinmetz, was not, and in the nature of things could
not be long maintained by the First Army. The
generals on the spot knew more accurately what had
occurred in the centre than the Great Staff when the
order to look on was written. General von Goeben,
knowing how deeply Manstein had committed the Ninth
Corps, felt bound to attack in order that he might detain
and provide employment for the French left. From a
point near Gravelotte he could see the masses of troops
held in reserve by Lebœuf and Frossard, and, with the
ready assent of his immediate chief he pushed forth
columns from both his divisions. On the south of the
high road the soldiers disappeared in the deep gully of
the Mance, their path marked by puffs of smoke as
they drove back the French skirmishers, and re-appeared
climbing the opposite slope leading to the huge quarries
below Point du Jour ; but here, struck and repelled by
the defenders, they vanished again into the depths,
where they held on to the gravel pits in the bottom.
Nearer the high road, one battalion wedged itself in to
the quarries close to St. Hubert ; while beyond the
highway, the Germans dashed through the wood, established themselves on its eastern border above and

about the farmstead, and stormed the stone parapets set up by the French foreposts at the confluence of the two streamlets which form the Mance. Farther they could not go, because Lebœuf's men stiffly held the eastern patch of woodland, while the open ground towards the Moscow farm was swept by musketry fire from the deep banks in the cross-roads, from the shelter trenches above, and from the loopholed buildings of the farm. But the attack on the Bois de Genivaux aided the men of the Ninth Corps who, from Chantrenne, had entered its northern border, and compelled the defenders of the lines in front of Moscow to turn upon the new assailants. Then the companies which had gathered about St. Hubert became engaged in a destructive contest, for the walls were high and well garnished, and the northern point of attack was more or less commanded by the higher ground towards Moscow. On the south front, however, there proved to be more chances of success.

Relying, perhaps, on Frossard's infantry and guns, the discharges from which commanded the high road, the garrison had forgotten to barricade the gates, doors, and windows; and when the place had been cannonaded by the southern line of guns, the assailants, who had suffered great loss with unflinching hardihood, came on with an irresistible rush, and carried the farm by storm. The feat was accomplished about three o'clock; and the work done gave a solid support to the German right wing. At this time, the German guns, so well fought, having taken more forward positions, had mastered the French artillery, which sank into comparative silence. There were seventy-eight pieces in action on the south of the high road, and fifty-four on the north, and their superiority is admitted and recorded by Frossard himself, who saw his batteries idle or withdrawn, his reserves smitten, and its defenders literally burnt out of the farm buildings at Point du Jour. Yet the French left was not shaken, it was hardly touched, by a vehement attack which had given the Germans a better defensive position, indeed, but still one only on the verge of Frossard's stronghold, and affording no facilities for a rush against the fortified lines occupied by the 3rd French Corps, in the thickets of Genivaux and on the brow of the bare hills.

The capture of St. Hubert was nearly coincident with that stage in the heady fight before Vernéville which saw the Hessians embattled on the Bois de la Cusse, the exposed artillery of the Ninth Corps in retreat from a false position, and the opportune appearance of the Guard about Habonville and of the Saxons to the north-west of St. Marie. In front of their main line the French held the latter village, were well forward in the hollows west of Amanvillers, stood fast in the farms of La Folie, Leipsic, Moscow, Champenois, and that portion of the Bois de Genivaux which covered the eastern arm of the Mance. The fight had raged for more than three hours, and they had only lost possession of the L'Envie and Chantrenne, places distant from their front, and St. Hubert, which, no doubt, was a dangerous-looking salient within a few hundred yards of the well-defended ridge where the high road turned at right angles towards the blazing farm of Point du Jour. From end to end, therefore, and it was between seven and eight miles in length, measured by an air-line, the whole of Bazaine's formidable position was intact. The Imperial Guard, the effective reserve, still stood on the heights east of Chatel St. Germain, behind the left, and six miles from the right where the battle was to be decided.

OPERATIONS BY THE GERMAN LEFT WING.

The two Corps, forming the left wing of the German Army, had been guided far more by the reports brought in by daring cavalry scouts, than by the orders received either from Prince Frederick Charles or von Moltke, because these latter were necessarily less well-informed than the Corps commanders who were the first to receive the information. Yet the latter, of course, while taking their own line conformed to the governing idea, which was that the French right flank, wherever it was, should be turned. Moving eastward from Jarny, with the Twelfth Corps the Crown Prince of Saxony learned before two o'clock, that Roncourt was the extreme northern limit of Canrobert's Corps, and he, therefore, varied a head-quarter's order to march upon St. Marie, by directing one division, the 23rd, under Prince George, to march down the right bank of the Orne, through Auboué, and turn to the right upon Roncourt. One brigade of the 24th division he directed on St. Marie, keeping the other back as a support. About the same time the whole of the Guard, except one brigade detached to back up the Ninth Corps, had formed up near Habonville, and their batteries, as we have seen, had taken up a position which enabled them to smite St. Privat. When, therefore, General Pape had moved up the Guards by the ravine west of St. Marie he found the Saxons ready to co-operate with him in driving out the French battalions occupying the pretty village which has the air of a small rural town. It sits at the foot of the long bare incline leading down from St. Privat, traversed by a straight road bordered, as usual, by tall scraggy trees ; and nestling amid gardens and walled enclosures shines out a cheerful white spot in the diversified landscape. From this point, St. Privat looms dark and large on the hill-top, larger and darker looking than it really is. To the southward of that village, beyond a dip, down and up which the cottages creep, stands the farmstead of Jerusalem, and further south the ground rolls away towards Amanvillers. More than a mile of open country separates St. Privat from St. Marie, affording no lurking places to either side, except such as can be found in the gentle swelling and falling of the fields; indeed, to the casual observer the smoothness of the surface seems broken only by the poplars on the highway. West of St. Marie there is a shallow ravine and beyond it copses, and south, as we know towards Vernéville, more copses, ruddy brown farmsteads, and white villages. At this moment the battle-smoke puffed out, curled, rose in fantastic clouds, or rolled along the ground, upon the hill sides and above the thickets and barns; about St. Marie, however, the air as yet was untainted by the sulphurous mists of combat so rank a mile away, but the garrison stood painfully expectant of the coming fray. For though the Guards were hidden the Saxon brigade to the north-west was visible, and the skirmishers driven from St. Ail, told how the " Prussians " were mustering for the onset.

Suddenly lines of skirmishers appear, gun after gun drives up, the Saxon artillery reinforcing the pieces which the Guard can spare, until three distinct lines of batteries are formed and open on the village. The German Generals, who judged the place to be stronger and more strongly garrisoned than it was, had brought to bear overwhelming forces—probably also to save time; so that, after enduring a hot cannonade from seventy-eight guns, the French battalions, who had borne the bombardment and had spent abundance of ammunition in return, did not await the shock of the storming columns sent against them, but fled by the eastern outlet to their main body. The Guard and the Saxons, who had come on with ringing hurrahs, swept into the place on all sides; some prisoners were taken, but the greater mass of the defenders and the French battery which had kept up a flank fire on the approach to the south face of the village, got safely up the hill. When they were inside St. Marie the assailants were able to see that "the adversary had done nothing to increase, by artificial means, the defensive value of a post, naturally strong; and had even neglected to barricade the roads and paths by which it is entered." The truth is that the occupation of St. Marie by the French was an after-thought, and that although defensible in itself the place was far too remote from the main French line of battle to be supported; and the garrison, which no doubt, in a different temper, might have died fighting in the streets and houses, yielded when they felt the hail of shells and saw the impending storm-cloud of infantry ready to burst upon them. The defenders hastened towards Roncourt and St. Privat, losing men from the fire of their exulting enemies, who followed on the eastern side until stopped by the Chassepot and the guns on the hill. Thus a point of support was secured in that quarter, about half-past three, but no advance could be made until the artillery had prepared the way, and the turning column had made further progress in its march.

Nevertheless, the Saxon troops on the north of St. Marie and some who had been engaged in its capture, carried away by their ardour and the sight of a retreating foe, pursued so far and were so promptly reinforced that a fierce infantry fight ensued. For a French brigade, led by General Péchot, dashed out of their lines, struck roughly on the front and turned the left flank of the Saxons who, being obstinate, held the slightly uneven meadow lands with great difficulty and much loss. Although they were aided by their own batteries and those of the Guard which had been moved forward on the front between St. Ail and Habonville, and whose fire smote diagonally the French columns rushing out of Roncourt and St. Privat, yet the Saxons were overmatched; and, after much labour, as they were nearly all spread out in skirmishing order, General Nehrdorff, who comprehended the situation, and saw the waste of effort, gradually drew them back to the original line. The French counter attack, swift and sharp, was well sustained, and the bold Saxons paid a heavy price for their temerity. While this combat was in progress, the Crown Prince of Saxony from a height in front of Auboué, gazing intently towards Roncourt, made an important discovery—he saw troops in movement to the north of that village, and, in fact, Canrobert's outposts extended nearly to the Orne. Thus, after a long search, yet not before four o'clock, the extreme right of the French Army was at length found, and thereupon the turning column of horse, foot, and guns, one-half Prince George's division, was ordered to take a still wider sweep northward ere it wheeled in upon the French rear. As it marched stealthily on its way, the Saxon artillery developed a long line of batteries pointing towards Roncourt, protected by Craushaar's brigade, which made a lodgment in the western block of a deep wooded ravine on the left of the guns, and stood ready to dash forward when their comrades emerged from the villages and copses behind the French right. In the centre the troops of the Ninth Corps had stormed and occupied the farm of Champenois, had tried again, without success, to win the eastern tracts of the Bois de Genivaux, and, supported by 106 guns, had maintained a sanguinary contest with Lebœuf's steady brigades, ensconced over against them in the farms, thickets, and hollow ways. About five o'clock the fury of the battle diminished for a moment, in the centre, on the left, and even on the right, where, down to that hour, it had raged with a spirit and vigour which must now be described.

GENERAL FROSSARD REPELS A FRESH ATTACK.

The enormous defensive strength of the position held by General Frossard's Corps does not seem to have been thoroughly understood by anyone except that accomplished engineer. Marshal Bazaine did not perceive its value, for he was perpetually afraid that the Germans would break in upon it, either from the Bois de Vaux or by the high road, and his apprehensions or prejudices were confirmed when a column of troops was seen to be ascending the river-road from Ars towards Jussy, near St. Ruffine. General von Steinmetz, on the other hand, who had peered out from every available height between the Bois des Ognons and Gravelotte, although each attack which he had directed had been repelled, thought he discerned symptoms of weakness and even of retreat. The truth is that Frossard's men were well hidden, not less by the natural features of the ground than by the trenches which he had dug and the breastworks which he had thrown up. If his batteries were silent or withdrawn it was because, although overpowered in the gun fight, they were yet still able to arrest the onsets of infantry; and if the French fantassins were invisible, it was because they were lying down or arrayed on the reverse of the ridge. The hot-tempered General of the First Army, however, surmised, after the capture of St. Hubert, that troops had been detached to aid the distant right, or that a moment had

come when, if pressed home by an attack of all arms,
Point du Jour could be carried and the French driven
headlong into Metz.   Under the influence of this delusion he rode up to General von Goeben, who was watching the battle, near Gravelotte.   Captain Seton, an
Indian officer who was present, noticed the violent.
gestures and rapid talk of Steinmetz because they
offered so strong a contrast to the steady coolness of
the younger warrior.   At that moment he was expound-
ing opinions and issuing orders which brought on one
of the most brilliant and destructive episodes in the
battle.   Goeben had already sent forward Gneisenau's
brigade, partly on and partly north of the road, but
they were needed to feed the combat, support the
weakened and scattered companies, and secure St.
Hubert.

What Steinmetz now designed was a home-thrust on
the French position ; and, accordingly, he ordered several
batteries of the Seventh Corps and von Hartmann's
cavalry division to cross the Gravelotte defile and
plant themselves on the gentle acclivities to the
south of the road.   Now the highway runs first through
a cutting, is then carried on an embankment, and only
near St. Hubert are the gentle southern slopes above
the gully accessible to horses and guns.   But this narrow
track swarmed with troops, into the midst of which
came the cavalry and artillery.   The infantry gave way
and four batteries arrived on the opposite side of the
defile, followed by the 9th Uhlans.   But so deadly was
the storm of shot which burst from the French position—
for cannon, mitrailleuse, and chassepot went instantly
to work—that two of the batteries were at once driven
into the ravine below.   The Uhlans actually rode out into
the open, took up a position, and remained until it was
plain to all that the lives of men and horses were being

uselessly sacrificed. The other regiments, " well pep-
pered," had already gone "threes about " before clearing
the defile, and the Uhlans, who were dropping fast, rode
back, as well as they could, to Gravelotte or the shelter-
ing woods. A more extravagant movement has rarely
been attempted in war, or one less justified by the
evident facts of the situation as well as by the deadly
results. Yet two batteries actually remained, one,
under Captain Hasse, in the open, about seven hundred
yards from the French lines of musketry; the other,
commanded by Captain Gnügge, covered in front by the
low wall of the St. Hubert garden, but lending a flank
to the adversary at the top of the road. Captain Hasse
and his gunners were stubborn men; they fought their
battery for two hours, in fact, until nearly all the men
and horses were down. Even then Hasse would not
retire, and one of his superiors was obliged to hurry up
fresh teams and forcibly drag the guns away. But the
battery under the wall held on, and did good service
by firing on the French about the Moscow farm.

The failure of these mistaken attacks and the retreat
of guns and horsemen seems to have shaken the constant
German infantry, for they gave ground everywhere but
at St. Hubert, and the French came on with such vigour
that General Steinmetz himself and his staff were under
a heavy fire. Fortunately three fresh battalions plunged
into the combat; but they could not do more than
sustain it; for every attempt made to approach the
French, either towards the Moscow farm or Point du
Jour, met with a speedy repulse. Indeed, down to
five o'clock, the point of time at which we have arrived,
along the whole line, no progress whatever had been
made by the German right wing, which held on to
St. Hubert, the ravine of the Mance, and the western
portion of the Bois de Genivaux, but could not show a

rifle or bayonet beyond in any direction. It was only the powerful German artillery which still remained the superb masters of the field, so far as their action was concerned.

It was at this time that King William and his staff, which included Prince Bismarck, rode up to the high ground above Malmaison, where he established his head-quarters in the field, and whence, until nearly dark, he watched the battle. Over against him, concerned respecting his left, and ignorant of the state of the battle on his right, was Marshal Bazaine, in the fort of Plappeville, whither he had returned from St. Quentin, which commanded a wide view to the south and south-west. He says that he gave General Bourbaki discretion to use the Guard wherever it might be wanted. But that officer knew little more than the Commander-in-Chief. An hour or two earlier, taking with him the Grenadier Division of the Guard, he had started towards the north, following a hilly road east of the St. Germain ravine. He had seen the immense mountain of white smoke which towered up in the north-west, but the current of air, hardly a wind, apparently blew from the south-east, since at Plappeville he could not hear the roar of the guns, and the view was so obstructed that he could not obtain even a glimpse of the country about St. Privat. He had to leave behind him the Voltigeurs and Chasseurs of the Guard, who were partly in reserve and partly posted to support Lebœuf, who called up one regiment from Brincourt's brigade. Bazaine had also sent some guns to support Lapasset in his contest with the troops which von Golz had marched up from Ars to the woodlands and vineyards opposite St. Ruffine. The French at this stage were still in good spirits. If Lebœuf was a little anxious behind his farmsteads, his woods, and skilfully-disposed re-entering echelons of

shelter trenches; Frossard, who soon after relieved his
front ranks from the reserve, was content; and de
Ladmirault, as was usual with him, believed that he
might be almost considered victorious, and only required
a few battalions of the Guard to ensure his success. The
ammunition on both sides was running out here and
there; indeed, Canrobert declares that he was compelled
to borrow from de Ladmirault; still there was enough to
last out the day. Over the seven or eight miles of
flame and smoke and tumult, for a brief interval, came
what may be called a lull compared with the deafening
tempest of sounds which smote on the ear when the
rival combatants raged most fiercely.

THE LAST FIGHTS NEAR ST. HUBERT.

For some time longer the German right wing did
little more than defend its somewhat irregular line of
front. The Second Corps, which had been marching
every day since it quitted the Saar, had attained Rezonville, and King William placed it under the orders of
von Steinmetz. As the minutes flew by, the head-
quarter staff on the hill near Malmaison were impressed
by a fact and an appearance—the increase of the vivacity
and volume of fire towards the North—where the
Guard had begun its onset on St. Privat—and the
symptoms of wavering which seemed, and only seemed,
to be visible on the French left. The King, therefore, sanctioned a fresh and formidable advance upon
Frossard's brigades by all the troops which von Steinmetz could spare for the enterprise. But the main
object of von Moltke, we infer, was to prevent, by
striking hard, the despatch of any assistance to Canrobert, and thus assist, by a resolute advance, upon one
wing, the decisive movement then approaching its
critical stage on the other. The Second Corps was,

therefore, brought up to Gravelotte, and all the available troops of the Seventh and Eighth were held in readiness to assail, once more, the enemies beyond the Mance.

But the French, who, though wearied, were still undaunted, anticipating their foes, became the assailants. Their silent guns spoke out in thunder, the heights were shrouded in a canopy of smoke, and the bolts hurled from the batteries fell like hail on the woods, and sent such an iron shower as far forward as the hilltop where the King and his great men stood that von Roon prevailed on the King to ride further back. The lively French skirmishers dashed forth into the open, strove hard to reach St. Hubert, drove the German foreposts headlong down the steeps into the Mance gully, filled the high road with a rushing, clamorous crowd of fugitives, and even caused terror and commotion in the rear of Gravelotte, so vehement and unexpected was the stroke. Fortunately for the Germans, the principal bodies of troops in St. Hubert and the woods were unshaken, and their rapid fire, as well as the responses sent from the artillery, checked the violent outfall. Then, as the sun was getting low, the fresh German brigades struck in. The men of the Seventh Corps went down into and over the Mance valley, and stormed up the eastern bank. The Second Corps, eager to win, pressed along the highway, with their drums and trumpets sounding the charge, or moved on the south side. They passed onward in a tumult, and boldly tried to grapple with the strong lines of the defence. Not only their commander, Fransecky, and Steinmetz, but von Moltke himself rode into the defile to witness and direct this huge and uproarious column of attack. But neither their numbers, and they were many, nor their valour, which was great, nor the

unfaltering devotion of their officers could resist the
smashing fire of cannon and mitrailleuse and chassepot
which the French brought to bear upon them.   Some
daring spirits pressed close up towards the ditches and
breastworks, a few clung to the banks and bushes on
the brow of the slope near Point du Jour.   A dense
mass collected near St. Hubert, where Fransecky and
Steinmetz, in the thick of the throng, saw the bands who
had hurried to the front break off, turn and hasten rearward, while fresh troops still pressed upward through
the confused crowds of fugitives.   So for some time,
in the twilight, the strange fight went on.   As it
grew darker, the outlines of Lebœuf's cleverly-designed
shelter trenches near the Moscow farm were drawn in
lines of musketry fire, and gradually nothing, save the
flashes of guns and rifles, could be seen in the gloom.
At length, when friend could not be distinguished from
foe, when no breach could be made in the French line,
which, except the outpost of St. Hubert, remained what
it had been in the morning, the Generals placed strong
guards on their front, and stood prepared to renew the
battle with the dawn.   General Frossard, who had engaged all his reserves, was proud of his achievement,
and not less of the foresight he displayed in providing
artificial cover for his men.   That had made the position,
from the Great Quarries to the farm and copse of La
Folie, impregnable, and renders it all the more difficult
to comprehend how Marshal Bazaine could have shown
such manifest distrust of the fastness which protected
his left wing.   The attack on St. Ruffine by von Golz
was merely a diversion shrewdly designed to increase
the Marshal's alarms, and its relative success shows how
correctly von Moltke estimated his adversary's abilities
as a soldier.   He reaped an ample reward, since long
before the last shot was fired in the neighbourhood of

St. Hubert, the French had been worsted at the other
and distant extremity of the vast field of battle.

THE PRUSSIAN GUARD ON THE CENTRE AND LEFT.

It may be said, indeed, that not one, but several
battles were fought on the 18th of August, in the long
space between the Bois de Vaux and the Forest of
Moyœuvre. They were inter-dependent, because one
mass of combatants held fast another, and the essence
of the German plan was that three-fourths of the French
Army should be nailed to the positions they had taken
up, while the remainder were crushed by the pressure
of superior forces. The original design of von Moltke
was framed on the supposition that the French right
stood near Amanvillers, and that he would be able to
fling upon an exposed flank two Corps d'Armée. Before
the error was discovered, several hours had been consumed; the Guard had been obliged to prolong the
front fighting line; only a part of the Saxon Corps
could be spared to engage in the turning movement,
and the ground which they had to traverse grew longer
and longer as the day waxed shorter. The extent of
country over which the various armies operated, and
the smoke which obscured the view, prevented a correct appreciation of the situation of affairs at a given
moment, and the German commanders were liable to
be deceived, and were deceived by appearances. The
knowledge that so brief an interval of daylight remained,
and an anxiety to make the most of precious moments,
quickened the tendency to decisive action, and thus
brought about the rash and premature attack which
was so destructive, and nearly proved so fatal to the
Prussian Guard.

Their magnificent divisions of infantry, it will be
remembered, stood between St. Ail and St. Marie,

except one brigade which had been annexed to the
Ninth Corps. It was intended that they should remain
quiescent until the Saxon column broke out upon the
French right in the direction of Roncourt, and for a
brief interval of time, after five o'clock, the action in
the centre as well as on the left was confined to a
deliberate cannonade. Prince Augustus of Würtemberg,
who was then near St. Ail gazing alternately on the
ebb and flow of Manstein's battle in the Bois de la
Cusse and towards the Bois de Genivaux, and on the
aspect of the field about St. Privat, thought he saw
French troops moving south from Roncourt. Com-
bining this impression with the fact that, as we have
already stated, a long line of Saxon guns had been
arrayed due north of St. Marie, he rapidly formed the
opinion that the turning column was on the point of
striking the enemy, and that the moment had come
when the Guard should be employed. He was also
somewhat affected by the condition of the combat in
the centre, and, perhaps, as much by the waning day
which left so narrow a margin of time for decisive
activity. He appealed to Prince Frederick Charles
and easily converted the Commander-in-Chief of the
Second Army to his views. So the order went forth
that the Guard should attack, and having set Budritzki's
division in motion from St. Ail, Prince Augustus rode
to St. Marie. There General von Pape revealed to him
his misconception—the turning column was not even
then in sight, and unless preceded by bombardment
from all the batteries, a front attack on St. Privat, Pape
said, would have but a slight chance of success. Why,
then, was it delivered ? Because the other division of
the Guard was actually at that moment under fire and
losing men by scores on the open slope. It was a
bitter moment for Prince Augustus, whose error was to

cost the Guard losses which are counted by thousands.
Moreover, General Manstein, seeing Budritzki in motion,
and de Cissey, whose division formed de Ladmirault's
right, wheeling up diagonally on the flanks of the new
foe, determined to despatch his Brigade of Guards, the
3rd, straight upon Amanvillers, to resume the offensive
with his Hessians, and support, by all the means he
possessed, the daring onset initiated on his immediate
left.   Practically, therefore, although other troops were
engaged at different points on the front of the Ninth
Corps, the battle on the northern half of the field was
thenceforth fought out by the Saxons and the Guard.

The character of the unequal combat was the same
from end to end of the line—superb, because it proved
the steadfast valour of Prussia's chosen infantry ; awful,
because the bare fields in the track of the onslaught
were soon literally strewed with thousands of dead and
wounded.   The charge of the 3rd Brigade towards
Amanvillers was pushed with such unwavering velocity
that, although the ranks were thinned at every stride,
the hardy survivors, spread out in skirmishing order,
carried their front to the brow of a hill within half a
mile of Amanvillers.   There they were stopped by the
fire which smote them in front and flank.   Yet there
they stayed undaunted, and maintained a steady contest
with antagonists who, if they tried to dash forward,
could not reach the unyielding line of the 3rd Brigade.
On their left the Hessians moved up on both sides of
the railroad cutting, and finally captured a house built
for the watchman at a level crossing.   Comrades of
the Ninth Corps, from the Bois de la Cusse, soldiers
who had been toiling for many hours, essayed to reach
the Guard, but they had not strength enough left, and
retired when they suddenly discerned, above Amanvillers, two regiments of Grenadiers—it was Bourbaki

who had led Picard's battalions on to the plateau, but who, distrusting appearances visible about and beyond St. Privat, feared to plunge into the fight at Amanvillers. Looking out from his hill, Bourbaki may have seen the devoted march of Budritzki's troops up the gentle slope in front of St. Ail; for these, what was left of them, were closing on the spur which lies south-west of St. Privat, and stretching out as far as the high road to St. Marie, a long dark streak of fire and smoke and the broad fields behind them black with the dying and dead. For the constant Guards, undismayed, the remnant of a splendid division, not only persevered and won the little rounded hill, but rooted themselves under its shelving terraces, while the left companies, next the high road, found shelter in its ditches. They had suffered most when beyond the effective range of the needle-gun, in the belt where the Chassepot had rained balls as thick as hail. They could now retort the fire, and at least keep their opponents at bay. These battalions, like those of the 3rd Brigade, had dared all the deadly perils of the open ground; they had bought a relative success at a heavy price, and were resolved to retain what they had won, their line of fire extending from the high road to the rounded eminence, or long hillock, south-west of Jerusalem. Three batteries had driven up to aid the infantry; the main body of the Guard Artillery had advanced eastward; and the Hessians and 3rd Brigade prolonged the front of combat to the south.

During part of the period thus occupied General Pape, holding one brigade in reserve at St. Marie, attacked with the other on the north of the high road. Starting at a quarter to six o'clock, this body of Guardsmen crossed the road facing north, and then wheeling in succession to the right, went obstinately forward.

The French fire, from the outset, was close and deadly;
officers of all ranks fell fast ; companies were reduced
to straggling groups or scattered files ; the whole line
was soon dispersed here and there ; but they still
pressed on.   One moiety trended to the right another
to the left, and General von Pape, watchful, active, and
fortunate, for he was not hit, led fresh battalions to
fill up the gaping intervals.   Soon after the foremost
bands had got within seven hundred yards of St. Privat,
where, in places, at least, the slope afforded shelter, the
reinforcements arrived ; and it may be said that thenceforth a continuous, yet thin line, curved inwards at the
northern end, and fringed with smoke and fire, stretched
irregularly over the vast glacis-like declivities from
opposite Amanvillers to the outskirts of Roncourt,
where the Saxons prolonged the ragged and shapeless,
but redoubtable array.   Against this mere thread of
riflemen, not even when they were weakest, the French
directed no bold attack, perhaps because they had no
reserves and stood in respectful awe of the hostile
artillery which drew nearer and nearer as the evening
wore on, until the black batteries formed a second line
to the intrepid infantry.

It was about seven o'clock.   St. Privat was in flames,
the black and tawny smoke of the burning village, boil-
ing upwards, stood out against the obscured sky in
strong contrast to the swelling clouds of white vapour,
through which leaped incessant sparkles from hundreds
of rifles, and the broader flashes of the cannon.   At no
preceding period of this dreadful day had the battle
raged with such intensity; for now along the whole
front of eight miles there was a deafening roar and
crash and tumult, and a murky atmosphere concealing
the ghastly sights which make these fields of carnage so
appalling to the lively imagination, which seeks in vain

to realize its multitude and variety of horror. Yet
there was an element of grandeur and sublimity in the
exhibition of courage, constancy and fortitude upon
such a stupendous scale.   " It is a good thing that war
is so terrible," said General Robert Lee, " otherwise we
should become too fond of it." Here, among these
woods and villages of Lorraine, war showed in abundance its attractive and repulsive forms.

THE CAPTURE OF ST. PRIVAT.

Marshal Canrobert had discerned the approaching
Saxons, who were now marching from the north upon
Roncourt, Montois, and Malancourt. He felt that his
right had been turned, and looked in vain for the
expected succour. Bazaine, he says, had promised to
send a division of the Guard. Bourbaki, astounded by
the spectacle which met his eyes, when he emerged from
the wooded defiles west of Saulny, had, as we have
seen, allowed himself to be attracted, for a moment,
towards de Ladmirault, had then retraced his steps,
and had taken a position to cover the high road to
Woippy, the so-called northern road from Metz which
goes to Briey. He had with him, according to his own
statement, three or four thousand Grenadiers and some
artillery ; but he did not arrive in time to frustrate
the Saxons and Prussian Guards. The Marshal, a little
after seven, or even before, felt that he could not stand.
He complains of failing ammunition, declares that the
German artillery had obtained a complete mastery over
his guns, and that his flank was turned. " At this
moment," he says in his own picturesque fashion, " a
valiant officer, who has since been killed before Paris,
and who was called Péchot, arrived at St. Privat [from
Roncourt] with the 9th battalion of Chasseurs, the 6th
and 12th of the Line. He dashed forward to stop the

enemy; but, as the enemy flung at us masses of iron, and did not come himself, as it was shells which came instead, we could not hold on. Péchot warned me, and we were obliged to retire. We did so by moving in echelon from the centre, and, in good order, I emphasize the phrase, we gained the heights beside the wood of Saulny." The German Staff acknowledge that the rearward movement was admirably done; but the succinct narrative vouchsafed by the Marshal to the Court which tried Bazaine, gives only a vague glimpse of the closing scene.

When the "valiant Péchot" retired from Roncourt before the Saxon inroad, he skilfully put his brigade into the forest of Jaumont, on the right rear of the original line. Colonel Montluisant, the gallant artilleryman, having received a welcome supply of ammunition, sent up from St. Quentin by the order of Bazaine, posting his batteries in lines one above the other on the terraces near the wood of Saulny, opened a sustained fire to cover the retreat. Bourbaki, although Canrobert did not know it at the time, such was the confusion and so thick was the air, had moved his batteries and Grenadiers near enough at dusk to bring both musketry and cannon-shot to bear upon the Germans. In St. Privat, glowing like a furnace, and as the darkness became deeper, shedding a wild light upon the scene, there were still stout and obstinate soldiers who either would not, or could not, follow the retiring brigades. Upon these devoted troops, as the sun went down behind the dark border of woods beyond the valley of the Orne, the much-tried Prussian Guards and the leg-weary Saxons threw themselves with all their remaining vigour; and in rear of them, yet far down the slope, stepped one Division of the Tenth Corps. The guns reinforced had again been dragged forward,

some overwhelming St. Privat, others pounding Montluisant, or facing south-east, and smiting the French
about Amanvillers. Then, with loud hurrahs, the
assailants broke into St. Privat, pursued the defenders
amid the burning houses, captured two thousand prisoners, who were unable to escape from the buildings,
and developed their lines in the twilight on the plateau
beyond. The capture of St. Privat enabled the German
artillery to press on once more, each battery striving
to gain the foremost place. For Canrobert's retreat
exposed the right flank of de Ladmirault's Corps, and,
under a scathing fire, he was obliged to throw it back,
protected by Bourbaki on the hill, and supported by
a brigade promptly despatched towards that side by
Lebœuf, who, all through the eddying fight, showed a
fine tactical sense and great decision. How far the
Germans were able to push their advantage it is difficult
to say, since General Gondrecourt, who was near the
place, maintains that some of de Ladmirault's soldiers
remained through the night in Amanvillers; whereas
the Germans assert that they broke into part of the
village. Be that as it may, Montigny la Grange, La
Folie, and the posts thence to Point du Jour, for certain, were held by the French until the morning. Marshal Lebœuf has stated that he summoned his Generals
in the evening, and said to them: " The two Corps on
our right, crushed by superior forces, have been obliged
to retire. We have behind us," he added, " one of the
defiles through which they ('cette troupe') may
retreat. If we give back a step the Army is lost. The
position, doubtless, is difficult, but we will remain."
He declares that the attack continued until midnight,
and that not one of his men budged a foot, which is
true; but Canrobert's men did fly in disorder to
Woippy, and de Ladmirault confessed that there was

" some disorder " in his Corps, and that what remained
of them in the wood of Saulny stood to their arms all
night.   The General states his case in an extraordinary
manner.   " Night," he says, " surprised us in this situation, having gained the battle, but not having been able
to maintain our positions."   What he meant to assert
was that he, de Ladmirault, had won the battle, but
that the defeat of Canrobert had obliged him to retire.
The truth was that some troops remained in Montigny
la Grange, but that the rest, or nearly all of them, were
huddled together in the wood of Saulny, whence they
retreated at dawn.

During the night each Corps commander received
from Marshal Bazaine an order to occupy certain positions under the guns of Metz.   Canrobert, de Ladmirault,
and the Guard, marched in the night, or very early in
the morning, to the places assigned them; Lebœuf
began his movement at dawn, but Frossard kept outposts on his front line long after daylight.   During the
forenoon, however, the Army of the Rhine had gained
the shelter of a fortified town, which they were not able
to quit until they marched off to Germany as prisoners
of war.

The effective strength of the German Armies present
on the field of Gravelotte was 203,402 men, and 726
guns; it would not be easy to calculate how many were
actually engaged in the fight, but the forces held in
reserve were considerable.   The number on the French
side has been put as low as 120,000, and as high as
150,000 men, and probably about 530 guns.   The loss
of the Germans in killed and wounded was 20,159, and
493 missing.   The French loss is set down at 7,853
killed and wounded, and 4,419 prisoners, many of whom
were wounded men.   The disproportion is tremendous,
and shows once again that, armed with the breechloader,

the defender is able to kill and injure nearly two to one. There were killed or mortally wounded in the German ranks no fewer than 5,237 officers and men, while the aggregate for the French is only 1,144.   The loss of officers and men in the Prussian Guards, nearly all inflicted in half an hour before St. Privat, reached the dreadful total of 2,440 killed or mortally injured, and of wounded 5,511!

CHAPTER X.

THE STATE OF THE GAME, AND THE NEW MOVES.

THE huge, stubborn, vehement and bloody conflict waged in the rural tract between the northern edges of the Bois de Vaux and the Forest of Jaumont, which the French Marshal called the "Defence of the Lines of Amanvillers," the French Army, "the Battle of St. Privat," and the Germans the battle of "Gravelotte-St. Privat," established the mastery of the latter over "the Army of the Rhine." Marshal Bazaine had not proved strong enough to extricate the Army he was suddenly appointed to command from the false position in which it had been placed by the errors and hesitations of the Emperor and Marshal Lebœuf. He had not been able to retrieve the time wasted between the 7th and 13th of August, by imparting, after that period, energy and swiftness to the movements of his troops, or, if he possessed the ability, of which there is no sign, he did not put it forth. Certain words imputed to General Changarnier, correctly or otherwise, hit the blot exactly. "Bazaine," the General is represented as saying, "was incapable of commanding so large an Army. He was completely bewildered by its great numbers. He did not know how to move his men. He could not operate with the forces under his orders." So simple an explanation did not, of course, satisfy those who could only account for a stupendous calamity by accusing the Marshal of treason. But on the 19th of August, the Emperor was still on the throne, and whatever thoughts may have passed through the mind of Bazaine after Sedan, it is inconceivable that he wilfully sacrificed the Army before that event. He was misinformed, he could not grasp the situation, he formed conjectures, without any solid basis, and acted on them; he was oppressed by the comparative want of provisions and munitions; and, above all, he could not resist the magnetism exerted by a stronghold like Metz, a magnetism which is likely to prove fatal to other weak captains who will have to handle armies, counted by hundreds of thousands, in the vicinity of extensive fortified camps. The consequences of the battles of Colombey, Vionville and Gravelotte are sufficiently accounted for by a recognition of the errors which, from the outset, placed the Army of the Rhine in a position whence it could have been extricated by a Napoleon or a Frederick, but not by a Bazaine; and only quenchless wrath, born of defeat, or " preternatural suspicion " too rife in the French Army, could seek an explanation in personal ambition or treason. The war was begun without the preparation of adequate means; the operations projected were based on miscalculations, political and military; the Generals were selected by favour; and when the collision of Armies took place, the French were out-numbered, out-marched, out-fought, and out-generalled. Bazaine was no more a traitor than Prince Charles of Lorraine in Prague, the King of Saxony in Pirna, or even poor Mack in Ulm. He was a brave soldier, and an excellent corps commander, but he was very far from ranking among those captains, and, according to the first Napoleon, they are few, who have the faculty and knowledge required to command 300,000 men. Upon his subsequent conduct, being beyond its scope, this history has nothing to say; moreover, it would acquire a volume to illuminate that dreadful labyrinth, the " Procès Bazaine." All we require to note is that, as a result of a series of errors, the whole of which did not fall to the Marshal's share, one French Army had been routed and driven headlong to Chalons, and another, the larger and better, had been worsted in combat and forced to seek shelter within the fortified area of Metz.

The German leaders forthwith resolved, and acted on the resolve, to take the largest advantage of success. When the broadening day showed that the French were encamped under the guns of the forts, and that they did not betray the faintest symptom of fighting for egress on any side, the place was deliberately invested. On the 18th, the cavalry had cut the telegraph between Metz and Thionville, and partially injured the railway between Thionville and Longuyon; and the French had hardly repaired the wire on the 19th before it was again severed. Soon the blockade was so far completed that only adventurous scouts were able at rare intervals to work their way through the German lines. As early as the forenoon of the 19th, the King had decided to form what came to be called the " Army of the Meuse " out of the Corps which were not needed to uphold the investment of Metz, and thus place himself in a condition to assail the French Army collecting at Chalons. The new organization was composed of the Guard, the Fourth and the Twelfth Corps, and the Fifth and Sixth Divisions of Cavalry; and this formidable force was put under the command of the Crown Prince of Saxony, who had shown himself to be an able soldier. Consequently, there remained behind to invest Bazaine, seven Corps d'Armée and a Division of Reserve under General von Kummer, which had marched up from Saarlouis, and was then actually before Metz on the right bank of the Moselle east of and below the town. The main strength, six Corps, were posted on the left or western bank, and the supreme command was entrusted to Prince Frederick Charles. Not a moment was lost in distributing the troops so that they could support each other, and in sealing up the avenues of access to the place. A bridge over the Moselle, covered by a tête de pont was constructed above and below Metz; defensive positions were selected and entrenched, and throughout the whole circuit, in suitable places, heavy solid works, as well as lighter obstructions, were begun. If the enemy tried to reach Thionville by the left bank he was to find an organized defensive position in his path, and the troops beyond the Moselle were to assail his right flank. If he endeavoured to pass on the other shore, similar means would be applied to bar his way. Field works would arrest his attack, and his left flank in that case would be struck. Egress to the west was to be opposed by abbatis, trenches and other obstacles. Remilly, then the terminus of the railway, and the site of a great magazine, was to be specially guarded; but if any "eccentric" movement were attempted on the eastern area, the Generals were to evade an engagement with superior forces. It is not necessary to enter more minutely into the blockade of Metz, which henceforth becomes subordinate to the main story. We have followed, so far, the fortunes or misfortunes of the Army now surrounded by vigilant, skilful and valiant foes; but the active interest of the campaign lies in other fields, and bears us along to an undreamed-of and astounding end.

THE KING MARCHES WESTWARD.

One Army had been literally imprisoned, another remained at large, and behind it were the vast resources

of France. Three Marshals were cooped up in the cage
on the Moselle; one, MacMahon, and the Emperor were
still in the field; and upon the forces with them it was
resolved to advance at once, because prudence required
that they should be shattered before they could be
completely organized, and while the moral effect of the
resounding blows struck in Alsace and Lorraine had
lost none of its terrible power.   Therefore the King and
General von Moltke started on the morrow of victory
to march on Paris through the plains of Champagne.
The newly-constituted Army of the Meuse, on the 20th,
was in line between Commercy and Briey, moving
towards Verdun on a broad front, with the cavalry
so well forward that on the 22nd the Guard Uhlans were
over the Meuse.   At the same time the Crown Prince
of Prussia, who had continued his march from the
Meurthe and Upper Moselle, was astride the Meuse
between Void and Gondrecourt, with infantry in front
at Ligny and a cavalry patrol as far forward as Vitry.
His columns had passed by roads south of Toul, from
the Moselle valley on to the Ornain, and as Toul refused
to surrender when, a little later, it was bombarded by
field guns, a small detachment was left to invest it until
captured French garrison guns could be hauled up from
Marsal.   On the 23rd the Meuse Army was up to the
right bank of the river, and the whole of the Third had
entered the basin of the Ornain.   Both Armies advanced
the next day further westward and continued the
movement on the 25th—a critical day on which they
attained positions it becomes necessary to note more
minutely. The Twelfth Corps, having failed on the 24th
to carry Verdun by a coup de main, halted at Dombasle
on the 25th, with its cavalry at Clermont in Argonne
and St. Menchould.   The Guard was on the Aisne at
Triaucourt, the Fourth near by at Laheycourt, the

Second Bavarians on their left front at Possesse, the Fifth Corps near Heiltz l'éveque, the Würtemberg Division at Sermaize on the Ornain, the Eleventh Corps close to Vitry on the Marne, the Sixth Corps at Vassy on the Blaise, and the First Bavarians at Bar le Duc, whither the King had come on the 24th, by way of Commercy, from Pont à Mousson. Thus the whole force was marching direct on Chalons, left in front; that is, the Third Army, as a rule, was a march in advance of the Saxon Crown Prince.

THE CAVALRY OPERATIONS.

During the period occupied in reaching these towns and villages the cavalry had been actively employed scouting far in advance and on the flanks; and what they did forms the most interesting and instructive portion of the story. As early as the 17th a troop of Hussars captured a French courrier at Commercy, and from his despatches learned that the cavalry of Can-robert's Corps had been left behind at Chalons, that Paris was being placed in a state of defence, that all men between 25 and 35 had been called under arms, and that a 12th and 13th Corps were to be formed. Another patrol was able to ascertain that at least part of de Failly's troops had retreated by Charmes, and that other hostile bodies had gone by Vaudemont and Neuf-chateau; they were hurrying to the railway station at the latter place and at Chaumont. At Ménil sur Saulx, on the 18th, the indefatigable horsemen seized many letters, and a telegram from M. Chevreau, Minister of the Interior, stating that the Emperor had reached Chalons on the 17th—he really arrived there on the evening of the 16th, having driven from Gravelotte in the morning—and that "considerable forces" were being collected in the famous camp on the dusty and windy plains of Champagne. Thus, day after day, the mounted parties preceded the infantry, spreading far and wide on all sides, so that as early as the 19th some Hussars actually rode within sight of French infantry retreating from St. Dizier, and on the 21st captured men belonging to the 5th Corps near Vitry. The next day the Second Cavalry Division rode out from four-and-twenty to six-and-thirty miles, entering, among other places, Chaumont, where, from the station books, they learned that de Failly's infantry had gone on, three days only before, in twenty trains, while Brahaut's Cavalry followed the road On the 23rd the Fourth Division of Cavalry had passed St. Dizier and ridden into the villages to the east of Chalons itself. Thence Dragoons were sent forward and these picked up information to the effect that the French Army had quitted the great camp. Reports to this effect had already reached headquarters, and had moved von Moltke to tell General von Blumenthal, the Crown Prince's chief of the staff, that it would be most desirable to have prompt information showing whither the enemy had gone. The Fourth Cavalry Division, which, on the 24th, was at Chalons camp, now abandoned, burnt, and desolate, pushed a party towards Reims, and there found that the French Army had departed in an easterly direction. Before this vital information arrived at the great head-quarters the King and von Moltke had determined that the two Armies should, at least for the time, still move westward on the lines appointed; and on the evening of the 25th, therefore, they occupied the positions already described. But at this moment the Army of MacMahon stood halted at Rhetel, Attigny, and Vouziers, within two marches of the Meuse, between Stenay and Sedan!

In order to learn why they were there we must turn to the camp at Chalons, which had been the scene of dramatic events, fluctuating councils, and fatal decisions, the fitting forerunners of an unparalleled disaster.

THE EMPEROR AT CHALONS AND REIMS.

Immediately after the first defeats befell the French Armies on the frontier, General Montauban, Comte de Palikao, summoned by the Empress, found himself abruptly made the head of a Government. He took, of course, the post of Minister of War. The Empress had been Regent from the day when the Emperor quitted Paris, and she exercised, or appeared to do so, a great influence on the course of events. The first act of the new Minister was to collect the materials out of which might be formed a fresh Army, a task in the execution of which he displayed considerable energy. The rapid march of the invader had intercepted, as we have related, one infantry division of Canrobert's Corps, all his cavalry "except a squadron," as he pathetically exclaimed, and more than half of his artillery. These remained in the camp of Chalons, and the Army formed was composed of these men, the 12th Corps, one division of which consisted of Marine Infantry; then the 1st and 5th Corps, which had come at racing speed from Alsace; and finally of the 7th from Belfort, which reached Chalons by way of Paris. There were in addition two regiments of Chasseurs d'Afrique, and subsequently a third—Margueritte's gallant brigade. General Lebrun estimates that the aggregates, including non-combatants, amounted to about 130,000 men. It will be duly noted that this Army came almost from the four winds, driven thither by the terrible pressure of defeat, and that many of the new troops were recruits, without discipline or training. They were collected together on an open plain, and had barely assembled before the vivacious German cavalry were reported to be and, though in small force, were

close at hand. When the Emperor arrived on the night
of the 16th, by far the greater part of the troops were
still distant; some speeding on their way from Chaumont
and Joinville, others travelling from Belfort, and some
from Cherbourg and Paris. They dropped into the
camp in succession after the 17th, and we may note
that the 7th Corps never entered Chalons at all, but
was sent on to Reims, which it reached on the 21st.
Out of this assembly of soldiers Marshal MacMahon had
to organize an Army. Moreover, the intendants, charged
with the duty of supplying the troops, had only just
come up. To increase the confusion many thousand
Mobiles, who had been at an early date sent thither from
Paris, behaved so badly—some reports of their ape-like
tricks are almost incredible—that they were speedily
returned to the capital, although the Emperor and
Marshal Canrobert, who had commanded them, would
have preferred, the former for political reasons, that
they should be distributed in the northern garrison
towns. Nothing more need be said of the Army of
Chalons except that, although it contained some admirable troops, none finer than the Marines, whose only
fault was that they could not march, yet that it was
unfit to engage in any adventure whatever, especially
one so perilous and toilsome as that into which it was
soon plunged.

Weary, perturbed, broken in health and spirits, yet
outwardly serene, Napoleon III. slept on the night of
the 16th in the pavilion of the camp, which he had
often visited when it was orderly and brilliant, which
he now revisited as a fugitive, passing silently, almost
furtively, through its disorder and gloom. With him
was Prince Jérome Napoleon, who saw the fortunes of
his house, like Balzac's *peau de chagrin*, shrinking
visibly day by day, and whose fertile mind was alive

with expedients to avert the fatal hour. He resented
the bigotry of the Empress, who would not surrender
Rome as a bribe to the Italian Court; he was pondering
over and, indeed, openly suggesting the abdication of
the Emperor. Sleeping also in that pavilion was the
youth, Louis, who is barely mentioned in the French
accounts after the 2nd of August; whose public life
began in the tumult of a national catastrophe and ended
so tragically among the savage Zulus.

Daylight brought no respite to the Emperor. He
saw around him silent and unsympathetic throngs of
soldiers bearing the marks of defeat and rout, and it is
said that he was even jeered by the Parisian Mobiles,
who had previously shouted in the ears of the astonished
Canrobert, " À Paris ! À Paris ! " instead of " À
Berlin ! "

Then came from the capital General Trochu, who
had been appointed to command the newly-formed
12th Corps, and was destined, in case of accident, to
succeed MacMahon. In conversing with the Emperor
the General developed a plan of action, which astonished
yet did not altogether displease his Majesty. Succinctly
stated it was this : That the Emperor and the Army
should return to Paris, and that General Trochu should
be named Governor of the capital. The Emperor, as
usual, listened, doubted, demurred, yet did not refuse
to contemplate a scheme which promised to place him,
once more, at the head of affairs, but he gave no decision. Marshal MacMahon was summoned; he was to
command the Army which, according to the plan, was
to be organized near Paris; and when consulted he
spoke favourably of Trochu as a man and a soldier, and
readily accepted the command of the Army. Prince
Napoleon, so soon to set out for Florence, if he did not
suggest, supported the nomination of Trochu, on the

ground that a revolution might break out at any moment
in Paris, and that the General was the man to put it
down.   It was during the prolonged debate on these
perplexing questions that some one said—" the Emperor
neither commands the Army nor governs the State; "
whether the words dropped from the lips of Napoleon III.
or his cousin, Marshal MacMahon, who was present,
could not remember; but whoever uttered them they
were true.   There was a subsidiary and much-disputed
question—what should be done with the noisy Mobiles,
who so eagerly desired to re-enter Paris?   In the end
it was agreed that, although the Emperor, for political,
and MacMahon, for military reasons, desired to give
them a taste of much-needed discipline in the northern
fortresses, these obstreperous battalions should be sent
to the capital.   Thus it came about that Marshal Mac-
Mahon took command of the Army and that Trochu became Governor of Paris.   The new Governor, with his
letter of nomination in his pocket, set out on his return
journey; but while he went slowly by rail, M. Pietri,
using the telegraph, informed the Empress of what had
been done, and alarmed her and the Minister of War by
reporting the intelligence that the Emperor and the
Army were to move on the capital.   Thereupon. two
hours before the luckless Trochu set foot in Paris,
Palikao had sent a remonstrance by telegram, dated
10.27 p.m. on the 17th.   " The Empress," he said, " has
communicated to me the letter in which the Emperor
announces that he wishes to move the Army from
Chalons to Paris—I implore the Emperor to give up
this idea, which will look like a desertion of the Army
of Metz."   If there was a "letter" Napoleon must have
written it on the 16th, during his journey, which is not
likely; but the document referred to was, no doubt,
Pietri's telegram to the Empress.   Some answer must

have been sent from the pavilion at Chalons, after
Trochu departed, for when he saw M. Chevreau, at
midnight, the Minister said promptly—" The Emperor
will not return"; and when the General exhibited his
proclamation to the Empress, beginning with " Preceded
by the Emperor," she instantly exclaimed, " You cannot
state that, because it is not a fact; the Emperor will
not come." Thus the Trochu plan was frustrated; yet
the remarkable thing is that the Emperor had not made
up his shifting mind; for on the 18th, as Marshal
MacMahon affirms, Napoleon intimated his intention to
start the next day. Still we find a telegram from him
to Palikao, dated the "18th, 9 h. 4 m.," presumably in
the morning, in which he says, "I give in to your
opinion," so that his resolutions fluctuated from hour
to hour. A most singular historical figure, at this
juncture, is the once-potent Napoleon III. Virtually
exiled from his capital, and not permitted, if he wished,
to command his troops, he was condemned to "assist,"
as the French say, at the capture of armies, the downfall of his dynasty, and the wreck of a nation.

These lugubrious debates, held almost within sight
of the battlefield of Valny, went on from day to day.
" What should be done with the Army?" was the
question which trod on the heels of " What shall be
done with the Emperor?" or rather both were discussed
together. On the 18th came a despatch from Bazaine,
stating that the Marshal had fought a battle two days
before, that he had " held his positions," yet that he
was obliged to fall back nearer to Metz in order that he
might replenish his supplies for men and guns. This
message had crossed one from MacMahon announcing
his appointment, conveying the important information
that he was still under the orders of Bazaine, and
asking for instructions. The answer came the next

evening, and it expressly declared that, being too remote
from Chalons, Bazaine left the Marshal free to act as
he thought fit.   That telegram, it was the last which
came direct by wire from Metz, raised the great military
question.   Palikao had already begun to insist that
Metz should be relieved.   The Marshal admits that he
was undecided for the moment; for if he started for the
Meuse Paris would be uncovered, and the sole remaining French Army put in great peril; whereas, if he did
not march eastward and Bazaine did march west, then
the latter might be lost.   In his anguish of mind, not
knowing that the wire had been cut, he appealed, by
telegram, to Bazaine for his opinion.   At the same time,
on the 20th, he forwarded a message to Palikao, which
stated the case most clearly.   His information, and it
was in substance correct, led him to believe that the
roads through Briey, Verdun, and St. Mihiel were
intercepted by the Germans; and he added that his
intention was to halt until he learned whether Bazaine
had moved by the north or the south—the idea that he
might be shut up closely in Metz had not then matured
in MacMahon's mind.   In the meantime he saw plainly
the dangers to which he was exposed by remaining on
the plain of Chalons; and, therefore, on the 21st moved
the whole Army to Reims, a long march, which tried
the inexperienced troops, and filled the country roads
with hundreds of stragglers.

MACMAHON RETIRES TO REIMS.

That very morning M. Rouher, inspired by a desire
to talk with his old master, arrived at Chalons, and proceeded with the soldiers to their new destination.   In
the evening, at the Imperial quarters, MacMahon was
summoned to consider afresh the oft-debated questions

of the hour. M. Rouher explained to the Marshal his
views, which were, in reality, those of Palikao, for the
President of the Senate was oppressed with the feeling
that Bazaine must be relieved. But at this moment
MacMahon was firmly resolved to march on Paris, and,
possessing exact information, he stated his case, on the
occasion, with great force and clearness. He was bound
to assume, he said, that Bazaine was surrounded in
Metz by 200,000 men; that in front of Metz, towards
Verdun, stood the Saxon Crown Prince with 80,000
men; that the Prussian Crown Prince was near Vitry
at the head of 150,000 men; and consequently that if he
risked a march eastward into the midst of these armies,
" I should," he continued, " find myself in a most difficult position, and experience a disaster which I desire
to avoid." A most just estimate, formed on reports
which were defective upon one point only—the Prussian Crown Prince was still about Ligny, but his
cavalry, as will be remembered, had looked in upon
Vitry. Moreover, the Marshal adhered to his opinion
that the Army of Chalons should be preserved, because
it would furnish the groundwork for an organized force
300,000 strong. M. Rouher, who acquiesced, then suggested that the Emperor should issue a proclamation
explaining the reasons why the Army of Chalons
moved on Paris; which, being done, Rouher went his
way, and MacMahon drew up the order of march
towards the capital.

THE CHALONS ARMY DIRECTED ON THE MEUSE.

The morning of the 22nd was spent in preparation,
but, before the final orders were issued, the Emperor
received the fatal despatch, dated Ban Saint Martin
[Metz], August 19, which Marshal Bazaine had been
able to send through the German lines. After a brief

description of the battle of Gravelotte, which ended, he
said, in a change of front by the 6th and 4th Corps, the
right thrown back, to ward off a turning movement, and
reporting that he had drawn in the whole Army upon a
curved line, from Longeville to Sansonnet, behind the
forts, he stated that the troops were wearied by incessant combats, and needed rest for two or three days.
" The King of Prussia, with M. de Moltke," he went on,
" were this morning at Rezonville, and everything
goes to show that the Prussian Army is about to feel
up to (va tâter) the fortress of Metz.   I count always
upon taking a northern direction, and turning, by
Montmédy, into the road from Sainte-Menehould to
Chalons, if it is not too strongly occupied.   In the contrary case, I shall continue upon Sedan, and even upon
Mézirères, to reach Chalons."   The Emperor sent this
despatch to MacMahon, who inferred from it that
Bazaine was about to start, and that, after crossing the
Meuse at Stenay, he should find him in the neighbourhood of Montmédy.   He, therefore, withheld the orders
directing the Army on Paris, and issued those which
turned its face to the East.   Further, he transmitted a
telegram addressed to Bazaine, stating that, in two
days, his Army would be on the Aisne, whence, in
order to bring succour, he would operate according to
circumstances.   Soon afterwards a despatch arrived from
Palikao, saying that the " gravest consequences " would
follow in Paris were no attempt made to help Bazaine;
but the Marshal had already taken his decision, though
with a dubious mind, because he knew better than the
Comte de Palikao, who was extremely ill-informed,
what dangers would beset his path, and how slight was
the chance that the Army enclosed in Metz would be
able to burst through the investing lines.   The Emperor
remained in a passive condition; he did not approve, he

did not oppose; but he shared, as a sort of interested spectator, in a venture determined by the operation of political motives, and devoid of a sound military basis.

For the moment, at least, Marshal MacMahon remained steadfast to his latest resolution; and on the 23rd the French Army moved out from its camp near Reims. It was not directed on the Verdun road, because the Commander-in-chief was well aware that if he was to gain Stenay, that goal could only be attained by evading the Saxon Prince's Army, which would necessitate a flank march on routes farther north. The first day's journey was short, for the Army halted on the river Suippe, facing north-east, with a cavalry division in front towards Grand Pré. At this early stage provisions were so scarce that Ducrot, commanding the 1st Corps, and Lebrun, who had the 12th, complained to the Marshal, who advised them to do as he did when retreating from Reichshofen—live upon the inhabitants. Yet the stress was severe, the country incapable of furnishing sufficient supplies, and MacMahon, yielding to the pressure, believed that the better course would be to follow the railway. He, therefore, moved next day to Rhetel with the 12th and 5th, while the 1st halted at Juniville, and the 7th near Vouziers, Margueritte's flanking cavalry remaining hard by on the left bank of the Aisne. A short march on the 25th brought all the Corps astride the river, between Rhetel and Vouziers, with cavalry outposts at le Chesne and Grand Pré. The movement had begun badly; but before following this Army farther on its devious path, we must return to the German head-quarters at Bar le Duc, where, at length, it had become known that the French were not retreating on Paris, but were advancing towards the Meuse!

CHAPTER XI.

THE GRAND RIGHT WHEEL.

IT has long been a well-authenticated fact that Mac-Mahon's march eastward from Reims took the German head-quarter staff by surprise. The reason was that they could not believe in the probability of a movement which, from their point of view, had no defence on military grounds. So that Marshal MacMahon with a fair, and General von Moltke with full knowledge of the facts, really arrived at identical conclusions when they surveyed the situation with what we may call cold scientific eyes. The influences which governed the Marshal's decision could not be known at Bar le Duc on the 25th of August; but it was none the less apparent to the cautious von Moltke that his adversary had committed a great error. The German was surprised, he was even somewhat embarrassed, but he never lost his presence of mind, and he was not unprepared.

Indeed, the subject had been discussed already by himself and his colleagues. As early as the 23rd, Prince Frederick Charles intercepted a letter from an officer of high rank belonging to the Metz Army. The writer expressed a confident hope that succour would soon arrive from Chalons. Thereupon the Saxon Prince was directed to keep a sharp look-out towards Reims, and break the railway between Thionville and Longuyon in more places than one.   The next day, at Ligny, the Great Staff met and conferred with the Crown Prince. It was then that Quartermaster-General von Podbielski was the first to suggest that if a march from Reims towards Bazaine was barely admissible on military grounds, it might be explained by political considerations, and consequently, the General thought, the German Armies should close to their right.   The reason was not deemed sufficient, and the Armies went on as pre-arranged.   Not until eleven in the evening of the 24th did the wary von Moltke consider that he had accumulated information sufficient to justify a tentative change of plans.   He learned from his own cavalry patrols that Chalons had been deserted ; from a Paris newspaper, captured on the 24th, that MacMahon was at Reims with 150,000 men ; and finally he got a telegram, dated Paris, the 23rd, and received at Bar le Duc viâ London.   " The Army of MacMahon," it said, " is concentrated at Reims.   With it are the Emperor Napoleon and the Prince.   MacMahon seeks to effect a junction with Bazaine."   Still von Moltke doubted. The straight line to Metz was barred, would the enemy venture to face the risks involved in a circuitous march close to the Belgian frontier ?   If he did the German Armies must plunge into the Argonne ; but at present the General decided that enough would be done were the Army turned to the north-west, and were a keen watch kept upon its own right by sending the cavalry, if possible, as far as Vouziers and Buzancy.   Such were the morning orders.   Here it may be noted that von Moltke spent the afternoon in framing a plan, solely for himself, based on the shrewd assumption that MacMahon might have quitted Reims on the 23rd, and might be over the Aisne already.   If he moved on continuously he could

not be caught on the left bank of the Meuse. Therefore
von Moltke drew out tables of marches which, had they
all been performed, as they easily might have been,
would have concentrated, in full time, 150,000 men at
Damvillers, east of the Meuse, and within easy reach of
the Army blockading Metz. Two corps, from that
force, were also called on to co-operate. They did
move out as far as Etain and Briey, but not being
wanted they soon returned to their cantonments on the
Orne and the Yron. Thus the plan was not carried
out, but it was prepared, indeed, served as a basis,
during the next two days, and was ready for execution;
and it reveals, once more, the astonishing foresight and
solid ingenuity which watched with sleepless eyes over
the conduct of the German Armies.

After he had finished the scheme by means of which
he intended to thwart MacMahon, in any case, fresh
intelligence arrived—newspaper articles and speeches
in the Chamber which declared that the French people
would be covered with shame were the Army of the
Rhine not relieved ; and above all a telegram from
London, based on a paragraph in *Le Temps*, of August
23rd, stating that MacMahon, although by such a movement he would uncover the road to Paris, had suddenly
determined to help Bazaine, and that he had already
quitted Reims, but that the news from Montmédy did
not mention the arrival of French troops, meaning
troops from Metz, in that region. Von Moltke was
not deeply impressed by the articles and speeches,
although he begun to give some weight to Podbielski's
shrewd remark ; but the positive statement in the telegram did move him, and he and the Quartermaster-
General hastened to lay the matter before the King.
The result was that those definite orders were issued
which produced the great right wheel and sent the

whole force towards the north.   Nevertheless, the
strategist still insists that, on the evening of the 25th,
he had no information which gave sure indications of
the enemy's whereabouts.

THE CAVALRY DISCOVER THE ENEMY.

These were soon forthcoming.   The cavalry, set in
motion at dawn, over a wide space and far in advance
of the new direction, were not long in regaining touch
of MacMahon's Army.   For the horsemen rode out
quickly, and speedily searched the country side from
Dun on the Meuse to the heart of the camp at Chalons,
accumulating in their excursions information almost
sufficient to convince the circumspect von Moltke.
This sudden display of activity and daring is a splendid
spectacle.   The wind howled through the woods and
swept the bare tracks, and heavy storms of rain deluged
the country from Bar le Duc to Rhetel, but the swift
march of these superb reiters was neither stayed by the
blast, the dripping woods, nor the saturated cross-roads.
No hardships, no obstacles slackened their speed, and
large were the fruits of their energy, endurance, and
astuteness.   Here we may observe, and it is a remarkable fact, that hitherto the Saxon leader's cavalry had
been directed only towards the west.   The horsemen
of the Third Army had ridden within sight of Reims
and on the south, or left flank, had approached closely
to the Aube.   Those attached to the Saxon Prince's
command had felt out to their immediate front and
towards the Prussian Crown Prince's left, but had not
examined the districts to their right front.   A cavalry
regiment had made a tiring forced march towards
Stenay, but not a trooper was directed on Grand Pré,
or on Varennes, until the 25th.   Yet there were French
horse on Grand Pré on the 24th, and it is evident that

had only one division been despatched towards and through Varennes immediately after the Saxon Prince's troops had crossed the Meuse, above and below Verdun, the presence of MacMahon's Army on the Aisne must have been discovered, and the report handed in at head-quarters on the morning, or at latest the afternoon, of the 25th. That would have been done had General von Schlotheim, the chief of the staff with the Meuse Army, been as careful to reconnoitre the country on his right as von Blumenthal was to send out horsemen to the flank as well as the front of the westward moving host. It was not done, and the error of judgment involved the loss of four-and-twenty hours.

The error was promptly and amply repaired. While each corps in the mighty Army, having wheeled to the right, was tramping north in the driving rain through the muddy forest roads to gain the distant bivouacs assigned them, the cavalry divisions had come up with, watched, touched, astonished, and bewildered the French, making the 26th of August a memorable day in their camps.

Near the Meuse the ubiquitous patrols discovered troops at Buzancy ; upon the central road which runs beside the Aire, the foremost squadron saw infantry and cavalry in Grand Pré ; upon the Aisne, two adventurous parties pressing up close to the flank and rear of Vouziers, were able to observe and report the presence of large bodies of all arms encamped to the east of the town, and to specify the positions which they held. No attempt was made to attack, and there was no firing except a sputter of carbine-shots discharged by a French at a German patrol which had approached the left bank of the Aire near Grand Pré. The whole line of horse-men, from the Meuse to the Aisne, was in constant communication, and their scouting parties, eager to see and not be seen, found their designs favoured by the abounding woods and the undulations of the land. Thus, in one day, a thick fringe of lynx-eyed cavalry was thrust in close proximity to the adversary many miles in front of the German Corps, plodding their arduous way along the plashy tracks and by-ways of the Argonne.

MOVEMENTS OF THE FRENCH.

No such bold and prudent use was made of the French cavalry by Marshal MacMahon, whom we left with his Army still lingering near the Aisne. The misgivings which oppressed him at Reims did not diminish during his halt at Rhetel; and they deepened as he moved towards the Meuse. But no doubts, based on the absence of intelligence from or concerning Bazaine and the difficulty of supplying the Army, will account for the misuse which he made of his cavalry. The danger he had to dread lurked in the region to the south, yet after the 24th the duty of covering the exposed right flank and of gleaning exact information was imposed upon the brigade attached to the 7th Corps. For Margueritte's division of Chasseurs d'Afrique was, on the 25th, suddenly drawn from the right and sent forward to le Chesne in front of the centre pointing towards Sedan or Stenay; while Bonnemains' division of heavy cavalry moved slowly close in rear of the 1st Corps, where it was useless. The incidents of the memorable 26th, when even minutes were priceless, quickly demonstrated the gravity of the error. On that day, at the close of a brief march, the 12th Corps stood at Tourteron, the 5th at Le Chesne, the 1st at Semuy, and the 7th a little east of Vouziers. Margueritte moved on to Oches, and Bonnemain's was at Attigny, on the left bank of the Aisne.

Now Douay, who commanded the 7th Corps, had become anxious, for he was on the outward flank. He sought some security by sending a brigade, under General Bordas, to Buzancy and Grand Pré, and his strongest regiment of Hussars to scout along the two rivers which unite at Senuc. The Hussar patrols came in contact with the German, and it was one of them which emptied its carbines at the hostile and inquisitive dragoons of the Fifth Cavalry Division. Retiring hastily on Grand Pré the French Hussars handed in reports which so impressed General Bordas that he at once contemplated a retreat on Buzancy, and forwarded the alarming message to his Corps Commander. General Douay instantly inferred that the dreaded German Army was not distant, and, ordering Bordas to retreat on Vouziers, he sent the baggage and provisions to the rear, and drew up his divisions in line of battle, at the junction of the roads from Grand Pré and Buzancy. Just before sunset a horseman rode up with a message that, after all, Bordas had not retired from the village which he occupied, though he believed the road to Vouziers was intercepted, and that the enemy might be upon him at any moment. The remedy applied was to send forth General Dumont with a brigade to bring him in. While Dumont marched in the darkness, Douay and his staff passed the night at a bivouac fire listening eagerly to every sound, and starting up when the step of a wayfarer or the clink of a horseshoe fell on their ears. About three in the morning of the 27th Dumont brought in Bordas and his brigade, together with a few Germans who, pressing too far forward at eventide, had been captured. Nor did the effect produced by the enterprising German cavalry end here. General Douay had sent in to MacMahon a report of the exciting incidents; and with the morning light came

the information that the Marshal had directed the whole
Army to draw near and support the 7th Corps. So it
fell out that the mere appearance of the German cavalry
had arrested the French. But at the same time their
leaders were also told by fugitive country folk—nothing
definite could be extracted from the prisoners taken at
Grand Pré—that the Prussian Crown Prince was at
St. Menehould, and that another army—whence derived,
in what strength, or by whom commanded they could
not imagine—was advancing from Varennes.

THE MARSHAL RESOLVES, HESITATES, AND YIELDS.

We now touch on the moment when the decision was
adopted which impelled the French Army on its final
marches towards defeat and captivity; a decision mainly
due to the extreme pressure exerted by the Comte de
Palikao and the Regency. Marshal MacMahon had
transferred his head-quarters to Le Chesne-Populeux,
a village on the canal which connects the Aisne and the
Meuse. The 12th Corps was there, with the 5th in its
front at Brieulles sur Bar; the 7th, as before, at
Vouziers, and the 1st in its rear at Voncq; Margueritte's
horse at Beaumont, and Bonnemains' still about Attigny.
The information placed before the Marshal by the inhabitants and his own officers, seemed to justify those
apprehensions which he had so strongly expressed at
Reims, and he began to feel again that he was marching
towards that " disaster which he wished to avoid." In
the midst of a prolonged survey of the position, he was
summoned by the Emperor who, having received some
authentic information, declared that the Prussian Crown
Prince had turned from the road to Paris and was then
advancing northwards. With Napoleon III. MacMahon
remained for a long time, and came back to his head-
quarters resolved to retreat upon Mézières. Indeed,

he issued orders on the spot, directing all the Corps to
retire behind the canal the next day, and take post at
Chagny, Vendresse, and Poix. Then, at half-past
eight in the evening of the 27th, he dictated to Colonel
Stoffel a telegram designed for the Minister, in which
he said that there was one hostile Army on the right
bank of the Meuse and another marching upon the
Ardennes. "I have no news of Bazaine," he went on.
"If I advance to meet him I shall be attacked in front
by a part of the First and Second German Armies,
which, favoured by the woods, can conceal a force
superior to mine, and at the same time attacked by the
Prussian Crown Prince cutting off my line of retreat.
I approach Mézières to-morrow, whence I shall continue
my retreat, guided by events, towards the west."
Colonel Stoffel relates that, just as he was about to
carry the telegram to Colonel d'Abzac, with orders to
forward it at once, General Faure, chief of the staff,
came in; and MacMahon, seizing the telegram, said,
"Here is a despatch which I have written to the
Minister." Faure read, and begged the Marshal not
to send it, for, said he, "You will get an answer from
Paris which, perhaps, will prevent you from carrying
out your new plans. You can transmit it to-morrow,
when we are already on the road to Mézières." The
Marshal answered, "Send it," and it was sent.

The reply, so shrewdly foreseen by General Faure,
was handed to the Marshal about half-past one on the
morning of the 28th. It was dated, "Paris, August 27,
11 p.m.," addressed to "the Emperor," and began with
these tell-tale words, "If you abandon Bazaine," wrote
the Comte de Palikao, 'la revolution est dans Paris,' or
Paris will revolt, and you will be attacked yourself by
all the enemy's forces." He asserted that Paris could
defend herself, that the Army must reach Bazaine; that

the Prussian Crown Prince, aware of the danger to which his Army and that which blockaded Metz, was exposed by MacMahon's turning movement, had changed front to the north. "You are at least six-and-thirty, perhaps eight-and-forty, hours in advance of him," the Minister continued. "You have before you only a part of the forces blockading Metz, which, seeing you retire from Chalons to Reims, stretched out towards the Argonne. Your movement on Reims deceived them. Everybody here feels the necessity of extricating Bazaine, and the anxiety with which your course is followed is extreme." The Marshal's will broke down under this strain. He could not bear the thought that men might in future point to him as one who deserted a brother Marshal. Against his better judgment he revoked the orders already issued, enjoining a retreat upon Mézières, and put all his Corps in motion for the banks of the Meuse. To complete the narrative of this decisive event, it may here be said that, on the 28th, at Stonne, as the Marshal himself has admitted, the Emperor made a last desperate appeal against the change of plan. Another despatch from Palikao, dated half-past one in the morning of the 28th, this time addressed to the Marshal, had come to hand at Stonne. "In the name of the Council of Ministers and the Privy Council," it said, "I request you ['je vous demande'] to succour Bazaine — profiting by the thirty hours' advance which you have over the Crown Prince of Prussia. I direct Vinoy's Corps on Reims."

It is probable that the purport, or a copy of this telegram, was sent to the Emperor, for he twice, through his own officers, reminded the Marshal that the despatches of a Minister were not orders, and that he was free to act as he thought expedient, and implored him to reflect maturely before he gave up his intention to

retreat. So much must be said for Napoleon III.—
that, at Metz, on the morrow of Woerth and Spicheren,
and at Stonne, when the toils were fast closing round
him, his military judgment was prompt and correct.
But the Marshal had decided; and the prayers of an
Emperor did not avail against the gloomy forecasts,
the impassioned language, and the formal request or
demand of a Minister of War whose telegrams exhibit
the depth of his ignorance concerning the actual situation. It is not surprising that he was ill-informed,
seeing how difficult it was for officers on the spot, German as well as French, to obtain exact knowledge; but
it is amazing that an experienced soldier and Minister
of War should not be aware of his own incompetence to
direct, from his closet in Paris, an army in the field.
Palikao combined the qualities of the Dutch Deputy with
those of the Aulic Councillor; and the troops of Marshal
MacMahon tramped on to meet their approaching
ruin. The positions they attained on the 28th will be
more conveniently specified later on; for it is time to
follow, once more, the footsteps of the hardy and far-
marching Germans, who were now across the direct
path of MacMahon's Army.

MOVEMENTS OF THE GERMANS.

How, by long and laborious marches, the tough foot
soldiers, almost treading on the heels of their mounted
comrades, gained ground on the adversary must now be
succinctly narrated. On the 26th, the Twelfth Corps
reached Varennes, and the Saxon Prince established his
head-quarters at Clermont in Argonne. The Guard
went on to Dombasle, and the Fourth Corps to a point
beyond Fleury. Such were the marches of the Army
of the Meuse. In the Third Army, the Bavarians made
a wet and weary night march in the wake of the Fourth

Corps, attaining Triaucourt and Erize la Petite; but for the moment, the Fifth, the Sixth, and the Würtembergers stood fast. The reason for this apparent hesitation was that von Moltke was not yet quite convinced. King William remained at Bar le Duc all the forenoon. Thither came the Crown Prince and General von Blumenthal from Ligny, and, at a council held in the great head-quarters, both of them declared unequivocally in favour of the northern march, urging that it would be wiser to delay the movement on Paris than run the risks of a battle in the north unless it could be fought by all the forces which could be got together. These opinions prevailed, and it was decided that the Bavarians should start at once, and that the next day the other Corps of the Third Army should proceed to St. Menehould and Vavray. General von Blumenthal, indeed, had formed a strong judgment on the situation. A few hours after the consultation at head-quarters, writes Dr. William Russell in his " Diary," " taking me into a room in which was a table covered with a large map on a scale of an inch to a mile, he (Blumenthal) said, ' These French are lost, you see. We know they are there, and there, and there—MacMahon's whole Army. *Where* can they go to? Poor foolish fellows! They must go to Belgium, or fight *there* and be lost;' and he put his finger on the map between Mézières and Carignan." It is a remarkable fact that General Longstreet, judging only from the telegrams which reached the United States about this time, arrived at the same conclusion.

King William, during the afternoon, journeyed to Clermont; while the Crown Prince drove to Revigny les Vaches, which he made his head-quarters until the 28th. Before losing sight of Bar le Duc, we may quote from Dr. Russell's pages one other sentence, which

affords a brief glimpse of the great political leader in
this war.   In the forenoon on the 26th, the graphic
Diarist "saw Count Bismarck standing in a doorway
out of the rain whiffing a prodigious cigar, seemingly
intent on watching the bubbles which passed along the
watercourse by the side of the street;" but probably
with his thoughts far away from the evanescent symbols
of men's lives.   He had entered the town with the King
on the 24th, and feared that the royal staff would linger
there for several days, "as in Capua;" yet, in a few
hours, this playful censor of delay was speeding North,
like the Armies, to play a conspicuous part in a sublime
tragedy at Sedan.

In his quarters at Clermont, General von Moltke still
disposed of the Meuse Army and the Bavarians in a manner which would enable him to effect, if necessary, that
concentration at Damvillers which we saw him meditating and devising on the afternoon of the 25th, at Bar
le Duc.   Thus, on the 27th, the Guard, which came up
to Monfaucon, and the 4th Corps to Germonville, were
each directed to throw bridges over the Meuse, so that
there should be four points of passage in case of need.
The Bavarians followed from the rear as far as Dombasle and Nixéville, and the other Corps of the Third
Army turned frankly northward, the Fifth pushing its
advance-guard to St. Menehould.   At the same time
the Saxon Corps had crossed the Meuse at Dun and
established a brigade firmly in Stenay.   The cavalry
had been as active and as useful as ever.   They had
covered the march of the Saxon Corps by occupying
Grand Pré, Nouart, and Buzancy, coming into contact
with the French at the last-named village.   General de
Failly, who, early in the morning, had moved to Bar,
observed hostile cavaliers beyond the stream, and sent
Brahaut's brigade to drive them off and seize prisoners.

That brought on a smart skirmish, during which de Failly received orders to retreat on Brieulles; but Brahaut was driven from Buzancy by the fire of a horse battery; and the unlucky French General made no prisoners.   There was no other rencontre during the day, but the German cavalry on all sides rode up close to the enemy's posts and kept the leaders well informed.   From the reports sent in, von Moltke inferred that there had been a pause in the French movements; at all events, that none of their troops had crossed the Meuse ; and, as he knew that the Saxons were in Dun and Stenay, he thought himself, at length, justified in believing it possible that he might strike MacMahon on the left bank.   Consequently, he abandoned the Damvillers plan, and sent back to Metz the two Corps which had been detached from the blockading army.   Therefore, while the Saxons stood fast, for one day, the Bavarians were directed to march, on the 28th, upon Varennes and Vienne le Chateau; the Guard upon Banthéville; and the Fourth Corps on Montfaucon—the general direction for all the Corps being Vouziers, Buzancy, and Beaumont.   During that day these orders were fulfilled, each Corps duly attaining its specified destination; the Guard and Fourth Corps, before they started, taking up the bridges thrown over the Meuse.   Four divisions of cavalry were out prying, through the mist, into every movement of the 5th and 7th French Corps, whose left flank, it was ascertained, was absolutely unguarded, so that the German horse looked on, and, in some cases, were misled by the astonishing confusion displayed by the enemy's vacillating motions.

EFFECTS OF MACMAHON'S COUNTER-ORDERS.

The fatal decision adopted at le Chesne on the night of the 27th brought disorder and disaster upon the

French Army. The wise resolve to retreat on Mézières, strangely as the statement may sound, had rekindled the fading spirits of the French soldiers. As soon as the fact was communicated to them they sprung with alacrity to perform the task of preparation. The officer who bore the order to the 7th Corps started from le Chesne at six o'clock, and by nine at night the baggage, the provision transport, the engineers' park, were actually in motion for Chagny, through the long defile which leads to le Chesne. The cavalry were despatched to watch the flanks, and the infantry in silence and darkness glided towards their first halting place, Quatre Champs. "Every man," says Prince Bibesco, who was an eye-witness, "marched with a firm step. All seemed to have forgotten the cold, the rain, and the anxiety of the preceding days." They drank in hope with the refreshing air, and then their hopes were suddenly extinguished; for as they were near Quatre Champs, at half-past five in the morning, an aide-de-camp from MacMahon rode up to General Douay and told him the latest decision—the Army was to move upon the Meuse.

The orders brought by the ill-omened messenger were that the 7th Corps, that very day, should move to Nouart, which it was not destined to reach; the 5th Beauclair, which it could not attain; that the 12th should gain La Besace, and the 1st le Chesne, both of which marches were duly performed. Bonnemains' heavy brigade of horse was sent to les Grands Armoises, and Margueritte's towards Mouzon, but afterwards to Sommauthe. The 7th Corps, fearing greatly for its baggage train, already far away, set out again and only reached Boult-aux-Bois, the men on short rations, the horses without a feed of oats. The same troubles beset the other corps which had despatched their trains

northward.   But the largest share of ill-fortune befell
de Failly.   He was ordered to march by way of
Buzancy upon Nouart and Beauclair—indeed, to get as
far forward as he could on the road to Stenay.   The
Marshal knew it was occupied, for he told de Failly
to expect a sharp resistance before he could carry it.
But when within sight of Harricourt and Bar his adventures began.   He discerned hostile cavalry in his path;
they were vigilant Uhlans of the Guard.   De Failly
halted; the cavalry increased, became enterprising, and
some shots were exchanged; but in the end the French
General, finding that he could not rely upon the support
of Douay, who was resting his wearied men at Boult-
aux-Bois, and believing that the direct road to Nouart
was commanded by the enemy, he turned aside and,
through narrow muddy lanes, made his way by Sommauthe to Belval and Bois les Dames, the last division
not arriving at the camp until eight in the evening.
Nevertheless, his appearance at and south of Bois les
Dames so imposed on the German cavalry scouts that
they retired from Nouart in the afternoon.   The movements and halts of both French corps had been observed, and when night fell the Germans at Bayonville
saw the French bivouac fires beyond Buzancy and in
the direction of Stenay.   At this time there were no
hostile German infantry west of the Meuse nearer than
Banthéville; for the troops on the flank of the French,
from Vouziers to the Dun, were wholly horsemen.   No
more valuable demonstration of the priceless value of
cavalry was ever made than that afforded by the Teutons
during this campaign.   They were more than the " eyes
and ears of the Army;" they were an impenetrable
screen concealing from view the force and the movements of the adversary, who was still engaged in pushing up his troops in the hope of compelling the French

to fight a decisive battle on the 30th. That hope, entertained by von Moltke on the 28th, was not fulfilled, because, at the last moment, MacMahon turned his Army from Stenay upon Mouzon. On that day the King moved on to Varennes, and the Prince, his son, to St. Menehould.

GERMAN AND FRENCH OPERATIONS ON THE 29TH.

The position of affairs on the evening of the 28th was somewhat perplexing, because the earlier reports sent in to head-quarters indicated, what was the fact for a brief interval, that the French were retiring northward. But no sooner had orders been issued to fit that state of things than certain information came to hand which showed that the Meuse was again their immediate objective; and it was then that, by abstaining from provocation, von Moltke judged it possible to move up troops sufficient to fight with advantage on the 30th, somewhere west of Stenay. The Saxon Prince, acting within the discretionary limits allowed him, decided to cross the Meuse with the Twelfth Corps, and bring up the Guard and Fourth to Buzancy and Nouart, but to evade a battle, and content himself with the fulfilling the task of obtaining intelligence. The orders were issued, and, while they were in execution, one body of cavalry tracked the 7th Corps during its painful march to Oches and St. Pierremont, and saw the divisions settling down in their bivouacs; and another made prize of le Capitaine Marquis de Grouchy bearing despatches from MacMahon to de Failly. This was an important capture, for it not only deprived the unfortunate General of vital orders, but it placed in the hands of von Moltke the arrangements which the Marshal had drawn up to guide the motions of his Corps. Out of this mishap grew a fresh misfortune for the French.

Marshal MacMahon, on the morning of the 28th,

framed his plans on the supposition that he would be able to pass the Meuse at Stenay, and kept the heads of his columns pointing south-west; but learning at a later period that the Saxons were posted at that place in force—his reports said 15,000 men—he was again, at midnight, obliged to change his scheme, and he resolved to pass the river at Mouzon and Remilly. He, therefore, sent out orders directing the 12th Corps and Margueritte's cavalry to Mouzon, for, having no pontoon train, he was compelled to seek permanent bridges; the 1st Corps and Bonnemains' horse to Roncourt; the 7th to La Besace, which, as we have seen, they did not reach, but halted at Oches and St. Pierremont; and the 5th to Beaumont, which place they entered after weary marches and a sharp action. These were the orders for the day which, with other useful documents, were found in the pockets of de Grouchy. No special interest pertains to the march of the 1st Corps. The 12th found its way safely to Mouzon, crossed the river, and occupied the heights on the right bank, while General Margueritte despatched some of his Chasseurs on the Stenay road. What then happened? The Chasseurs returned and reported that they had seen no enemy, although at that moment Stenay was held by the enemy's horse and foot. " They committed," writes General Lebrun, then commanding the 12th Corps, " the fault which in former wars was made a ground of reproach against the French cavalry." When in sight of Stenay they saw no Germans and turned back instead of pushing on to and beyond the town, or trying to do so; and the corps commander justly regards this laxity as a grave fault. So Lebrun, resting at Mouzon, could learn nothing, either from spies or his famous Chasseurs, respecting an enemy then within a few miles. The irony of the situation was complete when, a little later, the Zieten Hussars

from Stenay rode up to Margueritte's vedettes, and found
him although he could not find them. In that fashion
the French made war in 1870. General de Failly and
his 5th Corps were more severely treated, for their ill-
luck and misdirection brought upon them

THE COMBAT AT NOUART.

Acting on verbal instructions, given on the night of
the 28th, at Belval, by a staff officer from the head-
quarters at Stonne, de Failly set out the next morning
towards Beaufort and Beauclair, two villages a few
miles south-west of Stenay. He did not know, as we
do, that the Marshal had changed his plans, and that
the officer bearing the countermanding order had fallen
into the hands of a German patrol. The French General
did not break up his camp and quit Belval until ten
o'clock in the morning, which gave the Saxons, who
had been brought over the Meuse from Dun, plenty of
time to watch his movements. Indeed, he could see
them, troops of all arms, on the heights of Nouart,
moving, as he judged, in an easterly direction, which
was an error, possibly arising from some turn in the
road, for the whole Twelfth Corps were over the Meuse
between Dun and Nouart. General de Failly disposed
his troops in two columns, one of which marched towards
Beaufort by country roads; the other, with the General,
consisting of Guyot de Lespart's division and two regiments of Brahaut's cavalry, made for Beauclair. Their
road lay through the valley of the Wiseppe, a sluggish
stream meandering through a marshy bottom land and
passing Beaufort on its way to the Meuse. The route
through Nouart was barred by the Germans, and when
the leading French squadrons, crossing the valley to
gain the main road, began to ascend the slopes, they
suddenly came under a smart fire from infantry and

guns.   The French Hussars flitted fast back across the
meadows, and de Failly at once stopped the march of
both columns, putting his infantry and guns in position,
and resting them principally upon two small villages.
Then ensued, about noon, an indecisive but vexatious
combat, for the Germans did not intend to attack in
force, but simply harass and delay the 5th Corps; and
de Failly, uncertain respecting the numbers which
might be hidden by the woods, dared not retort, especially as he was remote from the French Army and without support from any other corps.   So, for several
hours, the fight went on.   The object of the Saxons, who
descended into the valley, was simply to detain the
French, and, although the assailants traversed the
brook and the high road, pushing forward a few companies and supporting them by an artillery fire from
the heights, they did not come to close quarters.   General
de Failly was of opinion that he had repelled an attack,
and that the enemy did not renew it because the French
were so strongly posted; but the truth is that Prince
George of Saxony not only held back his superior force
because he had been enjoined to abstain from a serious
engagement, but was himself misled by erroneous reports respecting the state of affairs towards Stenay.
Soon after four o'clock de Failly also drew off ; he had
then just received a duplicate of the order directing him
upon Beaumont.   He sadly deplores the mischance, and
pathetically relates how all his wearied troops reached
Beaumont " during the night," except the rear-guard,
which did not enter the camp until five o'clock on the
morning of the 30th.

THE STATE OF AFFAIRS AT SUNDOWN.

Thus, for the French, terminated another day of error
and loss, which left three Corps still on the left bank of

the Meuse. When the sun went down, the German horse were close to every one of them except the 12th, which, it will be remembered, was on the right bank near Mouzon. The active cavalry moved in the rear of the 1st Corps, seizing prisoners at Voncq, riding up to le Chesne, and keeping watch through the night upon the wearied 7th Corps, as it sought repose in the camps of Oches and St. Pierremont. The German Infantry Corps, meantime, had been closing up for the final on-slaught. The Twelfth Corps was in and about Nouart, covered by outposts and patrols, which stretched away to Stenay. The Guard was at Buzancy, the Fourth Corps at Remonville; the Fifth Corps was at Grand Pré, with the Würtembergers near at hand; the Bava-rians had come up to Sommerance and its neighbourhood on both banks of the Aisne; the Eleventh Corps stood at Monthois on the left, while the Sixth Corps was in the rear at Vienne le Chateau. The head-quarters of King William were set up in Grand Pré, under the old gloomy castle, the Prussian Prince was near by at the little village of Senuc, and the Saxon Prince at Bayon-ville. Thus, in three days, the whole Army had drawn together, facing north, and was ready, at a signal, to spring forward and grapple with the enemy who had committed himself so rashly to a flank march in the face of the most redoubtable generals, and the best in-structed, disciplined and rapidly-marching troops in Europe.

Examining attentively the reports which reached him from all points of the extensive curve upon which the cavalry were so active, and poring over the map, General von Moltke at length formed a definite judgment on the position as it appeared to him through this medium. He inferred that the Army of Chalons was marching in a north-west direction towards the Meuse; that its principal forces were then probably between le Chesne and Beaumont, with strong rear guards to the south; and the practical result of his cogitations was that the German Armies should move upon the line le Chesne-Beaumont in such a way as might enable them to attack the enemy before he reached the Meuse. Therefore, the Saxon Prince's Army, except the Guard, which was to become the reserve, was to march early on Beaumont, two Corps of the Third Army were to support the Saxon onset, but the left of that Army was to march on le Chesne. As a matter of fact, the French, in part at least, were nearer the Meuse than von Moltke supposed, for the 12th Corps was on the right bank, and the 1st at Roncourt; while the 7th was at Oches, the 5th at Beaumont, and there were no troops at le Chesne except stragglers. MacMahon took in the situation; he was resolved to pass the river " coûte que coûte " : and his chance of doing so, even then, depended on the rapidity with which his troops could march. The 5th Corps was struck and routed the next day, but the French Army did succeed in effecting a passage over the stream.

THE BATTLE OF BEAUMONT.

The German Armies had now fairly entered the Ardennes, formerly the northern district of the old province of Champagne. It is a land of vast woods which crowd one upon another between the Bar and the Meuse. Looking from some smooth hill-top, the landscape, in summer, wears the aspect of a boundless forest, the dark furrowed lines of shadow alone indicating the hollows, gullies, ravines, and defiles. Here and there may be seen a church or château, or a glimpse may be caught of a road bordered by tall trees. The woods are so dense that infantry, still less guns and horsemen, can-

not work through them, or move at all, except upon the
high roads, lanes and tracks, worn by the villagers and
farm people. Marshy brooks lurk under the green
covert, and rivulets burrow their way through steep
banks. Yet there are open spaces in the maze of verdure, farmsteads and fields, and rounded heights whence
the tourist may contemplate the extensive panorama.
It is not a country which lends itself easily to military
operations, but one more suitable to the sportsman than
the soldier. The boar of the Ardennes is still famous,
and it is on record that a certain Herr von Bismarck,
once upon a time, hunted the wolf through the snow in
the very region where he was hunting the French in
August, 1870.

It was amidst these thickets, dingles, and almost path-
less wilds that the French had to retreat and the Germans to pursue. We have seen that General de Failly's
Corps was struggling all night to reach what they hoped
would be a comparative haven of rest at Beaumont, a
bourgade upon the high road from le Chesne to Stenay,
planted down in a hollow, surrounded by gardens, and
having in its centre a fine church visible from afar.
Here he pitched his tents, so that his tired soldiers
might recover from the fatigues they had endured in
useless marches; and he thought, in his simple way,
that he might safely defer his march until the afternoon.
Yet Marshal MacMahon had visited the camp early in
the morning, and if he used language to de Failly, as he
probably did, similar to that which he employed at
Oches, it should have quickened the General's movements and saved him from defeat. For, after visiting
Beaumont, MacMahon, much concerned for the 7th as
well as the 5th Corps, rode into the camp at Oches.
The trains had entered the defile leading to Stonne, some
hours earlier, preceded and escorted by the brigades of

Conseil Dumesnil's Division, and the 2nd Division was just about to start, leaving the 3rd as a rear-guard. "You will have 60,000 men upon your hands, this evening," he said, "if you do not succeed in getting beyond the Meuse." Urging Douay to get rid of his heavy convoy, and " coûte que coûte," cross the river, he indicated Villers below Mouzon as the point of passage, and rode away. The misfortunes of the 7th Corps, also much tried, will be related later; but it may be said that they did not reach Mouzon, for their outlet from the toils proved to be the southern gate of Sedan !

THE SURPRISE OF THE 5TH CORPS.

Inspired by the hope of closing with the enemy, the German Armies were astir at dawn, and soon long columns of men and guns were tramping steadily northward; but, for the present the narrative is concerned only with the Saxon Twelfth, the Prussian Fourth, and von der Tann's Bavarians. These troops advanced through the forests, the Saxons near the Meuse, the Fourth in the centre by Nouart and Belval, and the Bavarians, from their distant bivouac at Sommerance, upon and beyond Sommauthe. Now it was originally designed that the two Corps, on the right and centre, should attack simultaneously, and to ensure this, each column, on arriving at the skirt of the forest, was directed to halt under cover until it had ascertained that the others on each flank had also gained the edge of the woods. But it turned out that the Saxons, from the start, were delayed by various obstacles which impeded not only the artillery, but the infantry. The leading division of the Fourth Corps met with fewer obstructions on its route through Belval, and thus arrived first on the scene of action. On the line of march in the forest, intelligence was picked up which quickened its

motions, and a squadron sent forward confirmed the
statement that the French about Beaumont reposed
in thoughtless security.   The Corps Commander, von
Alvensleben I.,—for there were two who bore the name
in this Army,—an officer ever ready to go forward, was
present with the advance-guard of the division, and not
likely to hold it back. So the soldiers advanced in
silence. On approaching the open country, the Hussars
in the front glided out of sight, and a company of
Jägers crept towards the selvage of the wood, and, from
a hillock near a farm, they saw, only six hundred paces
distant, a French camp, and beyond other camps.   The
cavalry horses were picketted, the artillery teams had
not returned from seeking water, the soldiers were either
resting or employed on the routine work of a camp.
What should be done?   Here was an absolutely unguarded Army Corps, ignorant that an enemy was within short musket range.   The divisional commander had
orders to await the arrival of lateral columns, but he
felt that the Frenchmen might discover his unwelcome
presence at any moment.   He had only a brigade on
the ground, yet the temptation to seize an opportunity
so unexpected, was almost irresistible.   He, therefore,
decided to attack as soon as his brigade could deploy,
and his batteries plant themselves in a favourable place.
Suddenly the men in the French camp were all in
motion.   General von Alvensleben inferred that the
proximity of his troops had been perceived, whereas
the activity displayed, as we learn from de Failly, was
caused by an order to fall in before starting for Mouzon.
Without waiting, however, until the battalions in rear
could reach the ground, Alvensleben opened fire, and
the shells bursting in their camp, gave the first warning
to the French that their redoubtable adversaries were
upon them.   General de Failly says that the grand-

guards had not had time to signal the enemy's presence, and that his own information led him to believe that the Germans had marched upon Stenay.   The verdict of Marshal MacMahon upon his subordinate is that " General de Failly was surprised in his bivouac by the troops of the Saxon Crown Prince."

The French soon recovered from their disorder, swarms of skirmishers rushed out towards the assailants, some batteries went rapidly into action ; and the combined fire of shells and bullets wrought havoc among the Prussian gunners and the infantry, hitting even those on the line of march.   They did not yield to the pressure ; and when the French delivered a determined attack it was repelled by volleys and independent firing. Then the French got several batteries into position on the hill side north of Beaumont ; the Germans were reinforced by the arrival of guns and foot, for the other division of the Corps came up and at once deployed on the right of its comrades.   At this time, a little after one o'clock, the Saxons on the right, next the Meuse, and the Bavarians on the left, who had been marching since five o'clock in the morning, had also begun to take part in the fight.   King William and his vast Staff, posted on a hill off the road from Buzancy, and his son, on a similar elevation near Oches, were closely watching the battle, discernible thence in its general smoky features, at least by the King.

General de Failly had no desire to fight a regular engagement.   His aim was to put his troops in order and offer as much resistance as might be required to cover his retreat upon Mouzon, distant only six miles. He, therefore, relied on his line of guns above the village, and they were effective, for some time ; but he showed great apprehension lest his left, or Meuse flank, should be turned.   Seeing the German lines develop and grow stronger, in men and guns, feeling the new power brought to bear by the Saxons, who, cramped for want of room, were pressed close to the river, and, hearing the Bavarian guns on his right, he made one more vigorous effort to arrest the Fourth Corps. Thick lines of skirmishers, followed by supports in close order, dashed forward with such valour and impetuosity that they drove in the covering infantry and charged to within fifty paces of the guns. The danger was great, but the Germans rapidly flung everything near into the contest, gained the mastery, compelled the gallant Frenchmen to wheel about, followed them promptly, captured the southern camp, and then poured into Beaumont itself upon all sides. But the Chassepot had told, and the Germans paid heavily, as they always did and were ready to do, for their persistent courage and well-tempered audacity. With the town fell the other camps; and then, for a time, the infantry combat ceased. But the artillery advanced, as usual, and engaged in a long duel with the powerful line of batteries established by the French to facilitate the retreat of their infantry and arrest pursuit. Although not able to stand up against 150 guns, they did not retire until their infantry had got into another position between the Yoncq brook and the Meuse. Then the batteries cleverly withdrew in succession, and before the Fourth Corps could advance, de Failly's troops disappeared in the woods, and were seen no more until they were reached beyond the hills and thrust headlong into Mouzon.

While the Fourth Corps was pulling itself together after the onset, de Failly had been compelled by the impenetrable wood of Givodeau to divide his forces, the left and the reserve artillery following the main route to Mouzon took post above Villemontrey, close to the Meuse, and derived support from guns and infantry which Lebrun had put into position on the high land in an elbow of the river on the right bank. The right wing hurried round the western side of the Givodeau thickets, and found a post upon a plateau beyond. In the meantime, General Lebrun had ordered two brigades of infantry, commanded by Cambriels and Villeneuve, and a cavalry division, to cross the river at Mouzon, but Marshal MacMahon, riding up, ordered back Cambriels, and all the horse except two regiments of cuirassiers. Those we shall presently meet again. The German right wing vainly endeavoured to drive de Failly from Villemontrey, and, after repeated attempts and much loss, desisted from the enterprise ; but kept a strong force at hand and a large number of guns in action.

Meantime a singular incident had occurred to the west of Beaumont. Just as the Bavarians were about to join in the attack on the camps by throwing themselves on the French flank, they were fired on from a farm called la Thibaudine and a hamlet named Warniforêt. They were astonished because the presence of an enemy there was not even suspected. The enemy was also astonished and still more frightened. The combat was caused by a French brigade, which had wandered from its line of march. It seems that the advance brigade of Conseil Dumesnil's division preceding the transport of the 7th Corps, a series of wagons, nine miles in length, had been ordered by MacMahon, who met them, to move by Yoncq instead of la Besace, and that, when the rear brigade came up to the point of divergence, the marker left to give information having disappeared, these unfortunate troops went forward on the great road to Beaumont. A staff officer arrived just as the action began, and he was leading the errant troops back, when the Bavarians emerged in

view. The conflict which ensued was sharp, but it
delayed the 7th Corps and ended in the rout of the
French, who fled as best they could through Yoncq
towards Mouzon. About this time Douay was at
Stonne ; the Uhlans of the Guard had followed him
step by step, and bringing a horse battery to bear on
his rear guard, had induced General Dumont to halt,
deploy the brigade, and in his turn open fire ; but
General Douay promptly appeared and stopped the
action, having made up his mind that the pressing duty
of the hour was to get over the Meuse in accordance
with the Marshal's desire. So the 7th, after some hesitation, retired upon Raucourt, hoping thence to gain
Villers below Mouzon ; yet, being pursued by the
Bavarians, they were overtaken and attacked outside
Raucourt, and, hearing that the bridge was broken,
they turned, some upon Remilly, and others through
Torcy into Sedan itself.

THE FLIGHT TO MOUZON.

When the left wing of the Fourth Corps, pressing
towards the defile of the Yoncq and the slopes above
it, sought to discover the French on that side, they
were at first sharply punished ; but, following on, they
came up and closed with their adversaries. One brigade
of Bavarians had been sent to the Fourth Corps and
moved on the left flank of the toilsome advance. For the
ground was difficult, the obstacles numerous, and the
French, though shattered and dispirited, still displayed
a fighting front. But at length, late in the afternoon,
the Germans mastered a hill-top whence adverse artillery had fired upon the assailants ; and then these fairly
entered the plain before Mouzon. Here, however, the
French occupied an isolated hill, called le Mont de
Brune, close to and almost overhanging the Faubourg

of Mouzon, from which its summit is less than a mile
distant. Unluckily for them they formed front facing
eastward, apparently anticipating an attack on that
side ; but the Germans promptly turned the flank from
the south and south-west, and drove the defenders down
the steep slopes towards Mouzon, capturing ten guns.
The victorious forward movement brought the leading
companies in front of Villeneuve's brigade and the
cuirassiers in the plain.   The Germans halted, and
opened a steady fire, when suddenly they beheld the
5th Cuirassiers coming down on their left flank and
rear.   Captain Helmuth, who commanded the three
companies exposed to this ordeal, made the left company face about in time, and then forbidding his men
to form rallying squares or groups, ordered them to
stand fast as they were, and only open fire when he
gave the signal.   The gallant French horsemen, as was
their wont, rode straight upon the infantry ; but the
independent firing opened on them at point blank range,
broke the impetus and crushed in the head of the
charging squadrons.   Colonel Contenson fell mortally
wounded within fifteen paces of the infantry line ; and,
although some fiery spirits dashed into their ranks, and
one engaged in single combat with Captain Helmuth
until he fell pierced by ball and bayonet, yet the whole
mass of cavalry was routed with immense loss, and
driven into the Meuse.

For, by this time, the wreck of de Failly's Corps was
in full retreat on all sides, and troops, artillery, transport trains, and stragglers, were crowding on towards
the bridge.   When his right was turned by the movement upon the Brune hill, and still further by the march
of the Bavarian brigade upon Pourron, de Failly quitted
his post at Villemontrey, which enabled the right division of the Fourth Corps, the Saxon regiments fighting

by its side, and the artillery to push on by the main
road to Mouzon.   After the first surprise of the Beaumont camp, the French had mainly stood, here and
there, to facilitate their retreat, and the contest, which
went on all the afternoon among the woods and hills
and ravines, was really a running fight.   The Germans
had pursued with relentless pertinacity.   Their soldiers
had been marching all day, but they seemed to be tireless, for they never halted until the fugitives were over
the Meuse, or the darkness forbade further motion.   De
Failly had been surprised and thrust in disorder over
the river, and when the evening closed the Germans
were in possession of the faubourg of Mouzon, and of
the bridge at its western end.   The 7th Corps, cut off
from Villers, had moved, in a state bordering on panic,
upon Remilly ; but there they found Bonnemains'
cuirassiers, the tail of a division belonging to the 1st
Corps, and a baggage column.   The Meuse had been
dammed to fill the ditches of Sedan, and not only were
the fords rendered useless, but the swelling stream
was unusually high.   Douay, halted at seven o'clock, became impatient after dark, and at ten rode down to the
bridge.   He found the cuirassiers engaged in passing
over the feeble construction.   " The horses," writes
Prince Bibesco, " affrighted, because they could not see
the shaking planks hidden by the water, and shifting
under their steps, moved with hesitation, their necks
extended, their ears erect.   Sitting upright, shrouded
in their large white cloaks, the cuirassiers marched on
silently, and appeared to be borne on the stream.   Two
fires, one at each end of the bridge, flung a ghastly light
on men and horses, and, flickering on the helmets, imparted a fantastic aspect to this weird spectacle."   At
length the white horsemen passed over; but when the
turn of the artillery came the horses were still more

recalcitrant, and the passage was so slow that, at two in the morning of the 31st, only three batteries and two regiments of foot had passed the Meuse. Douay then learned that the Marshal had ordered all the Army to assemble at Sedan, and he moved the rest of his Corps over the bridge at Torcy. These few details will give some idea of the terrible disorder which prevailed throughout the French Army.

On the evening of the 30th the Germans were upon the Meuse. The Fourth Corps was before Mouzon ; one Bavarian Corps at Raucourt, the other at Sommauthe ; the Fifth and Eleventh Corps about la Besace and Stonne; the Twelfth was near the Meuse in front of Beaumont, and the Guard just behind them; the Würtembergers were at Verrières, and the Sixth Corps well out to the west at Vouziers. On this flank also were the Fifth and Sixth Cavalry divisions threatening and watching the French communications; while the Twelfth Cavalry Division was astride the Meuse at Pouilly, and one of its squadrons, evading and passing through Margueritte's vedettes, had discovered and reported the presence of French troops on the Chiers near Carignan, and the movement of trains on the railway towards Sedan.

So ended this ominous day. The Army of the Meuse had lost 3,500 men in killed and wounded, but they had routed one French Corps, and fractions of two others, and they had captured forty-two guns. The French loss is set down at 1,800 killed and wounded, but the Germans aver that, included among the 3,000 acknowledged to be missing, there were 2,000 who bore no wounds.

CHAPTER XII.

Metz and Strasburg.

At the very moment when the Army of Chalons, instead of marching on its way to Montmédy, found its
Corps huddled together at Sedan, between the river and
the Belgian frontier, some information of the movement
undertaken by MacMahon, who yielded his better judgment to the importunate entreaties (les instances) of
Palikao, reached Marshal Bazaine in Metz.   He had already, on the 26th of August, collected a large mass of
troops upon the right bank, in order to break out towards
Thionville; but the rain poured down all day in torrents,
and, after a consultation at the Farm of Grimont with
his Marshals and Generals, whose opinions were adverse
to the sortie projected, he issued an order directing the
Army to resume its former quarters.   But, on the 29th,
a messenger who had crept through the German lines,
handed to the Marshal a despatch from the officer commanding in Thionville, Colonel Turnier, stating that
General Ducrot, with the 1st Corps, should be " to-day,
the 27th," at Stenay on the left of the Army, General
Douay on his right being on the Meuse.   Bazaine seems
to have had doubts respecting the authenticity of this
missive, the handwriting of which his staff did not
recognize ; but the next morning, about eleven, an

agent of his own came in from Verdun. He was the bearer of a telegram from the Emperor—it was really the message drawn up by MacMahon on the 22nd of August, copied, apparently, in cipher, by Napoleon, and entrusted to Bazaine's emissary. The despatch, which had no date, stated that the sender would march towards Montmédy, and when on the Aisne, would act according to circumstances, in order to succour the Metz Army. Regarding the second document, though antecedent in point of time, as a confirmation of the first which he had received, Marshal Bazaine, on the 30th, issued the orders which, the following day, led to

THE BATTLE OF NOISSEVILLE.

His plan, succinctly described, was to break through the line of investment on the right bank of the Moselle by directing three Corps, the 3rd, 4th, and 6th, principally upon St. Barbe, and he hoped, if successful, to march them forward upon Kedange, while the Guard and the 2nd Corps followed the track by the river. He estimates the force which was available for battle at 100,000 men, but he probably had more; at any rate, the delays which had occurred on the 14th of August, and were in part repeated on the 31st, shows how arduous is the task of issuing with such masses from a fortified town and position astride of a river. The weather was not favourable, for the continuous rain had soaked the ground, and at dawn a thick fog, which hung about for several hours, impeded the operations. The Germans had been more than usually on the alert since the abortive attempt on the 26th, and had thought it expedient to include Noisseville within the line of defence. The noise and preparations in Metz did not escape their notice, but the dense mist concealed much from their searching gaze. Yet they

saw and heard enough, both on the eastern and western
fronts of Metz, to warrant a belief that a resolute onset
was impending. As the fog bank rolled away, the
batteries and the massing of troops became visible, and
General von Manteuffel transmitted the results of his
careful observations to von Steinmetz and Prince
Frederick Charles, both of whom made instant arrangements to support the First Corps and the other troops
on the right bank. The forenoon passed by, and,
except some slight skirmishes and a brief artillery
duel, no action ensued. About midday the French sat
down to cook, and the smoke from their fires rose in
clouds, indicated their position, but hid them from
view; at the same time, although the sun was shining,
the culinary haze concealed the workmen engaged in
throwing up shelter for the heavy guns drawn from the
forts; and the German leaders arrived at the conclusion
that the onslaught would be deferred until the next day;
their soldiers also fell to cooking, and some fractions
recrossed the Moselle to join their main body ; but
their attention to the phenomena before them was not
relaxed.

Yet the afternoon began to wear away. It was not
until half-past two that Marshal Bazaine gave that
signal for attack which was nevertheless not obeyed
until another hour and a half had been consumed. The
signal was a salvo from the battery of heavy guns placed
behind the field works hastily thrown up in front of
Fort St. Julien. The battlefield of the 31st was one
with which we were made acquainted when von Golz
took upon himself to arrest the retreat of the French
over the Moselle on the 14th of August. It extended
from Mercy les Metz by Colombey, Noisseville and
Failly to Malroy on the Moselle. The French assailants,
therefore, had to cross the ravines east of Borny and

work up both banks of the Vallières brook which, rising near St. Barbe, enters the Moselle opposite the Isle Chambière. The 6th Corps, Canrobert's, was to attack by the river road towards Malroy; de Ladmirault, with the 4th, was to move by Failly and Vrémy to outflank St. Barbe on its right, while the left of that position was to be carried by Lebœuf's 3rd Corps; and Frossard, with the 2nd, was to follow and cover the right flank of Lebœuf. The Guard, the cavalry, and reserve artillery were to stand between Fort St. Julien and the Bois de Grimont, and all the baggage was to be ready in the Isle Chambière. The Germans were prepared to meet such an attack, but, as we have said, they had come to believe that it would be deferred.

Suddenly, about four o'clock, the dead silence was broken by a salvo from the heavy guns, followed by the fire of de Ladmirault's batteries. Then the action began along the whole front, the Germans at once developing a powerful line of fifty guns about Servigny and Poix, far in advance of the main line of defence, and bringing other pieces to bear from different points. Nevertheless, favoured by the broken ground and resolute to win, the French infantry persistently advanced until about six o'clock they had driven in all the foreposts, and had gained possession on their right of Noisseville, the garrison of which village they curiously complain held out longer than they were entitled to do. The capture of Noisseville facilitated the principal attacks which were directed upon Servigny and Poix, villages which served as redoubts guarding the avenues to St. Barbe, the culminating point in the region. At the same time the French right had pushed well forward towards Retonfay, the object being to protect the flank of the 3rd Corps, now in motion upon the central posts of the German line. Here the contest

was severe, and in the end the great line of guns which
had held de Ladmirault at bay so long, unable to bear
the musketry fire in front and flank, was compelled
to withdraw behind the villages. But, although the
French infantry came up boldly on both flanks, as well
as in front, they were unable to overcome the sturdy
defenders, in whose possession the villages remained at
dark. The French left under Canrobert had made
repeated attacks upon Failly, which met with no success,
and he halted at Chieulles and Vany; so that the movement near the Meuse had secured but little ground.
At dark the French had not done more than occupy a
line extending from Canrobert's right in front of Villers
l'Orme to Noisseville, and thence by Flanville to Château
d'Aubigny. By this time General von Manteuffel had
been reinforced by two brigades of Landwehr, and the
Twenty-fifth Division, under Prince Louis of Hesse,
which had crossed the Moselle, and considerably
strengthened his right wing. Then occurred a remarkable incident. General Aymard, about nine o'clock,
creeping silently up to Servigny, flung forward his
division and, without firing a shot, burst in upon the
surprised Germans, engaged in preparing the defences,
and carried the place. Astonished and enraged, General
von Gayl immediately gathered up a force, and breaking,
in his turn, upon the enemy, drove him out and
recovered possession before ten o'clock. Aymard's is
an example of a night attack well performed; but the
weak defence of what had been skilfully won, was not
so creditable to the French.

During the night General Manstein, with the other
half of the Ninth Corps, crossed the Moselle, halted in
rear of the German right wing, and thus enabled the
Hessian Division to take post behind St. Barbe. A
dense fog again filled the valley at dawn, but at an early

hour General von Manteuffel, holding his ground in the centre and on the right, brought his batteries to bear upon Noisseville and promptly assumed the offensive. The place was strongly occupied and stoutly defended. Although the Germans broke in for a moment they were speedily expelled, and several hours elapsed before the village fell into their hands. But throughout the day, except towards Rupigny and Failly, the French stood on the defensive. For the Germans arrayed 114 guns on the hills, crushed the adverse artillery, and prevented the French infantry from making any combined attack. The position on their right was soon rendered less safe by the arrival of a brigade of the Seventh Corps which, coming up from Laquenexy, drove the French out of Flanville. This demonstration on the right of Marshal Lebœuf's line, together with the terrible fire of the German artillery, induced him, about eleven o'clock, to draw back the whole of his troops and allow his adversary once more to occupy Noisseville. On the French left, Marshal Canrobert's soldiers had been forced back upon Chieulles, and the attacks upon Failly had wholly failed. Prince Frederick Charles who, at Malancourt, had heard the opening cannonade at Sedan on the morning of the 1st, took up his post of observation on a hill towards the Moselle before eight o'clock, and provided for the arrival of strong reinforcements, should they be needed, from the left bank, but only the Tenth Corps passed the Moselle and was stationed between Argancy and Antilly. The retreat of Marshal Lebœuf had been followed by that of the other corps, and a little after noon the French Army was marching back to the camps and bivouacs whence it had advanced on the 31st. The great sortie had signally failed in opening a road through the investing lines. The French had 3,547 officers and men killed and wounded, including in the latter category four Generals, one of whom, Manèque, mortally. The German loss was 2,976 killed and wounded. Marshal Bazaine estimates the number he put in the field at 100,000; the German authorities say they began the fight with 40,800 men and 138 guns; and at the end of the encounter had over the Moselle 73,800 men and 290 guns.

Marshal Bazaine and his troops re-entered their prison on the afternoon of the day when the white flag was hoisted on the Citadel of Sedan; and with his and their subsequent misfortunes we have nothing more to do in this work. Neither is it our business to consider whether by marching up instead of down the right bank he could have escaped with some portion of his Army safe and sound to the South of France. That he did his uttermost to push through on the 31st is the contention of the German staff, but it is doubtful whether on the second day the same spirit prevailed. All the knotty questions suggested by the military situation about Metz and elsewhere at the end of August could only be adequately discussed by entering upon a history of transactions with which we have no present concern. The essential fact is that the French Marshals tried to break the barrier and failed at a moment when even their success could not have prevented the capitulation at Sedan. The attempt demonstrated the immense advantages of a carefully prepared defensive position combined with a readiness to use artillery in the front line from the first, and an equal readiness to become the assailant whenever a useful opportunity occurred. But to the mind of this writer the moral of the Metz episode in the great war is the danger attending these large entrenched camps, which will certainly exert in the future, as they have in the past, an irresistible attraction upon inferior commanders, and

will task the intellect, and the ingenuity and the firmness of the greatest to put them to a proper use.
Neither Bazaine nor any colleague in superior command
could be described as a man of genius, and to such
soldiers, while war is conducted on a vast scale and
armies in the field are numbered by the hundred thousand, places like Metz will not cease to become traps in
which frustrated or beaten armies will be caught and
captured, sometimes, it may be, by force or stratagem;
usually by stress of famine.   Meantime the issue of the
war will be decided, as it always has been, by the belli-
gerent who is able to keep the field.

    Although huge Armies had penetrated so swiftly into
France on the morrow of the frontier victories, there
were still, besides the fortress of Metz, which was in an
exceptional case, several other strongholds which stood
out defiant upon the main lines of the German communications.   They were Verdun, Toul, Bitsche,
Phalsburg, Strasburg, and, at a later stage, Belfort.
Each of these, except the last-named, required to be,
and were, watched or invested by troops drawn from
the active Armies or the reserves in Germany; but they
had little or no influence upon the colossal events which
decided the issue of what we have called the Campaign
of Sedan.   Strasburg alone was a cause of any anxiety,
because the Germans were eager to obtain possession of
a fortress the fall of which would give them undis-
puted command of the Rhine, and become of great
value in the event of unlooked-for and improbable reverses.   General von Werder, with the Baden Division,
after the battle of Woerth, had been sent to invest the
town, and he arrived before it on the 11th.   It is not
intended to relate in these pages the siege of Strasburg,
which properly belongs to the story of the Franco-
German war as a whole.   The point to note is that the

regular siege was preceded by a useless bombardment. The engineer desired to proceed in the orthodox way; the chief of the staff wished to try the more violent method. He insisted that a bombardment would terrify the inhabitants, and make them exert such a pressure on the Governor, General Uhrich, a gallant veteran, as would compel him to surrender. The dispute was determined by an appeal to the Great Head-Quarters, then at Pont à Mousson, and General von Moltke, who desired that the place should be taken in the shortest possible time, and that the 40,000 men before it might be available for other operations, decided in favour of the bombardment. The consequence was that dreadful sufferings were inflicted upon the inhabitants of Strasburg, and terrible devastation brought upon the town, but that the cruelty did not attain the end in view; and that the wise engineer was permitted to apply his method at a moment when, had his advice been adopted, the besieging Army would have been near the success which was ultimately attained. The bombardment of Strasburg was not only an error regarded from a military point of view, it was a great political blunder; for who can doubt that the agonies endured in the last days of August, 1870, and the resentment created by the awful destruction of life and property, have materially helped to render inveterate that hostility to German rule which even now reigns in Strasburg as strong as ever. Strasburg would have been captured, probably at an earlier date, had there been no bombardment, humanity would have been spared a heart-rending spectacle, and Germany would have profited by showing some deference towards the feelings and some regard for the lives of the people whose town it was intended to restore to the Reich, and over whom she had determined to rule. It was

only on the 26th, when the King had just turned northward from the Ornain to hunt after MacMahon, that
von Werder, finding Uhrich resolute, decided to proceed by way of a regular siege.   After the end of the
month the fortress ceased to be, in any sense, a danger
to the German Armies, which, whether closed around
Metz or marching westward through France, could
afford to await, with calmness, the certain surrender of
Strasburg, an end which might have been attained just
as quickly had the wisdom of King William's statesmen
been called in to sustain the sound judgment of General
Schulz, the accomplished Engineer.

CHAPTER XIII.

Sedan.

GERMAN DECISION.

WHILE Strasburg was enduring the agonies of a siege and bombardment, and the " Army of the Rhine," already oppressed by " la question des vivres," was chafing in its restricted camps under the cannon of Metz; while Paris was quivering with excitement and barely restrained from bursting into open revolt, the victorious German host was closing steadily, yet swiftly, round the distracted and misguided Army of Chalons. It was pressed in so closely on the Belgian frontier that, during the afternoon of the 30th, before de Failly had been driven over the Meuse, Count Bismarck sent a formal communication to the German Minister at Brussels, in which he expressed a hope that, should MacMahon lead his soldiers across the boundary, the Belgian authorities would immediately deprive them of their arms.   At night, in his quarters at Buzancy, King William sanctioned a decisive order to his son and the Saxon Prince.   The troops were to march at dawn, attack the enemy wherever he could be found on the left and right bank of the Meuse, in order that he might be crushed up as much as possible between the river and the Belgian border.   The Saxon Prince was to operate beyond the Meuse, with two Corps; the Prussian Prince on the front and left ; movements designed to bar the road to Montmédy, prevent any attempt to recross the river, and, eventually, to interpose the German left wing between the French and Mézières. "Should the adversary enter Belgium and not be immediately disarmed, he is to be followed at once without waiting for fresh orders." These were not the final instructions which led to the investment of an Army, but they prepared the way towards, and foreshadowed the accomplishment of that astonishing result.

CONFUSION IN THE FRENCH CAMP.

Marshal MacMahon, perplexed, but not dismayed, by the events of the 30th, remained for some time in doubt. " I do not know what I shall do," said the Marshal early in the evening to Ducrot's aide-de-camp. " In any case, the Emperor should at once start for Sedan." At that time the Emperor was in the camp of Ducrot, who, instructed to protect the retreat of the Army either by Douzy or by Carignan, that is, towards Sedan or Montmédy, had divided his Corps between those two places. At a later period, when darkness had set in, MacMahon, seated at a bivouac fire, on the heights above Mouzon, sent for General Lebrun, and directed him to retreat, at once, upon Sedan, not by the highway, which was crowded with fugitives and wagons, but by cross roads leading upon Douzy. " We have had a bad time," said the Marshal, " but the situation is not hopeless. At the most, the German Army before us cannot exceed in numbers sixty or seventy thousand men. If they attack us, so much the better; we shall be able, doubtless, to fling them into the Meuse." The Marshal, who never spared himself, and seemed to live without sleep, rode back to Sedan, and Lebrun, stumb-

ling along devious tracks, in the darkness, and apparently
in dubious military array, fearing all the time that he
might be attacked, entered Douzy at eight in the morning, and did not reach Bazeilles, his destination, until
ten o'clock.

Meantime Ducrot, embarrassed by the presence of the
Emperor, awaited anxiously, at Carignan, the final
orders of MacMahon. He respectfully urged His
Majesty to depart by train for Sedan, but the Emperor
refused — "he wished to be with the Corps which
covered the retreat." He was astonished and incredulous when the rout before Mouzon was described. "It
is impossible," he repeatedly exclaimed, "our positions
were magnificent!" In the night he vanished from
Carignan ; and it was only some hours after he had
gone that Ducrot was informed of his departure by
train. The General then, in concert with Margueritte,
whose cavalry were on the Chiers, resolved to retreat
in the morning, without waiting longer for orders, and
to move upon Illy, because he assumed that MacMahon
would certainly direct the Army on Mézières. He was
mistaken. On reaching Villers-Cernay, about four in
the afternoon of the 31st, Ducrot learned that he was
to retire upon Sedan, and not upon Mézières, "whither
I have not any intention of going," said the Marshal's
despatch. In fact, the two Divisions of the 1st Corps,
left at Douzy on the 30th, had been already ordered to
retire on the Givonne. Lebrun, whom we saw follow in
their wake, after his painful night march, did not
destroy the bridge over the Chiers; so that, when he
was passing Francheval, Ducrot actually saw the enemy
—they were Saxon horsemen—issuing from the village,
and cutting in upon the baggage and transport trains.

On that memorable 30th, when the Emperor informed
the Empress by telegram, from Carignan, that there

had been an " engagement of no great importance," an
officer destined to be conspicuous, dropped in upon the
Army; it was de Wimpffen. He has been defined by
General Lebrun, who was with him at St. Cyr, as a man
of firm will, and " an unlimited confidence in his own
capacity." Indeed, he had come to restore victory.
When he passed through Paris, the Comte de Palikao
was good enough to tell him—so he writes, although
Palikao " thinks " he could not have so expressed himself—that MacMahon chimed in too easily with the sug-
gestions of the Emperor, which was not the fact; that
His Majesty was in a false position, and that he caused
the greatest embarrassment. " Send me to the Army,"
said de Wimpffen, " I shall impart the needed boldness
and decision." So he was sent to supersede de Failly
in command of the 5th Corps, carrying in his pocket a
letter which authorized him to succeed MacMahon in
command of the Army, should any accident befall the
Marshal. It was this audacious personage who super-
vened on the 30th, and to his horror, found the Army
he might have to guide and govern, falling to pieces
under his eyes. He met troops in flight from Mouzon;
they were frightened, famished, and could hardly
be persuaded that the " Prussians " were not at their
heels. As evidence of the reigning disorder, de Wimpffen says that he collected on the 30th, three regiments
belonging to the 5th, 7th, and 12th Corps, some squadrons of de Failly's cavalry, and several hundreds of
men belonging to the 1st Corps, who obeyed a non-
combatant officer. The General led them during the
night to Sedan. A like confusion prevailed on all sides,
as the soldiers, hungry and thoroughly wearied, fell
asleep as they dropped on the ground in their dreary
bivouacs.

The Emperor entered Sedan about midnight. The

Marshal urged him to embark afresh in the train, and seek security in Mézières, where General Vinoy was expected, and where he did, indeed, arrive that night with the advance guard of one division of the 13th Corps. The Emperor refused to quit Sedan, but the Prince Imperial had been sent away. The movement of Vinoy was delayed several hours, because a train running to Avesnes, and bearing the young Prince, " his baggage, his escort, and his suite," barred the way to Mézières.

When morning dawned upon the discomfited Army, Marshal MacMahon had not ceased to ponder. As he said before the Parliamentary Commission of Inquiry in 1872, he had no intention of fighting a battle at Sedan, but he wished to supply the Army afresh with provisions and munitions; and he spent part of the day in considering what he should do on the morrow, and in watching from the citadel the march of his foes. There were, he believed, a million rations in Sedan, but eight hundred thousand of these were stored in wagons at the station, and as shells reached them from beyond the Meuse, the station-master sent away the train to Mézières. With it went a company of engineers, instructed to blow up the bridge at Donchery; but frightened by the shells, the driver halted long enough to drop the engineers, and then hastily fled with the powder and tools. The Marshal did not hear of the mishap until ten o'clock at night, and when another company of engineers reached the bridge, they found it in possession of the enemy! Early in the morning, before that event occurred, Captain des Sesmaisons, carrying a message from Vinoy, entered Sedan, after having been fired on by a German battery established near Frenois. He saw the Emperor in the hotel of the Sub-Prefect, delivered his message, and received a despatch from His

Majesty directing Vinoy to concentrate his troops in
Mézières. Anxious that the Captain should return in
safety, the Emperor gave him a horse, and traced on a
map the road he should take, observing that the Army
would retire by that route the next day; that the road
would be open and safe, as it was new, had not been
marked on the map, and was unknown to the enemy.
But we learn from the German Staff history, that this
recently opened road, although not laid down on the
French, was duly figured in the German map, a contrast
between diligence and negligence not easily paralleled.
The Captain saw MacMahon, who then, nearly midday,
seemed resolved to march on Mézières, and believed
that he could crush any opposition.

At this moment General Douay arrived, and gave a
new turn to his thoughts. Douay had surveyed the
position in front of his camp with an anxious eye, and
had noted that, unless reinforced, he could not hold the
cardinal point—the Calvaire d'Illy. He got additional
troops in the end. " But," said the Marshal, who seemed
to share Douay's apprehensions, " I do not want to shut
myself up in lines; I wish to be free to manœuvre."
" M. le Maréchal, to-morrow the enemy will not leave
you the time," was the General's answer. According to
Captain des Sesmaisons, it was Douay's comments on
the position which made the Marshal modify his judgment, and think of fighting where he stood rather than
of retreating on Mézières. The Captain rode back to
his General, and carried with him a gloomy account of
the condition and outlook of the Army of Chalons. No
troops were sent forth to watch the Meuse below Sedan
and communicate with Vinoy. Later in the day, an old
soldier who lived in the neighbourhood, sought out
General Douay and told him that the enemy was preparing to pass the Meuse at Donchery—a fact, it might

be thought, which could not escape the notice of the watchers in Sedan—and then it was that the General occupied the position between Floing and Illy, and began to throw up entrenchments as cover for men and guns. He had not done so hitherto, because his soldiers, thoroughly exhausted by incessant marches, sleepless nights, want of food, and rear-guard combats, needed some rest. Enough has been said to indicate the lamentable weakness of mind at head-quarters, and the dire confusion prevailing throughout the limited area between the Belgian frontier and the Meuse, within which the French soldiers were now potentially enclosed. It is time to show a different example of the practice of war.

THE MOVEMENTS OF THE GERMANS.

The decision adopted by the Great Head-quarters at Buzancy were, as usual, anticipated, and the Commander-in-Chief of the Meuse Army, before the formal orders reached him, had directed the Guard and the Twelfth Corps to cross the river, by the bridge at Pouilly, constructed on the 30th, and a new one made at Létanne soon after daybreak on the 31st. The Saxon cavalry commander, indeed, taking with him a squadron at dawn, rode down the right bank, then shrouded in fog, as far as Mouzon, entered the town with four lancers, and crossed the bridge to the faubourg. Thereupon a Prussian battalion instantly passed over and took possession of the town. This adventurous squadron had actually captured prisoners and many wagons loaded with provisions. When the two divisions of cavalry, preceding the infantry advance, rode towards Douzy and Carignan, they struck the tail of Lebrun's Corps, and fired into the distant columns which Ducrot, on the other side of the Chiers, was leading by the hill roads to Francheval. In fact, by noon the Guard horsemen were masters of Carignan and such provision stores as the French had not time to destroy ; and the Saxons, passing through Douzy, had fallen upon a convoy on the right bank. The fire of infantry forced them back upon the town, but they held that and the unbroken bridge until the advance guard of the Twelfth came up in the afternoon and established themselves in the place. The Prussian Guard meanwhile, after a long march, had reached, with its leading battalions, Porru aux Bois and Francheval, the main body halting between Sachy and Missincourt, and the cavalry remaining in the rear. Thus, the Saxon Prince's Army had secured all the bridges over the Chiers and the important passage at Mouzon, where the Fourth Corps stood on both banks of the Meuse. The outposts formed a chain from the right bank of the river in front of Douzy, through Francheval to the Belgian frontier, at that point only nine miles from the Chiers, and sixteen from the Meuse. This narrow belt of territory was thus barred against French enterprise ; the road to Montmédy and Metz was definitely closed. The Saxon Prince did not push farther westward, because he knew that the Great Staff had planned a passage of the Meuse below Sedan for the next day, and, therefore, he did not wish to alarm the French. Enough had been done and his troops needed rest, especially the Guard, the whole of which had marched during the day upwards of thirty miles, and the advance guards more. No wonder the French were astounded at the "prodigious marches" made by Germans, whom they had considered to be incapable of such energy and endurance. Some share of the French disasters must be attributed to that fatal form of error —contempt for the enemy.

Not less success attended the operations of the

Prussian Crown Prince, whose business it was to secure possession of the left bank of the Meuse, and, if practicable, bring batteries to bear upon the French troops. We have already described the effect produced by the horse artillery batteries established under the protection of the cavalry at Frenois upon the railway officials who sent off the provision trains, and upon the drivers who ran away with the powder and tools required to destroy the bridge at Donchery. Behind the cavalry the whole Army was soon in motion. The Würtembergers marched from Verrières to the neighbourhood of Flize, where they became engaged with Vinoy's outposts, and induced them to burn the bridge over the Meuse. The Eleventh Corps moved upon Donchery, and, during the afternoon, not only secured the important bridge at that place, but constructed a second. The Fifth Corps stood close in rear of the Eleventh, and the Second Bavarians halted at Raucourt. On the extreme left the Sixth Corps, covering the rear, went to Attigny, Semoy, and Amagne; the Fifth Division of Cavalry was at Tourteron, and the Sixth at Poix, both scouting over the railway to Reims, and one breaking the line at Faux.

The First Bavarian Corps, which led the infantry advance upon the Meuse, moved early from Raucourt upon Remilly and Aillicourt. They had only started at eight o'clock, yet their guns were in position opposite Bazeilles before the last division of Lebrun's Corps, marching from Douzy, could gain the village. The guns opened at very long range, and Lebrun, who was on the watch, was so impressed that he ordered the division to turn back and enter the position by Daigny, where there was a bridge over the Givonne. The French drew out their guns, which led von der Tann to reinforce his own, so that there was soon a powerful line of batteries in action, and some houses in Bazeilles broke out into flames. Then the Bavarian infantry brigades arrived to support the advance guard, and the French threw out infantry to annoy the hostile gunners. Presently a sharp-eyed artilleryman observed that barrels of powder had been brought down to the railway bridge, apparently with intent to blow it up. Thereupon General von Stephan directed a Jäger battalion to frustrate this design ; and just as the French were lowering some barrels under the furthest arch, the Jägers, dashing on to the bridge, fell upon the working party, drove it off, and poured the powder into the Meuse. In this daring fashion was the railway viaduct saved from destruction under the noses of the 12th Corps. Von der Tann, having the fear of von Moltke before his eyes, desired to save the bridge but not engage beyond the stream. The Jägers, however, who, in the judgment of their comrades, held a post of peril, were promptly supported, and the forward spirit gaining the upper hand, the little troop, driving in the French skirmishers, actually held for some time the fringe of Bazeilles ; but not being supported by the General, who refused to disobey orders and bring on a premature engagement, the hardy adventurers had to retire with loss, to the right bank. Yet they secured the bridge from destruction, and to this day, apparently, General Lebrun cannot understand how it came to pass that MacMahon's orders were not executed. The French say that the powder was spoilt and that no fresh supply could be got from Sedan ; but no effort is made to explain why, when the Bavarians threw a pontoon bridge over the Meuse, just above the railway crossing, Lebrun's people did nothing to prevent it. The truth is that they could not prevent one bridge from being preserved, and the other from being built.

The gain on the day's resolute operations, therefore, was the acquisition of three permanent bridges over the Meuse, two above and one below Sedan ; the seizure of all the passages across the Chiers ; and the concentration of both Armies upon the right and left banks of the river within striking distance of the French troops packed up in a narrow area about Sedan. The Crown Prince brought his head-quarters to Chémery, and the King went through that place on his way to Vendresse. At Chémery, "a brief conference was held between the Generals von Moltke, von Podbielski, and von Blumenthal, relative to the general state of the campaign and the next steps which should be taken." It was a notable meeting, and few words, indeed, were required to indicate the finishing touches of an enterprise, so unexpectedly imposed on them, and so resolutely carried out by these skilful, far-seeing, and audacious captains. They had come to the conclusion that the French had before them only one of two courses—they must either retreat bodily into Belgium, or sacrifice the greater part of their Army in an endeavour with the remainder to reach Paris by way of Mézières. There was a third—to remain and be caught—but a finis so triumphant was not foreseen by the trio of warriors who met in the village of Chémery.

THE BATTLEFIELD OF SEDAN.

The battlefield of Sedan may be described as the space lying within the angle formed by the Meuse, and its little affluent, the Givonne, which flows in a southerly direction from the hills near the Belgian frontier. After passing Bazeilles and its bright meadows, the greater river meanders towards the north-west, making, a little below Sedan, a deep loop enclosing the narrow peninsula of Iges on three sides, and then running westward

by Donchery, Dom le Mesnil and Flize to Mézières.
From the northern end of the loop to the Givonne, the
ground is a rugged, undulating upland, attaining its
maximum of height a little south of the Calvaire d'Illy,
at a point where the Bois de la Garenne begins to clothe
the steep slopes on the south and east. Lower still is a
deep defile, called the Fond de Givonne, through which,
turning the wood, runs the highway from Sedan to
Bouillon, a town on the Semoy in Belgium. The eastern
face of the position, therefore, was the line of the Givonne,
a belt of cottages, gardens, factories and villages; the
southern and south-western was the fortress and the
Meuse; the north-western front was on the hills between Floing and Illy, and the lowlands on the loop of
the Meuse. The interval between Illy and the Givonne
was, at first, neglected because the French held that no
troops could work through the dense forest and broken
ground. The issues from this man-trap were the narrow
band of territory between the head of the Meuse loop
and the wooded Belgian frontier; the high road to
Bouillon; the routes eastward to Carignan up the Chiers,
and the gate of Torcy on the south. They were all
difficult, and in the nature of defiles which can only be
traversed slowly, even in time of peace, by large bodies
of men, horses, guns and wagons.

Within this remarkable enclosure the French Army
sat down on the 31st of August. The 12th and the 1st
Corps, Lebrun's and Ducrot's, held the line of the
Givonne, looking east and south-east, because Lebrun
had to guard the Meuse at Bazeilles. The 5th Corps,
now under de Wimpffen, was partly in the "old camp,"
close under the fortress, and partly behind the 7th,
which, as we have said, occupied the rolling heights
between Floing and Illy with a strong outpost in St.
Menges, at the head of the Meuse loop on the road which

led to Mézières through Vrigne aux Bois—the road supposed to be unknown to the Germans, because it was
not laid down on the French maps. The cavalry posted
in rear of the 7th were the divisions of Margueritte,
Bonnemains and Amiel, while Michel was behind Ducrot's left at the village of Givonne. The sun set, and
the night passed, yet Marshal MacMahon expressed no
decision. Believing that the enemy's numerical strength
had been exaggerated, or that he could break out in any
direction when he pleased, or trusting to fortune and
the opportunities which might offer during the conflict,
perhaps imagining that von Moltke would grant him
another day, the Marshal became the sport of circum-
stance which had escaped his control. " The truth is,"
he said to the Parliamentary Commission, " that I did
not reckon on fighting a battle on the ground we occupied. I knew already that we had no. provisions, and
that the place was barely supplied with munitions, but
I did not yet know on which side I ought, on the morrow (the 1st) to effect my retreat." The unfaltering
adversary had no such doubts, and his firm purpose
brought on not only the Battle, but the Investment of
Sedan. For the information which reached the Great
Head-quarters during the evening of the 31st, induced
von Moltke to quicken the operations. He inferred
that no attempt would be made by the French to break
out by Carignan; that they might try to reach Mézières
or pass into Belgium; and as he was eager to frustrate
their escape by any route, he instructed the Prussian
Crown Prince to set his Corps in motion during the
night. The Prince immediately issued the needful
orders, and directed von der Tann to attack with his
Bavarians at dawn, without awaiting the arrival of the
Twelfth Corps, so that Lebrun in Bazeilles being held
fast, the attention of the French might be attracted

towards that side. The Saxon Prince, being duly informed, entered with characteristic spirit and daring
into the plan, and not only determined to be early on
the scene of action with the Twelfth and the Guard,
but to push the latter well forward, so as to anticipate
the French should they endeavour to gain the Belgian
border. Thus a common motive animated the German
chiefs who, in taking firm steps to gain a decisive result,
were so well seconded by their tireless and intrepid
soldiers.

THE BATTLE OF SEDAN.

A thick white mist filled the valley of the Meuse on
the morning of the 1st of September, 1870, so thick
that von der Tann's Bavarians, marching towards the
railway bridge and the pontoons above it, could not see
many steps ahead, as in two columns they moved at four
o'clock in careful silence through the dense and clammy
atmosphere. At that very time General Lebrun, whose
anxieties kept him awake, started up, and rushing forth,
made the first bugler he encountered sound the call,
which roused the wearied troops sleeping on the hills
between Bazeilles and Balan. Yet it would seem that,
outside the former village, no adequate watch was kept,
for when the leading Bavarians emerged from the fog,
they gained at once possession of several houses, and
even entered the principal street without firing a shot.
It was only when the enemy were within the place, that
the gallant Marine Infantry, posted in the houses and
behind barricades, abruptly arrested the intruders by
opening a smart fire. Then began a sanguinary contest
for the possession of Bazeilles, which raged during many
hours; a series of street fights in which the inhabitants
took an active part; combats ebbing and flowing through
and round the market-place, the church, the larger
mansions, and the pretty park of Monvillers, washed

and beautified by the stream of the Givonne.   Without
a detailed plan, the incidents of this terrible episode in
the battle, are unintelligible.   Vassoigne and Martin des
Pallières, before the latter was wounded on the 31st,
had devised a plan of resistance worthy of the gallant
division they led, and it may be said that the defence of
Bazeilles was the most creditable feat of arms performed
by the French on that dreadful day.   During the earlier
hours, indeed, they kept the upper hand, driving the
Bavarians out of the village on all sides, but being
unable to eject them from two stone houses abutting on
the chief street.   The Bavarian batteries beyond the
Meuse could not open fire until six o'clock, because the
fog had shut out the view, which even then was indis-
tinct.   About this time General Lebrun, who was
quickly on the scene, had called reinforcements from
the 1st and 5th Corps; but then the Saxons had come
up opposite la Moncelle, where one battery, firing at
long range, astonished Lebrun, who saw that the shells
from his own guns fell short, or burst in the air.
When the Twelfth assailed la Moncelle fresh Bavarian
columns had crossed the Meuse, and the fierce conflict
which began in Bazeilles, had extended to the park of
Monvillers, where the French fought steadily.   After
four hours strenuous battle, no marked progress had
been made in this quarter, where three Bavarian
brigades had fallen almost wholly into skirmishing
order, scattered amidst the houses and lanes of the
villages, and some part of the park on the left bank of
the Givonne.   Von der Tann bringing over another
brigade and the reserve artillery from the left bank of
the Meuse, called up a division of the Fourth Corps
which he held back as a reserve.   During the course of
this stubborn combat, the Saxon Corps had seized la Moncelle, and had brought ten batteries to bear on that

village and Daigny, their left flank being prolonged by
two Bavarian batteries.   The accuracy of their fire still
further astonished General Lebrun, who confesses that
he had never seen such artillery.   He and his staff, six
or eight persons, were on an eminence above la Moncelle.
" The shells," he writes, " cut off one branch after another, from the tree at the foot of which I stood holding
my horse; " and he goes on to say that in quick succession, one officer was killed, two mortally wounded, and
two men who bore his fanion were hit.   He was as
much impressed by the " avalanche de fer " as Marshal
Canrobert himself.   The infantry in Bazeilles resisted
superbly, but the French General was none the less
amazed by the terrible fire of the German guns.   Between eight and nine the wave of battle was flowing up
the Givonne, for the Guard were now approaching from
Villers-Cernay.

MACMAHON'S WOUND AND ITS CONSEQUENCES.

Meanwhile, inside the French lines, the drama had
deepened, for the Commander-in-Chief had been wounded.
Marshal MacMahon has related how, before daybreak,
fearing lest the Germans should have moved troops over
the Meuse at Donchery, he had sent two officers to look
into matters in that quarter, and was awaiting their
return when, about five o'clock, he received a despatch
from Lebrun, which made him mount his ready-saddled
horse and ride towards Bazeilles.   Arrived there he saw
that the place was well defended, and went to the left
intending to examine the whole line of the Givonne,
especially as Margueritte had sent word that German
troops were moving towards Francheval.   Halting
above la Moncelle, not far from Lebrun, the Marshal
has stated that while he was gazing intently upon the

heights in front of the Bois Chevalier, and could not see anything, he was struck by the fragment of a shell. At first he thought that he was only bruised, but that being obliged to dismount from his horse, which was also wounded, he fainted for a moment, and then found that his wound was severe. Unable to bear up any longer he gave over the command of the Army to General Ducrot, and was carried to Sedan. That officer did not hear of the event until seven or later; it is impossible to fix precisely the moment when the Marshal was hit, nor when Ducrot learned his destiny, the evidence is so contradictory; but sometime between seven and eight Ducrot took the reins. His first act was to order a retreat on Mézières; Lebrun begged him to reflect and he did, but soon afterwards became positive. "There is not a moment to lose," he cried; and it was arranged that the retreat should be made in echelons, beginning from the right of the 12th Corps. Neither General knew the real facts of the situation, nor guessed even how vast were the numbers of the enemy.

The retreat began; it attracted the notice of Napoleon III., who had ridden on to the field above Balan; and it roused de Wimpffen. He carried in his pocket an order from Palikao authorizing him to succeed MacMahon, if the Marshal were killed or disabled. He had kept the fact secret; after the Marshal fell he still hesitated to use his letter, but not long. The combat about Bazeilles was well sustained; the cavalry had been out a little way beyond St. Menges and, as usual, after a perfunctory search, had "seen nothing," the attack on the Givonne even was not fully developed. General de Wimpffen, perhaps from mixed motives, resolved to interfere and show his old comrades how a man who really knew war could extricate a French

Army from perils in which it had been placed by weakness and incompetence. He certainly thought himself a great man, and he roughly stopped the retreat. Ducrot was indignant, but he obeyed. Lebrun was not more favourably affected by de Wimpffen's loud voice and overbearing manner. " I will not have a movement upon Mézières," he exclaimed. "If the Army is to retreat, it shall be on Carignan and not on Mézières." It should again be observed that the new Commander-in-Chief was quite as ignorant of the facts as his predecessors, and even when he wrote his book many months afterwards had not learned from sources open to all the world how many men stood at that moment between him and Carignan, nor was he at all acquainted with the difficult country through which he would have to move. Ducrot's plan, which would have placed the Army between the Meuse below Sedan and the forest on the frontier, leaving a clear sweep for the guns of the fortress, was far more sensible than that of his imperious rival. Still, to have a chance of success, it should have been begun early in the morning, when the Fifth and Eleventh German Corps were struggling towards the woods; even then it would have probably failed, but there would have been no capitulation of Sedan. General de Wimpffen, although he did not know it, was actually playing into the hand of von Moltke, who desired above all things that the French Corps on the Givonne should remain there, because he knew, so great were his means, so firm his resolution, and so admirable as marchers and fighters were his soldiers, that the gain of a few hours would enable him to surround the Army of Chalons.

How far the retreat from the front line was carried, when it was stayed, and in what degree it injured the defence, cannot possibly be gleaned from the French

narratives, which are all vague and imperfect in regard
to time and place. We know that the Germans did
not carry Bazeilles until nearly eleven o'clock, and then
only by dint of turning movements executed by the
Saxons and fresh Bavarian troops from the direction of
la Moncelle. General Ducrot, in his account, places
his stormy interview with de Wimpffen at a little after
nine; and he says that when it ended he spurred in
haste towards his divisions—Pellé's and L'Hériller's—
and made them descend a part of the positions which
they had climbed a few instants before. Lebrun is
equally vague. He says in one place that when de
Wimpffen came up his first brigades had " partly "
crossed the Fond de Givonne, and in another that the
Marine Infantry had abandoned Bazeilles, which they
had not done before nine o'clock. General de Wimpffen's
recollections are still more confused and his chronology
unintelligible; so that it is impossible to ascertain
precisely what happened beyond the Givonne after
Ducrot ordered and his successor countermanded the
retreat. If we take the German accounts, and try to
measure the influence of the much-debated retreat by
the resistance which the assailants encountered, we
may doubt whether it had much greater influence on
the issue than that which grew out of the impaired
confidence of the troops in their antagonistic and jealous
commanders. Nevertheless, it is probable that the
swaying to and fro in the French line between Bazeilles
and the village of Givonne, after nine o'clock, did, in
some degree, favour the assailants, and render the
acquisition of Bazeilles as well as the passage of the
brook less difficult and bloody. In any case, the intervention of de Wimpffen can only be regarded as a
misfortune for the gallant French Army, which can
hardly find consolation in the fact that within four-and-

twenty hours he was obliged to sign with his name the capitulation of Sedan.

This needful explanation and comment serves to illustrate the disorder, the infirmity of purpose, and the rivalries which existed in the French camp; and we may well agree with Marshal MacMahon when he says that the blow which obliged him to relinquish the command was a grievous event. Doubtless he would have taken a decided course had he not been wounded, and would have marched, if he could, with all his forces, either on Mézières or Carignan; and besides, he says, there was Belgium near at hand. He would not have tried to do all three at once. It is only an Army, well compacted and educated from the bottom to the top which can, without serious detriment, bear three successive commanders in three hours.

PROGRESS OF THE BATTLE ON THE GIVONNE.

While the French generals, almost in the presence of the helpless Emperor, were using high words and thwarting each other's plans, the German onset had proceeded on all sides with unabated vigour. But, about nine o'clock, or a little earlier, the French dashed forward so impetuously that the foremost German troops on the Givonne as far as Daigny, had to give ground ; and the batteries were so vexed by musketry fire that they also fell back on some points. In fact Lebrun's left and Ducrot's right came on with great spirit, and shook, but did not arrest long the hostile line. It was not until this period that the French in Daigny pushed a brigade on to the left bank of the Givonne and occupied ground which, by the confession of their staff officers, had never been reconnoitred. They brought over a battery, and General Lartigue rode with them. The brunt of the onslaught, falling upon the Saxon infantry

immediately in front, these were hard bested; but reinforcements arriving on either hand closed in upon the
enemy's flanks, and, not only was he routed from the
field, but, being swiftly pursued, his battery was captured, and the Saxons following the French into Daigny
wrested from them the village, the bridge, and the
opposite bank of the brook.   General Lartigue's horse
was killed by a shell, and he narrowly escaped capture,
and was then, or shortly afterwards, wounded.   His
chief of the staff, Colonel d'Andigné, hit twice, dropped
in a field of beet-root.   Shells from his own side fell
near him, and he was grateful to them because they
drove away a pig which came and sniffed at his wounds.
Saxon soldiers gave him wine and lumps of sugar, but
one of them stole his watch and cross ; in the end he
was tenderly carried to an ambulance.   Some of the
Zouaves engaged in this combat about Daigny, cut off
from the main body of fugitives, turned northward,
entered the woods, and reached Paris after traversing
the Belgian border.

The Germans owed their quick success at Daigny to
the fact that Lartigue was not supported, and to the
fortunate advent, at a critical moment, of the leading
troops of the Second Saxon Division, the whole of the
Twelfth Corps being now on the ground, engaged or in
reserve.   It need scarcely be remarked that the batteries,
as usual, preceded the bulk of the infantry, for it was
the Saxon guns which extorted the admiration of
Lebrun.   The attack, which had been made from his
side, upon the Saxons and Bavarians about la Moncelle,
was equally brilliant at the outset, for, as we have stated,
the German batteries were driven back by the close
musketry, and the French were advancing impetuously, when a Saxon regiment and part of a Bavarian
brigade striking into the fight, stopped the French and

drove them across the rivulet. Then the artillery
returned ; soon there were ninety-six guns in action ;
and the infantry pressing on, restored the battle. But
in Bazeilles itself the Marines had gained ground, and
fresh troops had to be poured into the village or upon
its outskirts to sustain the assailants, who were still
held at bay by the stout defenders. Yet the final
stroke at the village was delivered shortly after this
check. The troops in Monvillers and la Moncelle simultaneously swept forward from the orchards, and osier-
beds, and gardens, until they emerged on the heights
beyond, and showed a front which threatened the road
from Bazeilles to Balan.

The French stronghold in the place was a large villa
on the north, which had resisted all day ; but now the
freshly arrived Bavarians penetrated into the garden
and turned the building on one side ; while the Saxons
grouped in the park of Monvillers, cutting a path through
the hedges with their billhooks, appeared on the other.
The French then retreated ; but the splendid defence
of the whole position had inflicted a heavy loss on the
adversary.

In Bazeilles itself a conflict continued between the
armed inhabitants and the Bavarians, and soon after
the whole village was in flames. Whether it was set
on fire purposely or not is to this day a matter of bitter
controversy ; but it stands on record that only thirty-
nine lay persons met their deaths, during this long
contest, from fire or sword. It was not the interest of
the Germans to create a furnace across a line of road ;
and one effect of the conflagration was that the German
pioneers, unable to quench it, were compelled to open a
line of communication with the troops on the fighting
line outside the burning village.

The French retired and reformed between the Fond

de Givonne and Balan, whence their line ran northward,
no longer in the valley, but along the uplands to the
Calvaire d'Illy ; for the Prussian Guard, issuing from
Villers-Cernay and Francheval, had thrust the French
out of the village of Givonne, and, long before Bazeilles
was finally mastered, had established powerful lines of
guns which harassed the French troops in the Bois de
la Garenne. In fact, by nine o'clock, there were six
guard batteries in action, and two hours afterwards the
number was increased to fourteen. Givonne was seized
a little later, and infantry support afforded to the right
of the Twelfth Corps ; but Prince Augustus, in con-
formity with his instructions, held the main body of
the Guard ready to march towards Fleigneux, effect a
junction with the Third Army, and bar the road to
Bouillon. From an eminence a little east of Givonne
and just south of La Virée farm, whereon eighteen
guns stood, the Prince, looking westward about nine
o'clock, saw the smoke of that combat near St. Menges,
which he knew marked the formidable intervention of
the Fifth and Eleventh Corps, whose operations in the
forenoon must now be succinctly described.

THE MARCH ON ST. MENGES.

It will be remembered that, on receiving a pressing
order from von Moltke, the Prussian Crown Prince
directed the two Corps just named and the Würtemberg
division to move out in the dark and occupy the
Mézières road in order to intercept the French should
they endeavour to retire upon that town. They
promptly obeyed. The Würtembergers crossed the
Meuse on a bridge of their own making, at Dom le
Mesnil ; the Fifth and Eleventh at Donchery by the
permanent bridge and two improvised passages. The
object of the two Corps was to occupy the nearest

villages on the Mézières road, Vrigne aux Bois and
Vivier au Court, both which were attained about half-
past seven, when the contest was fierce on the Givonne.
Here the generals commanding, von Kirchbach and
von Gersdorf, received that despatch from the Prussian
Crown Prince which directed them to march on St.
Menges and Fleigneux, for at head-quarters a strong
hope had now arisen that the Army of Chalons could be
surrounded. The Eleventh moved on the right, next
the Meuse, the Fifth on the left ; but the roads were
few between the river and the forest—one column lost
its way, and both Corps at the head of the Loop had to
use the same road. No French scouts were out along
this important line of communication. Margueritte's
horsemen had patrolled a short distance, about six, but
neither saw nor heard of the approaching columns ;
nor until the German Hussars, leading the erring
column ascending the Meuse from Montimont, had got
close to St. Menges, were they discovered by a French
patrol sent out at the suggestion of de Wimpffen.

THE ELEVENTH AND FIFTH CORPS ENGAGE.

The shots exchanged by the hostile cavaliers aroused
the French infantry in St. Menges ; but they offered
no resistance when the nearest German battalion
attacked the village, which was immediately occupied.
Two companies, prolonging the movement, effected a
lodgment in Floing and could not be expelled ; while
three batteries, escorted by the Hussars, dashed upon
the ridge south of St. Menges, partly protected by a
copse, and opened fire on the French. It was this
initial combat which attracted the notice of Prince
Augustus of Würtemberg, who looked with interest,
from his hill above the Givonne, upon the white battle

smoke which curled up beyond the heights of Illy. Shortly afterwards seven additional batteries issued from the defile and formed in succession on the hill—the same which had filled General Douay with anxiety the day before—and some infantry battalions followed; but the body of the Eleventh Corps was only just clearing the pass, and the Fifth was still behind. In order to protect the batteries, infantry supports were advanced on either flank and in front towards the Illy brook. General Margueritte, on the Calvaire d'Illy, had watched this unwelcome development of artillery. Seeing the infantry spread out below, he thought that his horse might ride them down and then disable the line of batteries, which seemed to be without adequate support. Accordingly, by his order, General de Galliffet led forth three regiments of Chasseurs d'Afrique and two squadrons of Lancers against the intrusive foot and audacious gunners. But he never got near the batteries. Swooping down the slope upon the infantry below him, his men and horses soon fell fast, and although they swept through the skirmishers, they were crushed by the fire of the supports and the guns on the hill and the squads of infantry on either side. They endeavoured to ride in upon the flanks, but their bravery was displayed in vain, for nothing could live under the fire which smote them, and they rode back, frustrated, to the shelter of their own lines. The cavalry outburst had been repelled by a few companies of foot on an open hill-side. So puissant is the breech-loader in the hands of cool infantry soldiers. But the French foot took up the game, and the Chassepot, deftly plied, forced the forward German skirmishers to fall back on the villages and hills.

Gradually the two Corps arrived on the scene. Before eleven o'clock the artillery of the Fifth, preceding its infantry, went into line on a second ridge to the westward, and soon twenty-four batteries—that is, 144 guns—were pouring an "avalanche de fer" into the French position, and crossing their fire with that of the Guard batteries, which showered their shells into the right rear of Douay's men from the heights beyond the Givonne. About this time, also, as reinforcements came up to Fleigneux, the companies there moved westward towards Olly; captured, on their way, eight guns, many horses, much munition, and above a hundred officers and men, who seemed intent on escaping over the frontier, and finally entered Olly, where soon afterwards they were gratified by the arrival of a squadron of Prussian Hussars of the Guard. Thus was the circle completed which placed the two Armies in communication. In front of the right wing the two companies which at the outset obtained a lodgment in Floing, were at length supported and relieved. As the infantry from the wooded region north of the Meuse Loop arrived, they took the place of the battalions near the guns, and these then went forward upon Floing, one after the other, and by degrees got possession of the village. But the French delivered a counterstroke so well pushed that the defenders of Floing could not keep them back, and they were only thrust out by the timely intervention of three fresh battalions from St. Menges. The French retired towards the heights of Cazal, and for some time stopped the further advance of their foes.

The battle was now practically won; for the Germans held Balan as well as Bazeilles, supported by one-half the Second Bavarian Corps brought up to aid the First; one division of the Fourth Corps was deep in the fight, and the other in reserve, close at hand; the line of the Givonne, from end to end, was occupied on both banks; the Guard Cavalry, after vainly trying to

charge up the Calvaire d'Illy, were behind the Fifth
Corps; south of the Meuse a Bavarian division faced
the fortress; and to the west the Würtembergers interposed between Vinoy's troops in Mézières and Sedan.
Above all, a little after one o'clock, there were no fewer
than 426 guns hailing shells upon the unfortunate
French, who were almost piled one upon another in an
area which did not measure two miles either in depth
or breadth. It stands on record that there were in full
action twenty-six batteries on the North, twenty-four on
the East, ten to the West of la Moncelle, and eleven on
the South between Wadelincourt and Villette—an array
of force enough to crush out all resistance; but the
conflict still continued, for no one had authority sufficient to stop the awful carnage.

THE CONDITION OF THE FRENCH ARMY.

The main interest of the drama henceforth centres in
the despairing efforts of the French to avert the catastrophe of Sedan. Early in the morning the Emperor
Napoleon mounted his horse and rode out with his own
staff to witness the battle. On his way towards Bazeilles
he met and spoke to the wounded Marshal, who was
being carried to the hospital in Sedan. Then the
Emperor rode towards the hills above la Moncelle, and
for several hours he lingered on the field, well under
fire, for two officers were wounded near him; but he
had no influence whatever on the battle. Soon after
taking command, de Wimpffen, riding out of the Fond
de Givonne, came plump upon Napoleon as he watched
the fight near Balan. "All goes well, Sire," said the
General; "we are gaining ground;" and when His
Majesty remarked that the left, meaning the front
towards St. Menges, was threatened, the General replied, "We shall first pitch the Bavarians into the

Meuse, and then, with all our forces, fall upon the new foe." They parted, the Emperor returning to Sedan, whence he did not emerge again that day, and the General careering towards the fight. Then followed a sharp dispute between de Wimpffen and Ducrot, in the presence of Lebrun, ending in the order to stop the so-called retreat which had scarcely begun. It is impossible to reconcile the conflicting accounts of these officers; but de Wimpffen's own words show that, at the time, he did not attach great importance to the attack on Douay, for to that General he wrote, "I believe in a demonstration upon your Corps, especially designed to hinder you from sending help to the 1st and 12th Corps," and he asked him to aid Lebrun. Then he went himself to the position held by Douay, in order to expedite the despatch of reinforcements. "Come and see for yourself," said Douay, on reaching the heights. "I saw quite a hostile Army extending afar," writes de Wimpffen, "and a formidable artillery—"the big batteries of the Fifth and Eleventh Corps—firing with a precision which, under other circumstances," he adds, "I should have been the first to admire." Prince Bibesco says that de Wimpffen promised to send troops from the 1st Corps to occupy the Calvaire d'Illy, and then went away. As he was riding back, in that state of emotion which the French describe by the phrase, "le cœur navré," he encountered Ducrot. "The events which I predicted," said the latter, "have happened sooner than I expected. The enemy is attacking the Calvaire d'Illy. Douay is greatly shaken. Moments are precious. Hurry up reinforcements if you would keep that position." "Well," retorted de Wimpffen, still believing that he had only Bavarians to deal with, "look after that yourself. Collect what troops you can and hold the ground while I attend to the 12th

Corps." Thereupon Ducrot ordered up guns and infantry; while then, or shortly afterwards, de Wimpffen called for troops from Douay, who, believing the Calvaire was or would be occupied by Ducrot's people, sent off three brigades, and put his last division in front line. Apparently the cross currents of wandering battalions met in the wood of Garenne; and it is not easy to see how any advantages were obtained by the shifting to and fro which went on. Ducrot was anxious to defend the Illy plateau; de Wimpffen desired to break out towards Carignan. He fondled the idea at one o'clock, when neither object could possibly be attained; but if there had been a chance left, the conflict between the two Generals would have sufficed to destroy it.

That "Army" which de Wimpffen saw from the north-western heights came on in irresistible waves. The French infantry could not endure the thick and ceaseless hail of shells from the terrible batteries. The French artillery, brave and devoted, vainly went into action, for the converging fire from the hostile hills blew up the tumbrils, sometimes two at once, killed and wounded the gunners, and swept away the horses. Ducrot's reinforcements, despite his forward bearing and animated language, melted away into the woods, and the last battalions and the last two batteries led up by Douay were speedily forced to retire. The Germans, already in the village of Illy, advanced to the Calvaire, while the troops of the Eleventh Corps sallied out of Floing, deployed on both sides, and soon the interval between the two villages was full of hostile troops. General Ducrot pictures himself, and doubtless truly, as using every effort by word and example to rally and hold fast the foot; but they could not be held; they slipped off and vanished under the trees. At this time the only strong body of French was Liébert's division above the terraced hill which leads up to Cazal, and the cavalry of Margueritte and Bonnemains lurking in the hollows and under the cover of trees. To these men Ducrot appealed, and his appeal was nobly answered.

THE FRENCH CAVALRY CHARGE.

General Margueritte commanded five regiments of horse, principally Chasseurs d'Afrique. At the request of Ducrot he promptly moved out from cover, and prepared to charge; but wishing to reconnoitre the ground, he rode in advance, and was hit in the head by a bullet which traversed his face. Mortally wounded, he gave the command to de Galliffet, and rode off, supported by two men, and grasping the saddle with both hands, " the star of his arm," as Colonel Bonie poetically calls him. Then de Galliffet performed his task, and rode straight into the intrusive enemy. For half-an-hour, on the hill sides south of Floing, and even the lowlands bordering the Meuse, the dashing French horsemen dauntlessly struck at their foes. The German infantry scattered in lines of skirmishers, were just attaining the crest of the eminence, when the cavalry dashed upon them. They broke through the skirmishers, but fell in heaps under the fire of the compact bodies of supports. Failing to crush a front, they essayed the flanks and even the rear, and nothing dismayed, sought again and again to ride over the stubborn adversary, who, relying on his rifle, would not budge. The more distant infantry and the guns, when occasion served, smote these devoted cavaliers. Sometimes the Germans met them in line, at others they formed groups, or squares as the French call them, and occasionally they fought back to back. One body of horse rode into a battery, and was only repelled by the fire of a company of infantry. Another dashed through a village on the banks of the

river, and although they were hurried by infantry, and
turned aside and followed by some Prussian hussars,
several rode far down the river, and created some disorder in the German trains. There were many charges,
all driven home as far at least as the infantry fire would
permit, more than one carrying the furious riders up to
the outskirts of Floing. But, in the end, the unequal
contests everywhere had the same result—bloody defeat
for the horseman, who matched himself, his lance or
sword and steed against the breech-loader held by
steady hands in front of keen eyes. Yet it is not surprising that these daring charges excited the ungrudging
admiration and deep sympathy of friend and foe. They
did not arrest the march of the German infantry, or turn
the tide of battle, or even infuse new courage into the
French soldiers, who were exposed to trials which few,
if any, troops could bear. But they showed, plainly
enough, that the " furia francese " survived in the
cavalry of France, and that, if the mounted men refused
or disdained to perform more useful work by scouting
afar and covering the front of armies, they could still
charge with unabated heroism on the field of battle.
They were dispersed, and they left behind heaps of
dead and dying—one-half their strength resting on the
scene of their daring. Three Generals, Margueritte,
Girard and Tilliard, were killed, and Salignac-Fenelon
was wounded. The Germans say that their own losses
were small, but that among the Jägers a comparatively
large number of men were wounded by the sword.
These notable exploits were done about two o'clock or
a little later; and, with slight exceptions, they mark
the end of desperately offensive resistance on the part
of the French.

During the next hour the Germans pressed their adversaries close up to Sedan. " When the cavalry had

been driven back in disorder," says Ducrot in his sweeping style, " the last bodies of infantry which had stood firm broke and fled. Then on the right and left, with loud hurrahs, which mingled with the roar of cannon and musketry, the Prussian lines advanced." The statement is too superlative. The cavalry in squads, wandered, no doubt, from ravine to ravine, seeking an asylum, or tried to enter the fortress. The remains of several brigades were piled up in the wood of Garenne, and exposed to an incessant shell fire. But Liébert's division stoutly defended Cazal, and gave back, foot by foot, until they also were under the ramparts. Towards four o'clock the converging German columns, despite frantic onsets from bands of French infantry, especially on the Givonne front, had thrust these over the deep hollow way, and the victors were only halted when they came within range of the garrison guns.

GENERAL DE WIMPFFEN'S COUNTERSTROKE.

Throughout the battle General de Wimpffen cherished the idea that it would be feasible to crush " the Bavarians " and retreat on Carignan. At one o'clock he sent a despatch to General Douay, telling the General to cover his retreat in that direction. Douay received it an hour afterwards, and he then replied that " with only three brigades, without artillery, and almost without munitions," the utmost he could do would be to retreat in order from the field. That was near the moment when Liébert began to fall back, fighting stiffly, from Cazal. At a quarter past one de Wimpffen wrote a letter to the Emperor saying that " rather than be made prisoner in Sedan," he would force the line in his front. " Let your Majesty," he said, " place himself in the midst of his troops; they will hold themselves bound in honour to fray out a passage." His Majesty took no notice of this appeal, and de Wimpffen waited in vain for a reply; but he spent the time in an endeavour to dash in the barrier in his front, direct an attack on the Givonne, which failed; and to organize an onset on Balan, which partly succeeded. He went into Sedan and brought out troops, and gathered up all he could from the errant fragments of a broken Army. With these he fell fiercely and unexpectedly upon the Bavarians in Balan; refused to suspend the fight when ordered by the Emperor to open negotiations with the enemy; and by degrees became master of all the village except one house. But he could not emerge and continue his onslaught, for the hostile artillery began to play on the village; reinforcements were brought up, arrangements were made to frustrate the ulterior aim of the French and recover the lost ground. Against a resolute advance the infantry led by de Wimpffen could not stand, and possession of the village was regained just as the white flag went up over the nearest gate of Sedan. Suddenly the firing ceased on both sides. Although respectfully described by the Germans, General de Wimpffen's last charge is scoffed at by Ducrot and Lebrun, whom he had enraged by declaring both guilty of disobedience. Lebrun, who was an eye-witness as well as a gallant actor in the forlorn hope, says that they had not gone a quarter of a mile before the column broke and took refuge in the nearest houses. Looking back, de Wimpffen is reported by his comrade to have said, " I see we are not followed and that there is nothing more to do. Order the troops to retreat on Sedan." The battle had, at length, come to an end. The German infantry, both near Cazal and Balan were within a short distance of the fortifications; in the centre they stood south of the Warren Wood; to the eastward long lines of guns crowned the heights on both banks of the Givonne; on the south, the gate of

Torcy was beset, and behind all the foremost lines were ample reserves, horse as well as foot, which had never fired a shot. The number of batteries had increased during the afternoon, for the Würtemberg artillery was called over the Meuse and set in array at the bend of the river above Donchery. Even the high-tempered, if imperious, de Wimpffen was obliged to admit that through this dread circle, neither for him nor any other, was there an outlet. The agony had been prolonged, but enough had been done to satisfy the " honour " of the most obstinate and punctilious of generals. The wearied, wasted, famished, and unnerved French troops were thankful for the impressive stillness and unwonted rest which came abruptly with the declining sun, even though it set the seal on a horrible disaster.

THE EMPEROR AND HIS GENERALS.

Had Napoleon III. retained that Imperial authority which he had been supposed to possess, the slaughter might have been stayed some hours before. For early in the afternoon he became convinced that the Army could not be extricated, and that the time had come when it would be well to treat. His experiences, as a superfluous attendant on the battle-field, were dolorous. The first object which met his gaze was the wounded Marshal. The depressing incident may have called up visions of Italian triumphs; and, reflecting on the painful contrast, he may have remembered what he said after returning from the sanguinary victory of Solferino—that no more would he willingly lead great Armies to war; for the sight of its horrors had touched the chord of sympathy with human suffering which had always readily vibrated in his heart. During several hours he watched the tempest lower and break in fury; he saw and felt its effects, for two officers were shot at his side; wherever

he looked the clouds of encircling battle smoke rose in
the clear sunshine; and when he rode back into Sedan
the terrible shells were bursting in the ditches, and even
on the bridge which he traversed to gain his quarters.
As the day wore on his gloomy meditations took a more
definite shape; he wished to stop the conflict, and he
seems to have thought first that an armistice might be
obtained, and then that the King of Prussia, if personally besought, would grant the Army easy terms; for the
idea of a capitulation had grown up and hardened in his
mind.

At his instigation, no officer has come forward to
claim the honour, some one hoisted a white flag. As
soon as he heard of it, General Faure, Marshal Mac-
Mahon's Chief of the Staff, ascended the citadel and cut
down a signal so irritating to his feelings; but no one
told the Emperor that his solitary, independent, and
Imperial action, since he joined the Army of Chalons as
a fugitive, had been thus irreverently contemned. "Why
does this useless struggle still go on?" he said to General
Lebrun, who entered his presence some time before
three o'clock. "Too much blood has been shed. An
hour ago I directed the white flag to be hoisted in
order to demand an armistice." The General politely
explained that other forms were necessary—the Commander-in-Chief must sign a letter and send a proper
officer, a trumpeter, and a man bearing a white flag, to
the chief of the enemy. Lebrun drew out such a form,
and started forth. Faure, who had just pulled down
the white flag, would not look at it; de Wimpffen,
seeing Lebrun ride up followed by a horseman who
carried a rag on a pole, shouted out, "I will not have
a capitulation; drop that flag; I shall go on fighting;"
and then ensued their adventures about Balan, which
have been described. When Lebrun had gone, Ducrot,

and subsequently Douay, visited the Emperor. Ducrot found the interior of the fortress in a state which he qualifies as "indescribable." "The streets, the squares, the gates were choked up with carts, carriages, guns, the impedimenta and débris of a routed Army. Bands of soldiers, without arms or knapsacks, streamed in every moment, and hurried into the houses and churches. At the gates many were trodden to death." Those who preserved some remains of vigour exhaled their wrath in curses, and shouted " We have been betrayed, sold by traitors and cowards." The Emperor still wondered why the action went on, and rejected Ducrot's suggestion of a sortie at night as futile. He wished to stop the slaughter ; but he could not prevail on Ducrot to sign any letter. Douay at first appeared disposed to accept the burden, but de Failly or Lebrun induced him to revoke his consent by remarking that it entailed the duty of fixing his name to a capitulation. General de Wimpffen sent in his resignation, which, as the Emperor could not induce one of the other generals to take his place, was absolutely refused. The shells were bursting in the garden of the Sub-Prefecture, in the hospitals, the streets, and among the houses, some of which were set on fire. In these dire straits the Emperor at length resolved that the white flag should be again unfurled, and should, this time, remain aloft in the sunshine. Meantime, as evident signs indicating a desire to negotiate had appeared at various points, and as the white flag surmounted the citadel, the King directed Colonel Bronsart von Schellendorf and Captain von Winterfeld to summon the place to capitulate. When Bronsart intimated to the Commandant of Torcy that he bore a summons to the Commander-in-Chief, he was conducted to the Sub-Prefecture, " where," says the official narrative, " he found himself face to face with the Emperor Napoleon, whose presence in Sedan until that moment had been unknown at the German head-quarters." The arrival of the Prussian officer seems to have occurred just as the Emperor finished writing a letter to the King destined to become famous. But he answered Bronsart's request that an officer fully empowered to treat should be sent to the German head-quarters, by remarking that General de Wimpffen commanded the Army. Thereupon, Colonel Bronsart departed, bearing a weighty piece of intelligence indeed, but no effective reply ; and soon afterwards General Reille, entrusted with the Imperial letter, rode out of the gate of Torcy and ascended the hill whence the King had witnessed the battle.

KING WILLIAM AND HIS WARRIORS.

An eminence, selected by the Staff because it commanded an extensive view, rises a little south of Frenois —the site has been marked on the map with a small pyramid—and upon this, about seven o'clock, just as the fog was lifting, King William took his stand. When the mists vanished, the sun poured his dazzling splendour over the landscape, and the air was so lucid that everything could be seen distinctly through a powerful field-glass. "The sun shone out in full power," says Prince Bibesco. "The sun was exceedingly powerful," writes Dr. Russell. "The day had become so clear "—he is writing of the same period as the Prince—"that through a good glass the movements of individual men were plainly discernible." And, a little earlier, he says, "on the hills, through wood and garden," he was looking towards the Givonne, "and in the valleys, bayonets glistened, and arms twinkled and flashed like a streamlet in moonlight." And so it continued to the end. "The hills of the battlefield," writes Dr. Moritz Busch, "the gorge in its midst, the villages, the houses and the towers of the fortress, the suburb of Torcy, the ruined [railway] bridge to the left in the distance, shone bright in the evening glow, and their details became clearer every minute, as if one were looking through stronger and stronger spectacles." Through such a rich and transparent atmosphere the King gazed from his height upon the city wherein Turenne was born, in September, 1611, and on the battle which has made the little town on the Meuse, which Vauban fortified, still more memorable. A glimpse of the group on the hill is fortunately afforded by Dr. Russell, whose keen eyes on a battlefield seem to overlook nothing. "Of the King, who was dressed in his ordinary uniform, tightly buttoned and strapped," it is noted that he "spoke but little, pulled his moustache frequently, and addressed a word to von Moltke, Roon, or Podbielski," who looked frequently through a large telescope mounted on a tripod. "Moltke," he goes on, and the touch is characteristic, "when not looking through the glass or at the map, stood in a curious musing attitude, with his right hand to the side of his face, the elbow resting on the left hand crossed towards his hip." A picture of von Moltke, which, taken with what another observer calls his "refined and wrinkled face," deserves to live in the memory. Count Bismarck, we are told, "in his white cuirassier flat cap with the yellow band and uniform, stood rather apart, smoking a good deal, and chatting occasionally with a short, thick-set, soldierly-looking man in the undress uniform of a United States' Lieutenant-General." It was Sheridan. And near these were many less famous personages, but representative of "all Germany," as one writer puts it. On another hill a little further west, whither Dr. Russell transferred himself, was a second and notable group, which he sketches. "The Crown Prince with his arms folded, and his flat cap, uniform frock, and jack boots ; Blumenthal so spruce and trim ; half-a-dozen princes and many aides-de-camp," were all sharply and well-defined on the sky-line. Thus these two groups, " from morn to dewy eve," looked down, on, and into a scene which nature and man had combined to make at once beautiful and sublime.

It was towards the King's hill that General Reille turned when he rode out of the Torcy gate. Walking his horse up the steep, he dismounted, and taking off his cap, presented a letter to his Majesty. King William, breaking the Imperial seal, read these phrases, which, if somewhat dramatic, are striking in their brevity :— [1]

Monsieur mon Frère,

  N'ayant pu mourir au milieu de mes troupes, il ne me reste qu' à remettre mon epée entre les mains de Votre Majesté.

I suis de Votre Majesté,
  le bon Frère,
    NAPOLÉON.

Sédan, le 1er Septembre, 1870.

Only one half hour earlier had Colonel Bronsart brought the startling information that the Emperor was in Sedan ! The King conferred with his son, who had been hastily summoned, and with others of his trusty servants, all deeply moved by complex emotions at the grandeur of their victory. What should be done? The Emperor spoke for himself only, and his surrender would not settle the great issue. It was necessary to obtain something definite, and the result of a short conference was that Count Hatzfeldt, instructed by the Chancellor,

---

[1] " Not having been able to die in the midst of my troops, nothing remains for me but to place my sword in the hands of your Majesty."

retired to draft a reply. " After some minutes he brought it," writes Dr. Busch, " and the King wrote it out, sitting on one chair, while the seal of a second was held up by Major von Alten, who knelt on one knee and supported the chair on the other." The King's letter, brief and business-like, began and ended with the customary royal forms, and ran as follows:—

" Regretting the circumstances in which we meet, I accept your Majesty's sword, and beg that you will be good enough to name an officer furnished with full powers to treat for the capitulation of the Army which has fought so bravely under your orders. On my side I have designated General von Moltke for that purpose."

General Reille returned to his master, and as he rode down the hill the astounding purport of his visit flew from lip to lip through the exulting Army which now hoped that, after this colossal success, the days of ceaseless marching and fighting would soon end. As a contrast to this natural outburst of joy and hope we may note the provident Moltke, who was always resolved to " mak siker." His general order, issued at once, suspending hostilities during the night, declared that they would begin again in the morning should the negotiations produce no result. In that case, he said, the signal for battle would be the reopening of fire by the batteries on the heights east of Frenois. The return of peace, so fervently desired by the Army, was still far off in the distance when the tired victors bivouacked in quiet, and dreamed of home through the short summer night.

HOW THE GENERALS RATED EACH OTHER.

While General Reille, who performed his part with so much modesty and dignity, rode back over the Meuse, the Emperor still awaited, in the Sub-Prefecture, the advent of General de Wimpffen, who was fretting and fuming at the Golden Cross within the walls. According to his own confession he had become convinced that the refusal of his sovereign to head a sally from Balan had delivered over the Army to the mercy of the Germans, and violent despair had taken possession of his soul. For had not the Comte de Palikao sent him to overbear Napoleon III. and the set who surrounded him, and had he not failed to bend the monarch to his will? Twice, he repeats, with pride, "I obstinately refused to obey" the Emperor's invitation to treat with the enemy; and because Napoleon III. had authoritatively interfered with his command he sent in that letter of resignation which the Emperor refused to accept. At first he seemed inclined to resist as well as resent the conduct of his master, who had presumed to consult others and, by hoisting the white flag, to take, as the General haughtily says, "a decision contrary to my will." Let the Emperor sign the capitulation. Such were the first thoughts of a man whose temper was imperious, but whose better nature was not insensible to reason. He quelled his wrath and threw off his despair, moved, as he says, by the feeling that in defending the interests of the Army he would be rendering a last service to his brave companions in arms, and to his country. So he went from the Golden Cross to the Sub-Prefecture. Still angry, he loudly asserted as soon as he entered the room that he had been vanquished in battle because, addressing the Emperor, "your Generals refused to obey me." Thereupon Ducrot started up, exclaiming, "Do you mean me? Your orders were only too well obeyed, and your mad presumption has brought on this frightful disaster." "If I am incapable," retorted de Wimpffen, "all the more reason why I should not retain the command." "You took it this morning,"

shouted Ducrot, also a violent man, " when you thought
it would bring honour and profit.   You cannot lay it
down now.   You alone must bear (endosser) the shame
of the capitulation."   " Le General Ducrot etait trés
exalté," he says in his narrative, and he calls on his
brother officers who were present to testify that he
used these brave words, which, in substance, appear in
de Wimpffen's account ; but the latter adds that he
threw back the accusation, saying, " I took the command to evade a defeat which your movement would
have precipitated ;" and that he requested General
Ducrot to leave the room, as he had not come to confer
with him ! What the quiet and well-mannered Emperor
thought of his two fiery and blustering Generals is
nowhere stated.   The calm language in the pamphlet
attributed to Napoleon III., which shows, nevertheless,
how deeply he was vexed by de Wimpffen's selfish wish
to shirk his responsibilities at such a moment, takes
no note of the quarrel, and simply tells us how " the
General understood that, having commanded during the
battle, his duty obliged him not to desert his post in
circumstances so critical."   Thus, when General Reille
returned with King William's letter, he found de
Wimpffen in a reasonable frame of mind and ready to
perform, with courage and address, the hard task of
obtaining the best terms he could for the French Army
from the placidly stern von Moltke, in whose heart there
were no soft places when business had to be done.

THE GENERALS MEET AT DONCHERY.

Late on the evening of September 1st a momentous
session was held in Donchery, the little town which
commands a bridge over the Meuse below Sedan.   On
one side of a square table covered with red baize sat
General von Moltke, having on his right hand the

Quartermaster-General von Podbielski, according to one account, and von Blumenthal according to another, and behind them several officers, while Count von Nostitz stood near the hearth to take notes. Opposite to von Moltke sat de Wimpffen alone; while in rear, " almost in the shade," were General Faure, Count Castelnau, and other Frenchmen, among whom was a Cuirassier Captain d'Orcet, who had observant eyes and a retentive memory. Then there ensued a brief silence, for von Moltke looked straight before him and said nothing, while de Wimpffen, oppressed by the number present, hesitated to engage in a debate " with the two men admitted to be the most capable of our age, each in his kind." But he soon plucked up courage, and frankly accepted the conditions of the combat. What terms, he asked, would the King of Prussia grant to a valiant Army which, could he have had his will, would have continued to fight? "They are very simple," answered von Moltke. " The entire Army, with arms and baggage, must surrender as prisoners of war." " Very hard," replied the Frenchman. " We merit better treatment. Could you not be satisfied with the fortress and the artillery, and allow the Army to retire with arms, flags and baggage, on condition of serving no more against Germany during the war ? " No. " Moltke," said Bismarck recounting the interview, "coldly persisted in his demand," or as the attentive d'Orcet puts it, " von Moltke was pitiless." Then de Wimpffen tried to soften his grim adversary by painting his own position. He had just come from the depths of the African desert; he had an irreproachable military reputation ; he had taken command in the midst of a battle, and found himself obliged to set his name to a disastrous capitulation. " Can you not," he said, " sympathise with an officer in such a plight, and soften, for me, the bitterness of my situation by granting more

honourable conditions?" He painted in moving terms
his own sad case, and described what he might have
done; but seeing that his personal pleadings were un-
heeded, he took a tone of defiance, less likely to prevail.
"If you will not give better terms," he went on, "I
shall appeal to the honour of the Army, and break out,
or, at least, defend Sedan." Then the German General
struck in with emphasis, "I regret that I cannot do what
you ask," he said; "but as to making a sortie, that is
just as impossible as the defence of Sedan. You have
some excellent troops, but the greater part of your infantry is demoralized. To-day, during the battle, we
captured more than twenty thousand unwounded
prisoners. You have only eighty thousand men left. My
troops and guns around the town would smash yours
before they could make a movement; and as to defending
Sedan, you have not provisions for eight-and-forty hours,
nor ammunition which would suffice for that period."
Then, says de Wimpffen, he entered into details respecting our situation, which, "unfortunately, were too true,"
and he offered to permit an officer to verify his statements, an offer which the Frenchman did not then
accept.

Beaten off the military ground, de Wimpffen sought
refuge in politics. "It is your interest, from a political
standpoint, to grant us honourable conditions," he said.
"France is generous and chivalric, responsive to gener-
osity, and grateful for consideration. A peace, based
on conditions which would flatter the amour-propre of
the Army, and diminish the bitterness of defeat would
be durable; whereas rigorous measures would awaken
bad passions, and, perhaps, bring on an endless war
between France and Prussia." The new ground broken
called up Bismarck, "because the matter seemed to
belong to my province," he observed when telling the

story; and he was very outspoken as usual. " I said to him that we might build on the gratitude of a prince, but certainly not on the gratitude of a people—least of all on the gratitude of the French. That in France neither institutions nor circumstances were enduring; that governments and dynasties were constantly changing, and the one need not carry out what the other had bound itself to do. That if the Emperor had been firm on his throne, his gratitude for our granting good conditions might have been counted upon; but that as things stood it would be folly if we did not make full use of our success. That the French were a nation full of envy and jealousy, that they had been much mortified by our success at Königgratz, and could not forgive it, though it in nowise damaged them. How, then, should any magnanimity on our side move them not to bear us a grudge for Sedan. This Wimpffen would not admit. " France," he said, " had much changed latterly; it had learned under the Empire to think more of the interests of peace than of the glory of war. France was ready to proclaim the fraternity of nations; and more of the same kind." Captain d'Orcet reports that, in addition, Bismarck denied that France had changed, and that to curb her mania for glory, to punish her pride, her aggressive and ambitious character, it was imperative that there should be a glacis between France and Germany. " We must have territory, fortresses and frontiers which will shelter us for ever from an attack on her part." Further remonstrances from de Wimpffen only drew down fresh showers of rough speech very trying to bear, and when Bismarck said " We cannot change our conditions," de Wimpffen exclaimed, " Very well; it is equally impossible for me to sign such a capitulation, and we shall renew the battle."

Here Count Castelnau interposed meekly to say, on

behalf of the Emperor, that he had surrendered, personally, in the hope that his self-sacrifice would induce the
King to grant the Army honourable terms.   " Is that
all? " Bismarck inquired.   " Yes," said the Frenchman.
" But what is the sword surrendered," asked the Chancellor; " is it his own sword, or the sword of France? "
" It is only the sword of the Emperor," was Castelnau's reply.   " Well, there is no use talking about other
conditions," said von Moltke, sharply, while a look of
contentment and gratification passed over his face, according to Bismarck; one " almost joyful," writes the
keen Captain d'Orcet.   " After the last words of von
Moltke," he continues, " de Wimpffen exclaimed, ' We
shall renew the battle.'   ' The truce,' retorted the
German General, ' expires to-morrow morning at four
o'clock.   At four, precisely, I shall open fire.'   We
were all standing.   After von Moltke's words no one
spoke a syllable.   The silence was icy."   But then
Bismarck intervened to soothe excited feelings, and
called on his soldier comrade to show, once more, how
impossible resistance had become.   The group sat down
again at the red baize-covered table, and von Moltke
began his demonstration afresh.   " Ah," said de Wimpffen, " your positions are not so strong as you would
have us believe them to be."   " You do not know the
topography of the country about Sedan," was von
Moltke's true and crushing answer.   " Here is a bizarre
detail which illustrates the presumptuous and incon-
sequent character of your people," he went on, now
thoroughly aroused.   " When the war began you supplied your officers with maps of Germany at a time when
they could not study the geography of their own country for want of French maps.   I tell you that our
positions are not only very strong, they are inexpugnable."   It was then that de Wimpffen, unable to reply,

z

wished to accept the offer made, but not accepted at an earlier period, and to send an officer to verify these assertions. "You will send nobody," exclaimed the iron General. "It is useless, and you can believe my word. Besides, you have not long to reflect. It is now midnight; the truce ends at four o'clock, and I will grant no delay." Driven to his last ditch, de Wimpffen pleaded that he must consult his fellow-Generals, and he could not obtain their opinions by four o'clock. Once more the diplomatic peacemaker intervened, and von Moltke agreed to fix the final limit at nine. " He gave way at last," says Bismarck, "when I showed him that it could do no harm." The conference so dramatic broke up, and each one went his way; but, says the German official narrative, " as it was not doubtful that the hostile Army, completely beaten and nearly surrounded, would be obliged to submit to the clauses already indicated, the Great Head-quarter Staff was occupied, that very night, in drawing up the text of the capitulation "—a significant and practical comment, showing what stuff there was behind the severe language which, at the midnight meeting, fell from the Chief of that able and sleepless body of chosen men.

NAPOLEON III. SURRENDERS.

General de Wimpffen went straight from the military conference to the wearied Emperor who had gone to bed. But he received his visitor, who told him that the proposed conditions were hard, and that the sole chance of mitigation lay in the efforts of His Majesty. " General," said the Emperor, " I shall start at five o'clock for the German head-quarters, and I shall see whether the King will be more favourable;" for he seems to have become possessed of an idea that King William would personally treat with him The Emperor

kept his word. Believing that he would be permitted
to return to Sedan, he drove forth without bidding fare-
well to any of his troops; but, as the drawbridge of
Torcy was lowered and he passed over, the Zouaves on
duty shouted " Vive l'Empereur! " This cry was " the
last adieu which fell on his ears " as we read in the
narrative given to the world on his behalf. He drove
in a droshki towards Donchery, preceded by General
Reille who, before six o'clock, awoke Count Bismarck
from his slumbers, and warned him that the Emperor
desired to speak with him. " I went with him directly,"
said Bismarck, in a conversation reported by Busch;
"and got on my horse, all dusty and dirty as I was, in
an old cap and my great waterproof boots, to ride to
Sedan where I supposed him to be." But he met him
on the high road near Frenois, " sitting in a two-horse
carriage."   Beside him was the Prince de la Moskowa,
and on horseback Castelnau and Reille. " I gave the
military salute," says Bismarck. " He took his cap off
and the officers did the same; whereupon I took off
mine, although it was contrary to rule. He said,
' Couvrez-vous, donc.' I behaved to him just as if in
St. Cloud, and asked his commands." Naturally, he
wanted to see the King, but that could not be allowed.
Then Bismarck placed his quarters in Donchery at the
Emperor's disposal, but he, thinking, as we know, that
he would return to the Sub-Prefecture, declined the
courtesy, and preferred to rest in a house by the way-
side. The cottage of a Belgian weaver unexpectedly
became famous; a one-storied house, painted yellow,
with white shutters and venetian blinds. He and the
Chancellor entered the house, and went up to the first
floor where there was "a little room with one window.
It was the best in the house, but had only one deal
table and two rush-bottomed chairs." In that lowly

abode they talked together of many things for three-quarters of an hour, among others about the origin of the war which, it seems, neither desired, the Emperor asserting, Bismarck reports that "he had been driven into it by the pressure of public opinion," a very inadequate representation of the curious incidents which preceded the fatal decision. But when the Emperor began to ask for more favourable terms, he was told that, on a military question, von Moltke alone could speak. On the other hand Bismarck's request to know who now had authority to make peace was met by a reference to "the Government in Paris;" so that no progress was made. Then "we must stand to our demands with regard to the Army of Sedan," said Bismarck. General von Moltke was summoned, and "Napoleon III. demanded that nothing should be decided before he had seen the King, for he hoped to obtain from His Majesty some favourable concessions for the Army." The German official narrative of the war states that the Emperor expressed a wish that the Army might be permitted to enter Belgium, but that, of course, the Chief of the Staff could not accept the proposal. General von Moltke forthwith set out for Vendresse where the King was, to report progress. He met His Majesty on the road, and there "the King fully approved the proposed conditions of capitulation, and declared that he would not see the Emperor until the terms prescribed had been accepted;" a decision which gratified the Chancellor as well as the Chief of the Staff. "I did not wish them to come together," observed the Count, "until we had settled the matter of the capitulation;" sparing the feelings of both and leaving the business to the hard military men.

The Emperor lingered about in the garden of the weaver's cottage; he seems to have desired fresh air after his unpleasant talk with the Chancellor. Dr.

Moritz Busch, who had hurried to the spot, has left a
characteristic description of the Emperor. He saw
there "a little thick-set man," wearing jauntily a red
cap with a gold border, a black paletôt lined with red,
red trousers, and white kid gloves. "The look in his
light grey eyes was somewhat soft and dreamy, like that
of people who have lived hard. His whole appearance,"
says the irreverent Busch, "was a little unsoldierlike.
The man looked too soft, I might say too shabby, for the
uniform he wore," phrases which suggest a lack of sympathy with adversity, and severe physical as well as
mental suffering. But imagination can realize a picture
of the fallen potentate, whose dynasty, crashing down,
drew so much with it, as he was seen by the cynical
German, talking to his officers, or to the burly Chancellor, or walking alone up and down a potato field in
flower, with his white-gloved hands behind his back,
smoking a cigarette; "betrayed by fortune" or fate, as
he believed, but pursued, as others might say, by the
natural consequences of his marvellous adventures, and
of a strange neglect of the one source of strength on
which he relied, the Army. He had failed in the business upon the conduct of which he prided himself; he
was a bankrupt Emperor.

THE FRENCH GENERALS SUBMIT.

While one scene in the stupendous drama was
performed at the weaver's cottage, another was acted
or endured in Sedan, where de Wimpffen had summoned
the generals to consider the dreadful terms of capitulation. He has given his own account of the incident;
but the fullest report is supplied by Lebrun. There
were present at this council of war more than thirty
generals. With tearful eyes and a voice broken by
sobs, the unhappy and most ill-starred de Wimpffen

described his interview and conflict with von Moltke and Bismarck, and its dire result—the Army to surrender as prisoners of war, the officers alone to retain their arms, and by way of mitigating the rigour of these conditions, full permission to return home would be given to any officer, provided he would engage in writing and on honour not to serve again during the war. The generals, save one or two, and these finally acquiesced, felt that the conditions could not be refused; but they were indignant at the clause suggesting that the officers might escape the captivity which would befall their soldiers, provided they would engage to become mere spectators of the invasion of their country. In the midst of these mournful deliberations Captain von Zingler, a messenger from von Moltke, entered, and the scene became still more exciting. "I am instructed," he said, "to remind you how urgent it is that that you should come to a decision. At ten o'clock, precisely, if you have not come to a resolution, the German batteries will fire on Sedan. It is now nine, and I shall have barely time to carry your answer to head-quarters." To this sharp summons de Wimpffen answered that he could not decide until he knew the result of the interview between the Emperor and the King. "That interview," said the stern Captain, "will not in any way effect the military operations, which can only be determined by the generals who have full power to resume or stop the strife." It was, indeed, as Lebrun remarked, useless to argue with a Captain, charged to state a fact; and at the General's suggestion de Wimpffen agreed to accompany Captain von Zingler to the German head-quarters.

These were, for the occasion, the Chateau de Bellevue, where the Emperor himself had been induced to take up his abode, and about eleven o'clock, in a room under the

Imperial chamber, de Wimpffen put his name at the foot of the document drawn up, during the night, by the German Staff. Then he sought out the Emperor, and, greatly moved, told him that "all was finished." His Majesty, he writes, "with tears in his eyes, approached me, pressed my hand, and embraced me ;" and "my sad and painful duty having been accomplished, I remounted my horse and rode back to Sedan, 'la mort dans l'âme.'"

So soon as the convention was signed, the King arrived, accompanied by the Crown Prince. Three years before, as the Emperor reminds us in the writing attributed to him, the King had been his guest in Paris, where all the sovereigns of Europe had come to behold the marvels of the famous Exhibition. "Now," so runs the lamentation, "betrayed by fortune, Napoleon III. had lost all, and had placed in the hands of his conqueror the sole thing left him—his liberty." And he goes on to say, in general terms, that the King deeply sympathized with his misfortunes, but nevertheless could not grant better conditions to the Army. "He told the Emperor that the Castle of Wilhelmshöhe had been selected as his residence ; the Crown Prince then entered and cordially shook hands with Napoleon; and at the end of a quarter of an hour the King withdrew. The Emperor was permitted to send a telegram in cipher to the Empress, to tell her what had happened, and urge her to negotiate a peace." Such is the bald record of this impressive event. The telegram, which reached the Empress at four o'clock on the afternoon of the 3rd, was in these words : "The Army is defeated and captive ; I myself am a prisoner."

For one day more the fallen sovereign rested at Bellevue to meditate on the caprices of fortune or the decrees of fate. But that day, at the head of a splendid

company of princes and generals, King William, crossing
the bridge of Donchery, rode throughout the whole vast
extent of the German lines, to greet his hardy warriors
and be greeted by them on the very scene of their
victories.   And well they deserved regal gratitude, for
together with their comrades who surrounded Metz, by
dint of long swift marches and steadfast valour, they had
overcome two great Armies in thirty days.

During the battle of Sedan, the Germans lost in killed
and wounded 8,924 officers and men.   On the other
hand, the French lost 3,000 killed, 14,000 wounded,
and 21,000 captured in the battle.   The number of
prisoners by capitulation was 83,000, while 3,000 were
disarmed in Belgium, and a few hundreds, more or less,
made their way by devious routes near and over the
frontier, to Mézières, Rocroi, and other places in France.
In addition, were taken one eagle and two flags, 419
field guns and mitrailleuses, 139 garrison guns, many
waggons, muskets, and horses.   On the day after the
surrender, the French soldiers, having stacked their
arms in Sedan, marched into the peninsula formed by
the deep loop of the Meuse—"le Camp de Misère" as
they called it—and were sent thence in successive
batches, numbered by thousands, to Germany.   Such
was the astonishing end of the Army of Chalons, which
had been impelled to its woful doom by the Comte de
Palikao and the Paris politicians.   Directed by General
Vinoy, who was an able soldier, the troops brought to
Mézières, escaped by rapid and clever marches from the
German cavalry and the Sixth Corps, and formed the
nucleus of the improvised Army which afterwards
defended the capital.

THE END.

On the 3rd of September the Emperor Napoleon III.

departed from Bellevue on his journey to the Castle of Wilhelmshöhe, near Cassel. The morning was wet and gloomy, and a thunderstorm was gathering among the hills of the Ardennes. The Imperial baggage-train had been permitted to leave Sedan, and was drawn up on the road ready to start. Columns of prisoners also were moving out of the fortress and marching towards the peninsula formed by the Meuse. It was a lugubrious scene, and the superstitious might remark that as the sun shone resplendently on the German victory, so his light was obscured when the captive Emperor drove through the muddy streets of Donchery and thence to the northward, wrapped in the sombre mist and thickly falling rain. And as he journeyed, disconsolately, in the forenoon, upon the road to Bouillon, orders went forth from the German head-quarters, where time was never lost, directing the conquering generals to leave the Eleventh and one Bavarian Corps on guard over Sedan and the thousands of unhappy prisoners, and resume, with all the rest, that march on the capital of France which had been so abruptly interrupted only eight days before. So the victors and the vanquished went their different ways.

The Emperor travelled without haste, and on the evening of the 4th he slept at Verviers. The next morning he learned, in common with all Europe, indeed all the civilized world, that the fires which seethe under the bright surface of society in Paris had once more burst through the thin crust of use and wont, and that the dynasty of the Bonapartes had been utterly overthrown at a blow to make way for the Republic. Like intelligence reached the King of Prussia, also, at his head-quarters, which, on the 5th, were already in Reims. The contrast is painful. The King saw his hopes of an early peace destroyed; but his was a solidly planted throne and he was the leader of irresistible armies. The Emperor knew that his fond dream of founding an Imperial House had been dispelled in an hour by a blast of national wrath ; and, being a kindly man, his agony was the keener because, as he pathetically says, "he was separated from his son, and knew not what fate had befallen the Empress." Racked by such sad reflections, at the very time when his wife was escaping to England, Louis Napoleon Bonaparte went, by railway, from Verviers to Wilhelmshöhe. There, during a luxurious captivity of six months, he had ample leisure to meditate on the causes which led to the catastrophe of Sedan and the surrender of Metz ; and to ascertain, if he could, why, after a second trial, ending in the third entry of hostile troops into Paris, the French nation had lost its belief in the saving qualities of a family bearing a name which, if associated with undying "glory," has also become indissolubly linked with bitter memories of lost provinces and gigantic military disasters.

FINIS.

APPENDICES.

I.

THE GERMAN FIELD ARMIES.

COMMANDER-IN-CHIEF, KING WILLIAM OF PRUSSIA ; Chief of the Staff, General Baron von Moltke ; Quartermaster, General Podbielski ; Inspector-General of Artillery, General von Hindersin.

Present with the Great Head Quarters were the Minister of War, General von Roon ; and the Federal Chancellor and Minister President, General Count von Bismarck-Schönhausen.

FIRST ARMY.

COMMANDER-IN-CHIEF, General von Steinmetz ; Chief of the Staff, Gen. von Sperling ; Chief Quartermaster, Col. Count von Wartensleben.

First Corps.[1]

COMMANDER-IN-CHIEF, General Baron von Manteuffel ; Chief of the Staff, Lieut.-Col. von der Burg. 1st Div., Lieut.-Gen. von Bentheim ; 1st Brig., Major-Gen. von Gayl ; 2nd Brig., Major-Gen. Baron von Falkenstein. 2nd Div., Major-Gen. von Pritzelwitz ; 3rd Brig., Major-Gen. von Memerty ; 4th Brig., Major-Gen. von Zglintski ; Commander of Artillery, Major-Gen. von Bergemann.

Strength of Corps : 25 battalions, 25,000 men ; 8 squadrons, 1,200 horses ; 14 batteries, 84 guns ; 3 companies of Pioneers.

---

[1] This Corps did not arrive until August 5.

Seventh Corps.

COMMANDER-IN-CHIEF, General von Zastrow; Chief of the Staff, Col. von Unger. 13th Div., Lieut.-Gen. von Glümer; 25th Brig., Major-Gen. Baron von Osten-Sacken; 26th Brig., Major-Gen. Baron von Golz. 14th Div., Lieut.-General von Kameke; 27th Brig., Major-Gen. von François; 28th Brig., Major-Gen. von Woyna. Commander of Artillery, Major-Gen. von Zimmermann.

Strength of Corps: 25 battalions, 25,000 men; 8 squadrons, 1,200 horses; 14 batteries, 84 guns; and 3 companies of Pioneers.

Eighth Corps.

COMMANDER-IN-CHIEF, General von Goeben; Chief of the Staff, Col. von Witzendorff. 15th Div., Lieut.-Gen. von Weltzien; 29th Brig., Major-Gen. von Wedell; 30th Brig., Major-Gen. von Strubberg. 16th Div., Lieut.-Gen. Barnekow; 31st, Major-Gen. Count Neidhard von Gneisenau; 32nd, Col. von Rex. Commander of Artillery, Colonel von Kameke.

Strength of Corps: 25 battalions, 25,000 men; 8 squadrons, 1,200 horses; 15 batteries, 90 guns; and 3 companies of Pioneers.

First Cavalry Division.

COMMANDER, Lieut.-General von Hartmann. Brigadiers: 1st Brig., Major-Gen. von Lüderitz; 2nd Brig., Major-Gen. von Baumgarth (each was composed of one Cuirassier and two Uhlan regiments, and accompanied by a Horse Artillery Battery).

Strength: 24 squadrons, 3,600 horses, and 6 guns.

Third Cavalry Division

COMMANDER, Lieut.-Gen. Count von der Gröben. Brigadiers: 6th Brig., Major-Gen. von Mirus (one Cuirassier and one Uhlan regiment); 7th Brig., Major-Gen. Count von Dohna (two Uhlan regiments).

Strength: 16 squadrons, 2,400 horses, one Horse Artillery battery, 6 guns.

Strength of First Army.

	Battalions.	Squadrons.	Batteries.	Guns.
1st Corps	25	8	14	84
7th Corps	25	8	15	90
8th Corps	25	8	14	84
1st Cav. Div. . . .		24	1	6
3rd Cav. Div. . . .		16	1	6
Total	75	64	45	270

THE SECOND ARMY.

COMMANDER-IN-CHIEF, H.R.H. Prince Frederick Charles of Prussia; Chief of Staff, Major-Gen. von Stiehle; Chief Quarter-master, Colonel von Hertzberg; Commander of Artillery, Lieut.-Gen. von Colomier.

The Guard Corps.

COMMANDER-IN-CHIEF, Prince Augustus of Würtemberg; Chief of the Staff, Major-Gen. von Dannenberg. 1st Div., Major-Gen. von Pape; 1st Brig., Major-Gen. von Kessel; 2nd Brig., Major-Gen. Baron von Medem. 2nd Div., Lieut.-Gen. von Budritzki; 3rd Brig., Colonel Knappe von Knapp-städt; 4th Brig., Major-Gen. von Berger. Commander of Artillery, Major-Gen. Kraft, Prince of Hohenlohe Ingelfingen.

CAVALRY DIVISION:—Commander, Major-Gen. Count von der Golz; 1st Brig. Major-Gen. Count von Brandenburg I. (Life Guards and Cuirassiers); 2nd Brig., Lieut.-Gen. Prince Albert of Prussia (two Uhlan regiments); 3rd Brig., Lieut.-Gen. Count von Brandenburg II. (two Dragoon regiments).

Strength of Corps: 29 battalions, 29,000 men; 32 squadrons, 4,800 horses; 15 batteries, 90 guns; and 3 companies of Pioneers.

Second Corps.[1]

COMMANDER-IN-CHIEF, General von Fransecky; Chief of the Staff, Colonel von Wichmann; Commander of Artillery, Major-Gen. von Kleist. 3rd Div., Major-Gen. von Hartmann; 5th

[1] Came up to the front at the battle of Gravelotte.

Brig., Major-Gen. von Koblinski; 6th Brig., Colonel von der Decken. 4th Div., Lieut.-Gen. Hann von Weihern; 7th Brig., Major-Gen. du Trossel; 8th Brig., Major-Gen. von Kettler.

Strength of Corps: 25 battalions, 25,000 men; 8 squadrons, 1,200 horses; 14 batteries, 84 guns; and 3 companies of Artillery.

Third Corps.

COMMANDER-IN-CHIEF, Lieut.-Gen. von Alvensleben II.; Chief of the Staff, Colonel von Voights Rhetz; Commander of Artillery, Major-Gen. von Bülow. 5th Div., Lieut.-Gen. von Stülpnagel; 9th Brig., Major-Gen. von Döring; 10th Brig., Major-Gen. von Schwerin. 6th Div., Lieut.-Gen. Baron von Buddenbrock, 11th Brig., Major-Gen. von Rothmaler; 12th Brig., Colonel von Bismarck.

Strength of Corps: 25 battalions, 25,000 men; 8 squadrons, 1,200 horses; 14 batteries, 84 guns; and 3 companies of Pioneers.

Fourth Corps.

COMMANDER-IN-CHIEF, General von Alvensleben I.; Chief of the Staff, Colonel von Thile; Commander of Artillery, Major-Gen. von Scherbening. 7th Div., Lieut.-Gen. von Schwarzhoff; 13th Brig., Major-Gen. von Worries; 14th Brig., Major-Gen. von Zychlinski. 8th Div., Lieut.-Gen. von Schöler; 15th Brig., Major-Gen. von Kessler; 16th Brig., Colonel von Scheffler.

Strength of Corps: 25 battalions, 25,000 men; 8 squadrons, 1,200 horses; 14 batteries, 84 guns; and 3 companies of Pioneers.

Ninth Corps.

COMMANDER-IN-CHIEF, General von Manstein; Chief of the Staff, Major Bronsart von Schellendorf; Commander of Artillery, Major-Gen. von Puttkammer. 18th Div., Lieut.-Gen. Baron von Wrangel; 35th Brig., Major-Gen. von Blumenthal; 36th Brig., Major-Gen. von Below. The Hessian Division (25th): Commander, Lieut.-Gen. H.R.H. Prince Louis of

Hesse; 49th Brig., Major-Gen. von Wittich; 50th Brig., Colonel von Lyncker.

Strength of Corps: 23 battalions, 23,000 men; 12 squadrons, 1,800 horses; 15 batteries, 90 guns; 3 companies of Pioneers.

Tenth Corps.

COMMANDER-IN-CHIEF, General von Voigts-Rhetz; Chief of the Staff, Lieut.-Col. von Caprivi; Commander of Artillery, Colonel Baron von der Becke. 19th Div., Lieut.-Gen. von Schwarz Koppen; 37th Brig., Colonel von Lehmann; 38th Brig., Major-Gen. von Wedell. 20th Div., Major-Gen. Kraatz Koschlau; 39th Brig., Major-Gen. von Woyna; 40th Brig., Major-Gen. von Diringshofen.

Strength of Corps: 25 battalions, 25,000 men; 8 squadrons, 1,200 horses; 14 batteries, 84 guns; 3 companies of Pioneers.

Twelfth (Royal Saxon) Corps.

COMMANDER-IN-CHIEF, General H.R.H. the Crown Prince of Saxony; Chief of the Staff, Colonel von Zezschwitz; Commander of Artillery, Major-Gen. Köhler. 1st. Div., Prince George of Saxony; 1st Brig., Major-Gen. von Craushaar; 2nd Brig., Colonel von Montbé. 2nd Div., Major-Gen. Nehrhoff von Holderberg: 3rd Brig., Major-Gen. von Leonhardi; 4th Brig., Colonel von Schulz. [N.B. The Infantry Divisions were also numbered 23 and 24, and the brigades 45, 46, 47, and 48, to fit them into the general system.]

Strength of Corps: 29 battalions, 29,000 men; 24 squadrons, 3,600 horses; 16 batteries, 96 guns; 3 companies of Pioneers. [The cavalry formed the 12th Division, commanded by the Count of Lippe; Brigadiers, Major-Gen. Krug von Nidda and Major-Gen. Seufft von Pilsach.]

The Fifth Cavalry Division.

COMMANDER, Lieut.-Gen. Baron von Rheinbaben; 11th Brig., Major-Gen. von Barby (a cuirassier, a Uhlan, and a dragoon regiment); 12th Brig., Major-Gen. von Bredow (similarly formed); 13th Brig., Major-Gen. von Redern (three hussar regiments).

Strength of Division: 36 squadrons, 5,400 horses; 2 batteries, 12 guns, Horse Artillery.

The Sixth Cavalry Division.

COMMANDER, Duke William of Mecklenburg-Schwerin; 14th Brig., Major-Gen. Baron von Diepenbroick-Grüter (a cuirassier and two Uhlan regiments); 15th Brig., Major-Gen. von Rauch (two hussar regiments).

Strength of Division: 20 squadrons, 3,000 horses; and 1 Horse Artillery battery, 6 guns.

Strength of Second Army.

	Battalions.	Squadrons.	Batteries.	Guns.
Guard	29	32	15	90
2nd Corps	25	8	14	84
3rd Do.	25	8	14	84
4th Do.	25	8	14	84
9th Do.	23	12	15	90
10th Do.	25	8	14	84
12th Do.	29	24	16	96
5th Cav. Div. . . .		36	2	12
6th Do. . . .		20	1	6
Total	181	156	105	630

THE THIRD ARMY.

COMMANDER-IN-CHIEF, H.R.H. the Crown Prince of Prussia; Chief of the Staff, Lieut.-Gen. von Blumenthal; Chief Quartermaster, Colonel von Gottberg; Commander of Artillery, Lieut.-Gen. Herkt.

Fifth Corps.

COMMANDER-IN-CHIEF, Lieut.-Gen. von Kirchbach; Chief of the Staff, Colonel von der Esch; Commander of the Artillery, Colonel Gaede. 9th Div., Major-Gen. von Sandrart; 17th Brig., Colonel von Bothmer; 18th Brig., Major-Gen. Voigts-Rhetz. 10th Div., Lieut.-Gen. von Schmidt; 19th Brig., Colonel von Henning auf Schönhoff; 20th Brig., Major-Gen. Walther von Montbary.

Strength of Corps; 25 battalions, 25,000 men; 8 squadrons, 1,200 horses; 14 batteries, 84 guns; 3 companies of Pioneers.

Sixth Corps.[1]

COMMANDER-IN-CHIEF, General von Tümpling ; Chief of the Staff, Colonel von Salviati ; Commander of Artillery, Colonel von Ramm. 11th Div., Lieut.-Gen. von Gordon; 21st Brig., Major-Gen. von Malachowski; 22nd Brig.,Major-Gen. von Eckartsberg. 12th Div., Lieut.-Gen. von Hoffmann ; 23rd Brig., Major-Gen. Gündel; 24th Brig., Major-Gen. von Fabeck.

Strength of Corps : 25 battalions, 25,000 men; 8 squadrons, 1,200 horses : 14 batteries, 84 guns; 3 companies of Pioneers.

Eleventh Corps.

COMMANDER-IN-CHIEF, Lieut.-Gen. von Bose ; Chief of the Staff, Major-Gen. Stein von Kaminski ; Commander of Artillery, Major-Gen. Hausmann. 21st Div., Lieut.-Gen. von Schachtmeyer ; 41st Brig., Colonel von Koblinski ; 42nd Brig., Major-Gen. von Thile. 22nd Div., Lieut.-Gen. von Gersdorff ; 43rd Brig., Colonel von Konski ; 44th Brig., Major-Gen. von Schkopp.

Strength of Corps : 25 battalions, 25,000 men : 8 squadrons, 1,200 horses; 14 batteries, 84 guns ; 3 companies of Pioneers.

First Bavarian Corps.

COMMANDER-IN-CHIEF, General von der Tann-Rathsamhausen; Chief of the Staff, Lieut.-Col. von Heinleth ; Commander of Artillery, Major-Gen. von Malaisé. 1st Div., Lieut.-Gen. von Stephan ; 1st Brig., Major-Gen. Dietl; 2nd Brig., Major-Gen. von Orff. 2nd Div., Major-Gen. Schumaker; 3rd Brig., Colonel Heyle ; 4th Brig., Major-Gen. Baron von der Tann.

Strength of Corps : 25 battalions, 25,000 men ; 20 squadrons, 3,000 horses (Cuirassiers and Light Horse) ; 16 batteries, 96 guns ; 3 companies of Pioneers.

[1] This Corps did not cross the frontier until the 6th of August.

Second Bavarian Corps.

COMMANDER-IN-CHIEF, General Ritter von Hartmann ; Chief of the Staff, Colonel Baron von Horn ; Commander of Artillery, Major-Gen. Lutz. 3rd Div., Lieut.-Gen. von Walther ; 5th Brig., Major-Gen. von Schleich ; 6th Brig., Colonel Borries von Wissel ; 4th Div., Lieut.-Gen. Count von Bothmer ; 7th Brig., Major-Gen. von Thiereck ; 8th Brig., Major-Gen. Maillinger.

Strength of Corps : 25 battalions, 25,000 men ; 20 squadrons, 3,000 horses (Cuirassier, Uhlan, Light Horse) ; 16 batteries, 96 guns ; 3 companies of Pioneers.

The Würtemberg Division.

COMMANDER-IN-CHIEF, Lieut.-Gen. von Obernitz ; Chief of the Staff, Colonel von Bock ; Commander of Artillery, Colonel von Sick ; 1st Brig., Major-Gen. von Reitstenstein ; 2nd Brig., Major-Gen. von Starkloff ; 3rd Brig., Majer-Gen. Baron von Hügel.

Strength of Division : 15 battalions, 15,000 men ; 10 squadrons, 1,500 horses ; 9 batteries, 54 guns ; 2 companies of Pioneers.

Baden Division.

COMMANDER-IN-CHIEF, Lieut.-Gen. von Beyer ; Chief of the Staff, Lieut.-Col. von Leszczynski ; Commander of Artillery, Colonel von Freydorf ; 1st Brig., Lieut.-Gen. du Jarrhs, Baron von la Roche ; 2nd Brig., Major-Gen. Keller.

Strength of Division : 13 battalions, 13,000 men ; 12 squadrons, 1,800 horses ; 9 batteries, 54 guns ; 1 Pioneer company.

Second Cavalry Division.[1]

COMMANDER, Lieut.-Gen. Count Stolberg-Wernigerode ; 3rd Brig., Major-Gen. von Colomb (two regiments, cuirassier and Uhlan) ; 4th Brig., Major-Gen. Baron von Barnekow (two regiments of Hussars) ; 5th Brig., Major-Gen. von Baumbach (two regiments of Hussars).

Strength : 24 squadrons, 3,600 horses ; 2 Horse Artillery batteries, 12 guns.

---

[1] This Division came up after the 4th of August.

Fourth Cavalry Division.

COMMANDER, General H.R.H. Prince Albert of Prussia, senior; 8th Brig., Major-Gen. von Hontheim (two regiments, cuirassier and Uhlan); 9th Brig., Major-Gen. von Bernhardi (two Uhlan regiments); 10th Brig., Major-Gen. von Krosigk (two regiments, hussar and dragoon).

Strength: 24 squadrons, 3,600 horses; 2 Horse Artillery batteries, 12 guns.

STRENGTH OF THIRD ARMY.

	Battalions.	Squadrons.	Batteries.	Guns.
5th Corps	25	8	14	84
6th Do.	25	8	14	84
11th Do.	25	8	14	84
1st Bavarian	25	20	16	96
2nd Bavarian	25	20	16	96
Würtemberg Div.	15	10	9	54
Baden Div.	13	12	9	54
2nd Cav. Div.	—	24	2	12
4th Cav. Div.	—	24	2	12
	153	134	96	576

TOTAL OF THE THREE ARMIES.

	Battalions.	Squadrons.	Batteries.	Guns.
First Army	75	64	45	270
Second Army.	181	156	105	630
Third Army	153	134	96	576
Grand Total	409	354	246	1,476

By the end of August the 17th Division of Infantry and the 2nd Division of Landwehr, under the Grand Duke of Mecklenburg-Schwerin, in addition to the 3rd Reserve Division already on the spot under General Kunsmor, were brought up to take part in the investment of Metz. The troops sent forward to reinforce the Baden Division before Strasburg were the Landwehr Division of the Guard, the 1st Reserve Division, and the 1st brigade of reserve cavalry. During August, counting all ranks, sick or well, and including every species of non-combatant, the mean strength of the Armies in the field was 780,723 men, and 213,159 horses.

II.

THE FRENCH ARMY.

COMMANDER-IN-CHIEF, THE EMPEROR NAPOLEON III.; "Major-General" or Chief of the Staff, Marshal Lebœuf, assisted by General Lebrun and General Jarras. Commander of Artillery, General Soleille; of Engineers, General Coffinières de Nordeck.

IMPERIAL GUARD.

COMMANDER-IN-CHIEF, General Bourbaki; Chief of the Staff, General d'Auvergne; Commander of Artillery, General Pé d'Arros; Divisional Commanders, 1st Div. (Voltigeurs), General Deligny; Brigadiers: 1st Brig., General Brincourt; 2nd Brig., General Garnier. 2nd Div. (Grenadiers), General Picard; Brigadiers: 1st Brig., General Jeanningros; 2nd Brig., General Le Poitevin de Lacroix.

Strength of Corps: 24 battalions; 24 squadrons—(Desvaux's Div. of three brigades, commanded by Halna du Fretay, de France, and du Preuil, consisting of guides, chasseurs, lancers, dragoons, cuirassiers, and carbineers)—60 guns, and 12 mitrailleuses; 2 companies of Engineers.

1st Corps.

COMMANDER-IN-CHIEF, Marshal MacMahon, Duke of Magenta; Chief of the Staff, Gen. Colson; Commander of Artillery, Gen. Forgeot. Divisional Commanders: 1st Div., Gen. Ducrot; 1st Brig., Gen. Wolff; 2nd Brig., Gen. de Postis du Houlbec; 2nd Div., Gen. Abel Douay; 1st Brig., Gen. Pelletier de Montmarie; 2nd Brig., Gen. Pellé; 3rd Div., Gen. Raoult; 1st Brig., Gen. L'Hériller; 2nd Brig., Gen. Lefebvre; 4th Div., Gen. Lartigue; 1st Brig., Lieut.-Gen. Fraboulet de Kerléadec; 2nd Brig., Gen. Lacretelle.

Strength of Corps: 52 battalions—45 deducting the regiments left in Strasburg; 28 squadrons—Duhesme's brigade of cuirassiers, hussars, chasseurs, lancers, and dragoons—96 guns and 24 mitrailleuses; 5½ companies of Engineers.

2nd Corps.

COMMANDER-IN-CHIEF, General Frossard; Chief of the Staff, Gen. Saget; Commander of Artillery, Gen. Gagneur. 1st Div., Gen. Verge; 1st Brig., Gen. Letellier Valazé; 2nd Brig., Gen. Jolivet. 2nd Div., Gen. Bataille; 1st Brig., Gen. Pouget; 2nd Brig., Gen. Fauvart-Bastoul. 3rd Div., Gen. de Laveaucoupet; 1st Brig., Gen. Doëns; 2nd Brig., Gen. Micheler.

Strength of Corps: 39 battalions; 16 squadrons—(Valabrègue's Division, 4 regiments of chasseurs and dragoons)— 72 guns, 18 mitrailleuses; 5 companies of Engineers.

3rd Corps.

COMMANDER-IN-CHIEF, Marshal Bazaine; Chief of the Staff, Gen. Manèque; Commander of Artillery, Gen. de Rochebouët. 1st Div., Gen. Montaudon; 1st Brig., Gen. Baron Aymard; 2nd Brig., Gen. Clinchant. 2nd Div., Gen. de Castagny; 1st Brig., Gen. Nayral; 2nd Brig., Gen. Duplessis. 3rd Div., Gen. Metman; 1st Brig., Gen. de Potier; 2nd Brig., Gen. Arnaudeau. 4th Div., Gen. Decaën; 1st Brig., Gen. de Brauer; 2nd Brig., Gen. Sanglé-Ferrière.

Strength of Corps: 52 battalions; 28 squadrons—(de Clérambault's Div., 3 regiments of chasseurs, 4 of dragoons, organized in 3 brigades)—96 guns, 24 mitrailleuses and 5½ companies of Engineers.

4th Corps.

COMMANDER-IN-CHIEF, General de Ladmirault; Chief of the Staff, Gen. Osmont; Commander of Artillery, Gen. Lafaille. 1st Div., Gen. Courtot de Cissey; 1st Brig., Gen. Count Brayer; 2nd Brig., Gen. de Golberg. 2nd Div., Gen. Grenier; 1st Brig., Gen. Bellecourt; 2nd Brig., Gen. Pradier; 3rd Div., Gen. Count de Lorencez; 1st Brig., Gen. Count Pajol; 2nd Brig., Gen. Berger.

Strength of Corps: 39 battalions; 16 squadrons—(Legrand's Div., one brigade of hussars and one of dragoons)— 72 guns, 18 mitrailleuses; 4 companies of Engineers.

5th Corps.

COMMANDER-IN-CHIEF, General de Failly; Chief of Staff,

Gen. Besson; Commander of Artillery, Gen. Liédot. 1st
Div., Gen. Goze; 1st Brig., Gen. Sauron; 2nd Brig., Gen.
Nicolas-Nicolas. 2nd Div., Gen. de l'Abadie d'Aydrein; 1st
Brig., Gen. Lapasset; 2nd Brig., Gen. de Maussion. 3rd Div.,
Gen. Guyot de Lespart; 1st Brig., Gen. Abatucci; 2nd Brig.,
Gen. de Fontanges.

Strength of Corps: 39 battalions; 16 squadrons—(Brahaut's Div., brigade of hussars and chasseurs, and one of
lancers)—72 guns, 18 mitrailleuses; 4 companies of Engineers.

6th Corps.

COMMANDER-IN-CHIEF, Marshal Canrobert; Chief of the
Staff, Gen. Henri; Commander of Artillery, Gen. Labastie.
1st Div., Gen. Tixier; 1st Brig., Gen. Péchot; 2nd Brig.,
Gen. Le Roy de Dais; 2nd Div., Gen. Bisson; 1st Brig., Gen.
Archinard; 2nd Brig., Gen. Maurice; 3rd Div., Gen. Lafont
de Villers; 1st Brig., Gen. Becquet de Sonnay; 2nd Brig.,
Gen. Colin. 4th Div., Gen. Levassor-Sorval; 1st Brig., Gen.
de Marguenat; 2nd Brig., Gen. Comte de Chanaleilles.

Strength of Corps: 49 battalions; 24 squadrons—(Div. of
Salignac-Fénelon, three brigades lancers, hussars, chasseurs,
and cuirassiers)—114 guns, 6 mitrailleuses, and 5 companies
of Engineers.
[Only 40 battalions and 36 guns were able to reach Metz.]

7th Corps.

COMMANDER-IN-CHIEF, General Félix Douay; Chief of the
Staff, Gen. Renson; Commander of Artillery, Gen. de Lié-
geard. 1st Div., Gen. Conseil Dumesnil; 1st Brig., Gen.
Nicolaï; 2nd Brig., Gen. Maire. 2nd Div., Gen. Liébert; 1st
Brig., Gen. Guiomar; 2nd Brig., Gen. de la Bastide. 3rd Div.,
Gen. Dumont; 1st Brig., Gen. Bordas; 2nd Brig., Gen. Bittard
des Portes.

Strength of Corps: 38 battalions; 20 squadrons—(Amiel's
Div., five regiments, in two brigades, lancers, hussars, and
dragoons)—72 guns, 18 mitrailleuses, and 4 companies of
Engineers. [One cavalry brigade of two regiments never
joined the 7th Corps.]

Reserve Cavalry.

1st Div., Gen. du Barail; 1st Brig., Gen. Margueritte; 2nd Brig., Gen. de Lajaille; 16 squadrons, Chasseurs d'Afrique, and 12 guns. [Three regiments reached Metz on the 10th of August, and the 4th at Mouzon on the Meuse.]

2nd Div., Gen. Viscomte de Bonnemains; 1st Brig., Gen. Girard; 2nd Brig., Gen. de Brauer; 16 squadrons, all cuirassiers.

3rd Div., Gen. de Forton; 1st Brig., Gen. Prince Murat; 2nd Brig., Gen. de Gramont; 16 squadrons—(one brigade of dragoons, the other cuirassiers)—and 12 guns.

Artillery Reserve: Gen. Canu, 126 guns, 6 mitrailleuses, and 3 companies of Engineers.

STRENGTH OF ARMY.

	Battalions.	Squadrons.	Batteries.	Guns.	Mitrailleuses.
Guard . . .	24	24	12	60	12
1st Corps . .	52	28	20	96	24
2nd Do. . . .	39	16	15	72	18
3rd Do. . . .	52	28	20	96	24
4th Do. . . .	39	16	15	72	18
5th Do. . . .	39	16	15	72	18
6th Do. . . .	49	24	20	114	6
7th Do. . . .	38	20	15	72	18
Reserve Cav. .	—	48	6	30	6
Reserve Art. .	—	—	16	96	—
	332	220	154	780	144

It is not possible to do more than guess at the numerical strength of the French Corps, and consequently of the French Army; so great is the variation in the strength of battalions and squadrons. The infantry of the several Corps was continually augmented by the arrival of reserves, so that, the losses at Spicheren notwithstanding, the 2nd Corps was stronger by more than 2,000 men, five days after the battle than it was on the morning of the 6th; Marshal Lebœuf told the Parliamentary Commission that, on the 1st of August, according to the " states " sent in to the head-quarters, the effective of the Army of the Rhine, including all the Corps in the field, was 243,171 men. But " the real effective," he adds, " was greatly superior." For by the 1st of August, no fewer than " 278,882 men had been sent to the Army of the Rhine," and subsequently, until the 14th, "numerous detachments." It is plain that no precise information can be obtained, but it seems probable that the strength was always greater than that reported at the time. Similar uncertainty prevails respecting the effective strength of the "Army of Chalons." The only authentic figures extant are those supplied by the German account of the capitulation, from which the original strength, increased by additions on the line of march, may be inferred.

III.

THE PROTOCOL OF CAPITULATION.

Between the undersigned, the Chief of the Staff of His Majesty the King of Prussia, commanding in chief the German Army, and the General, commanding in chief the French Army, each having received full powers from their Majesties, King William and the Emperor Napoleon, the following Convention has been concluded:

Article 1.—The French Army, placed under the orders of General de Wimpffen, finding itself actually surrounded in Sedan by superior forces, is prisoner of war.

Article 2.—Having regard to the brave defence of this Army, an exception is made for all the generals and officers, as well as for the functionaries, having the rank of officer, who shall give their word of honour, in writing, not to bear arms against Germany, and not to act in any other manner against her interests until the end of the present war. The officers and functionaries who may accept these conditions, shall preserve their arms and personal property.

Article 3.—All other arms, as well as the *matériel* of the Army, consisting of flags (eagles and standards), cannons, horses, military chests, army equipages, munitions, etc., shall be surrendered at Sedan to a Military Commission, appointed by the French Commander-in-Chief, to be given over immediately to the German Commissioner.

Article 4.—The fortress of Sedan shall be immediately placed in its actual state, and, at the latest, by the evening of September 2, at the disposal of His Majesty the King of Prussia.

Article 5.—The officers who shall not have subscribed the engagement mentioned in Article 2, and the men, after having been disarmed, shall be ranked in regiments and conducted in good order into the peninsula formed by the Meuse near Iges. The groups thus constituted shall be handed over to the German Commissioners by the officers, who will immediately give over the command to the sous-officers. This arrangement will begin on the 2nd of September and should be finished on the 3rd.

Article 6.—The military medical men, without exception, will remain behind to take care of the wounded.

Done at Frénois, September 2, 1870.

(Signed)   Von Moltke.

De Wimpffen.

IV.

A LIST OF THE PRINCIPAL WORKS CONSULTED FOR THE CAMPAIGN OF SEDAN.

Der Deutsch-Französiche Krieg, 1870-71. Redigirt von der Kriegsgeschichtlichen Abtheilung des Grossen Generalstabes.

The German Artillery. Captain Hoffbauer.

Operations of the First Army. Major A. von Schell.

Operations of the Bavarian Army. Captain H. Helvig.

Tactical Deductions from the War 1870-71. Captain A. von Boguslawski.

Our Chancellor; Sketches for a Historical Picture. By Moritz Busch.

Bismarck and the Franco-German War, 1870-71. By Dr. Moritz Busch.

My Diary during the last Great War. By W. H. Russell.

L'Armée du Rhin. Par le Maréchal Bazaine.

Episodes de la Guerre de 1870 et le Blocus de Metz. Par l'Ex-Maréchal Bazaine.

Affaire de la Capitulation de Metz. Procès Bazaine.

Metz, Campagne et Negociations. Par un Officier supérieur de l'Armée du Rhin.

Journal d'un Officier de l'Armée du Rhin. Par Ch. Fay.

Œuvres Posthumes autographe inédits de Napoleon III.
Collected and published by the Comte de la Chapelle.

Sedan. Par le Général de Wimpffen.

La Journée de Sedan. Par le Général Ducrot.

Guerre de 1870. Bazeilles-Sedan. Par le Général Lebrun.

Campagne de 1870. Belfort, Reims, Sedan. Le 7ᵉ Corps de l'Armée du Rhin. Par le Prince Georges Bibesco.

Journal d'un Officier d'Ordonnance, Juillet 1870—Février 1871. Par le Comte d'Hérisson.

Campagne de 1870. La Cavalerie Française. Par le Lieut.-Col. Bonie.

Campagne de 1870-71. Siége de Paris. Operations du 13ᵉ Corps at de la Troisième Armée. Par le Général Vinoy.

Documents Relatifs au Siége a Strassbourg. Publiés par le Général Uhrich.

Un Ministère de la Guerre de vingt quatre jours. Par le Général Cousin de Montauban Comte de Palikao.

Enquête Parlementaire sur les Acts du Gouvernement de la Defense National.

Papiers et Correspondances de la Famille Impériale.

Ma Mission en Prusse. Par le Comte Benedetti.

France et la Prusse avant la Guerre. Par le Duc de Gramont.

The Times, October 25, 1871. Translation of Prince Bismarck's Reply to Count Benedetti's "Mission en Prusse."

La Politique Française en 1866. Par G. Rothan.

L'Affaire du Luxembourg: le prélude de la Guerre de 1870. Par G. Rothan.

Les Coulisses de la Diplomatie. Quinze Ans à l'Etranger. 1864-1879. Par Jules Hansen.

Révue des Deux Mondes. Avril, 1878, and 1886-7.

Papers presented to Parliament Respecting the War between France and Germany, 1870.

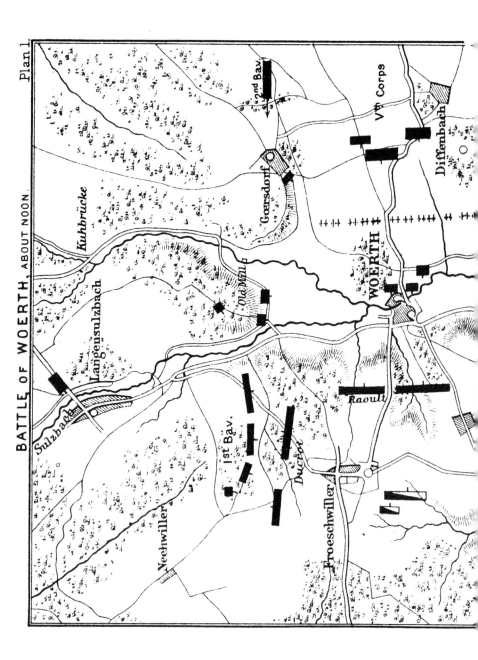

BATTLE OF WOERTH, ABOUT NOON.

Plan 1.

Kuhbrücke

Langensulzbach

Goersdorf

2nd Bav.

Old Mill

V.th Corps

Diffenbach

WOERTH

Sulzbach

Raoult

1st Bav.

Neehwiller

Ducrot

Froeschwiller

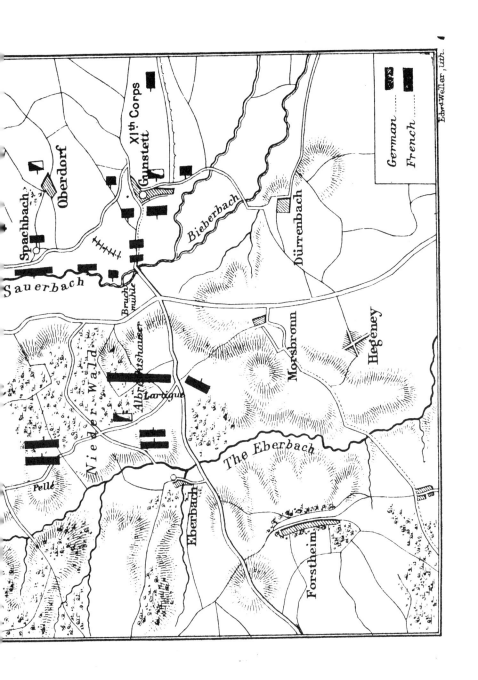

Spachbach

Oberdorf

XIᵗʰ Corps

Gunstett

Sauerbach

Bieberbach

Bruch mühle

Dürrenbach

Morsbronn

Hegeney

Nieder Wald

Albrechtshauser

Lartigue

The Eberbach

Pellé

Eberbach

Forstheim

German ......
French ......

Eckstweiler, lith.

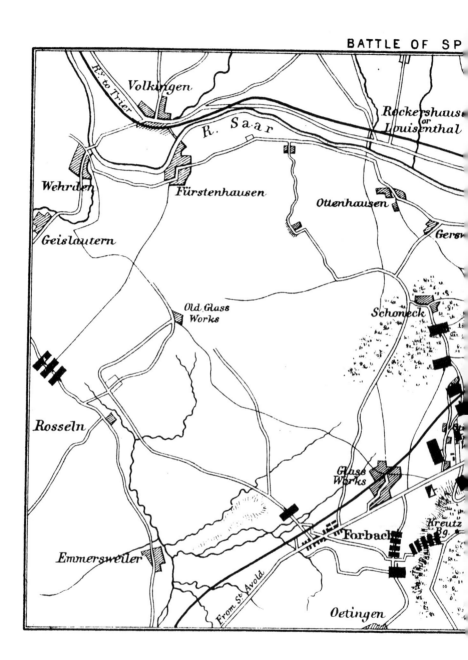

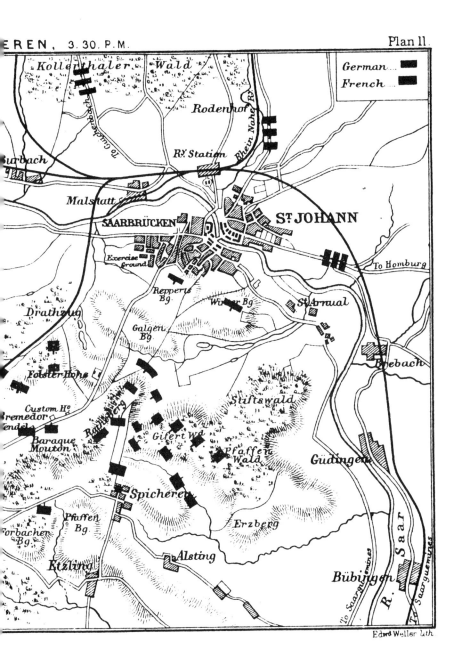

German
French

Kollerthaler Wald
Rodenhof
Ry. Station
Burbach
Malstatt
SAARBRÜCKEN
St. JOHANN
To Homburg
Exercise ground
Repperts Bg.
Winter Bg.
St. Arnual
Drathzug
Galgen Bg.
Brebach
Folster Höhe
Stiftswald
Custom Ho
Bremedorf
endel
Baraque Mouton
Gifert wd.
Pfaffen Wald
Güdingen
Spicheren
Pfaffen Bg.
Erzberg
Forbacher Bg.
Etzling
Alsting
Bübingen
R. Saar

Edwd Weller Lith.

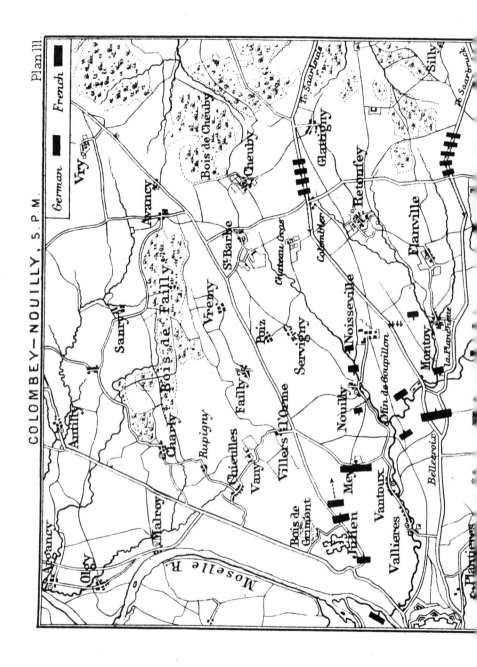

COLOMBEY–NOUILLY, 5 P.M.

Plan III.

German ▮ French ▮

Vry

Bois de Cheuby

Cheuby

Glatigny

To Saarlouis

Silly

To Saarbruck

Avancy

St Barbe

Château Gros

Colombey

Retonfey

Flanville

Amanvillers

Sanry

Bois de Failly

Vremy

Poix

Servigny

Noisseville

Montoy

la Planchette

Antilly

Charly

Rupigny

Failly

Quieulles

Vany

Villers l'Orme

Nouilly

Min de Goupillon

Belleeroix

Malroy

Olgy

Moselle R.

Bois de Grimont

Mey

Julien

Vantoux

Vallières

Ars-laquancy

Plantiěres

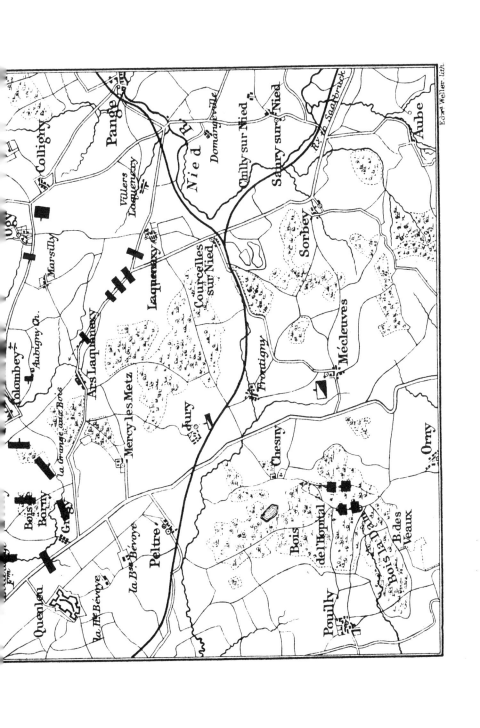

Colligny
Pange
Villers Laquenexy
Nied R.
Domangeville
Chilly sur Nied
Saury sur Nied
Aube
Ugy
Marsilly
Laquenexy
Courcelles sur Nied
Sorbey
R. de Saarbruck
Colombey
Aubigny Gr.
Ars Laquenexy
Mécleuves
la Grange aux Bois
Mercy les Metz
dury
Frontigny
Bois
Borny
Gr.
Chesny
Orny
la H.te Bevoye
Peltre
la B.te Bevoye
Bois
de l'Hôpital
B. des Veaux
Bois la D.
Queuleu
Pouilly

Edwrt Weller lith.

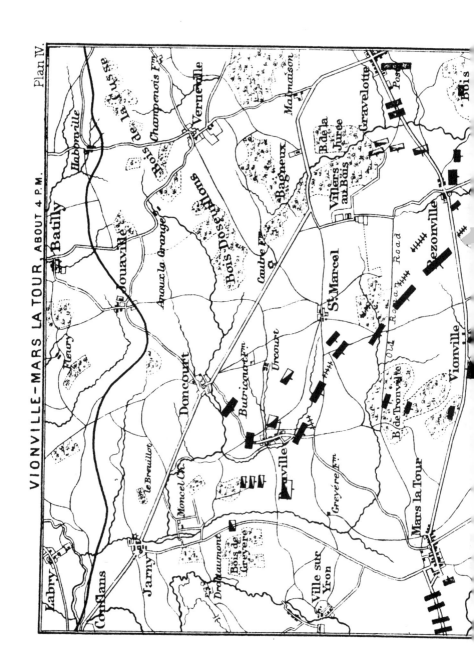

Plan IV.

VIONVILLE—MARS LA TOUR, ABOUT 4 P.M.

Labry
Conflans
Jarny
Batilly
Fleury
Habonville
Bois de la Cusse
Bois Champenois Fm
Vernéville
Doncourt
le Breuillot
Moncel Chx.
Dx. Beaumont
Bois de Greyère
Ville sur Yron
Greyère Fm
Mars la Tour
Vionville
B. de Tronville
Rezonville
Old Roman Road
St. Marcel
Urcourt
Butricourt Fm
Tronville
Caulre Fm
Bois Doseuillons
Anoux la Grange
Bruville
Malmaison
Bagneux
B. de la Justice
Villers aux Bois
Gravelotte
Post
Bois

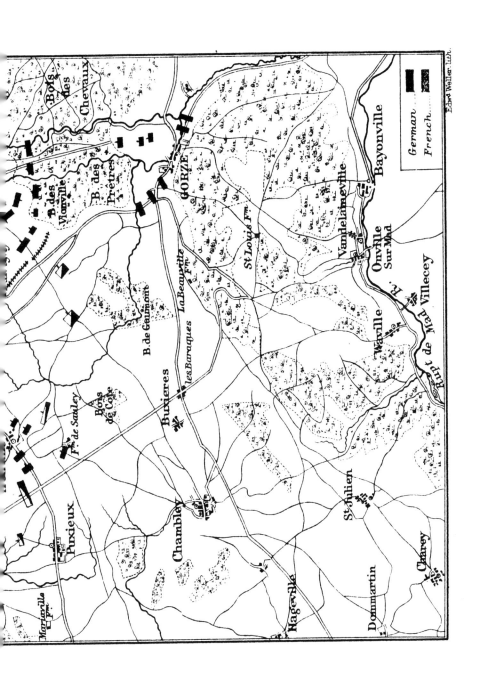

Bois des Chevaux

Bois des Prêtres

B. des Vionville

GORZE

St Louis Fm

La Beauville Fm

B. de Geaumont

les Baraques

Buxieres

Bois de Sabley

Fm de Sabley

Bois de Coin

Chambley

Puxieux

Marianville Fm

Nageville

St Julien

Dommartin

Charey

Vanlelameville

Onville Sur Mad

Bayonville

Waville

Villecey

Rupt de Mad R.

German

French

Edwd Weller lith.

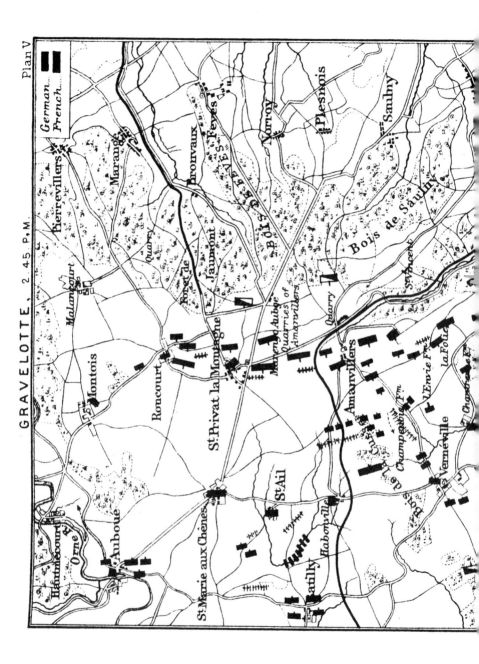

GRAVELOTTE, 2.45 P.M.

Plan V

German.
French.

Pierrevillers
Marange
Montois
Malancourt
Quarry
Roncourt
St Privat la Montagne
St Marie aux Chênes
Auboué
Hautménicourt
Orne R.
St Ail
Habonville
Batilly
Hatrize
Forêt de Jaumont
Brouvaux
BOIS DES FEVES
Norroy
Plesnois
Saulny
Bois de Saulny
Maison Aubé
Quarries of Amanvillers
Quarry
St Vincent
Amanvillers
Le Champenois Fm.
La Cusse
Bois de Jaum
Envie Fme.
la Folie
Chantrenne Fm.
Verneville

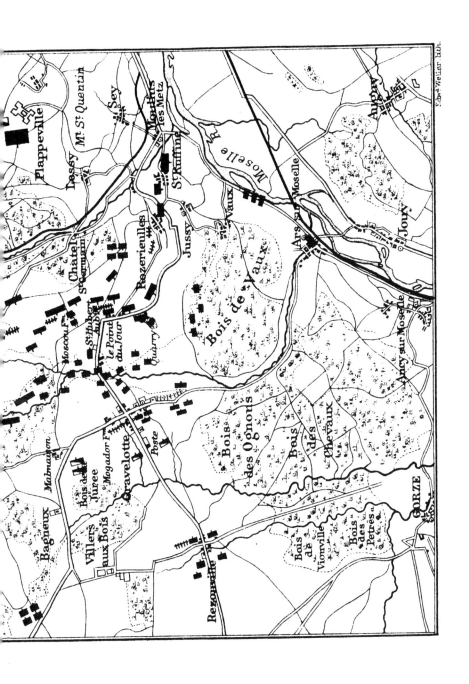

Edw.ᵈ Weller lith.

Plappeville

Lassy Mt St Quentin

Sey

Moulins les Metz

St Ruffine

Châtel St Germain

Fezerieulles

Jussy

Moselle R.

Vaux

Ars sur Moselle

Jouy

Bois de Vaux

Moscou Fe

St Hubert Aubé

Le Point du Jour

Quarry

Bagneux

Malmaison

Gravelotte

Poste

Mogador Fe

Bois de Jurée

Villers aux Bois

Bois des Ognons

Bois des Chevaux

Ancy sur Moselle

Bois de Vionville

Bois des Petres

GORZE

Rezonville

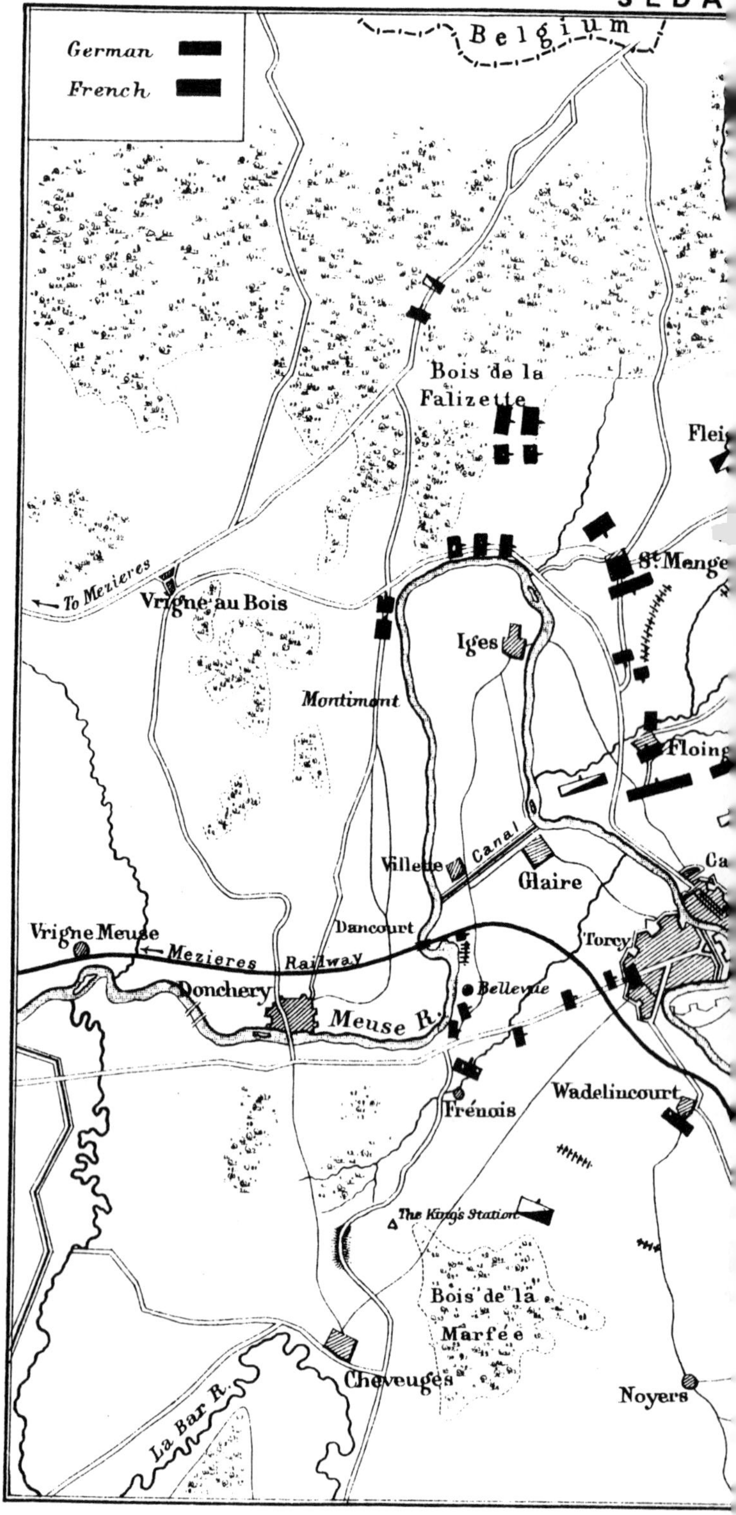

Belgium

German

French

Bois de la
Falizette

Fleï

St. Menge

← To Mezieres

Vrigne au Bois

Iges

Floing

Montimont

Villette Canal

Glaire

Ca

Vrigne Meuse

Dancourt

Torcy

← Mezieres Railway

Donchery

Meuse R.

Bellevue

Frénois

Wadelincourt

The King's Station

Bois de la
Marfée

Cheveuges

Noyers

La Bar R.

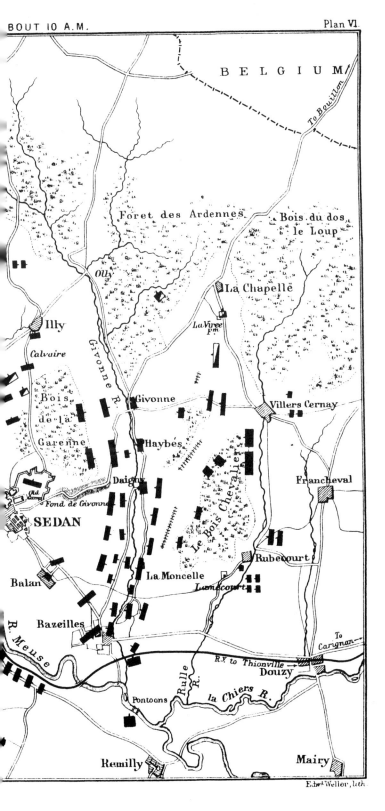

BELGIUM

To Bouillon

Foret des Ardennes

Bois du dos
le Loup

Olly

La Chapelle

La Viree
Fm.

Illy

Calvaire

Givonne

Villers Cernay

Bois
de la
Garenne

Haybes

Le Bois Chevalier

Francheval

Daigny

Old

Fond de Givonne

SEDAN

Rubecourt

Balan

La Moncelle

Lamecourt

Bazeilles

To
Carignan

R. Meuse

Rulle R.

RY to Thionville

la Chiers R.

Douzy

Pontoons

Remilly

Mairy

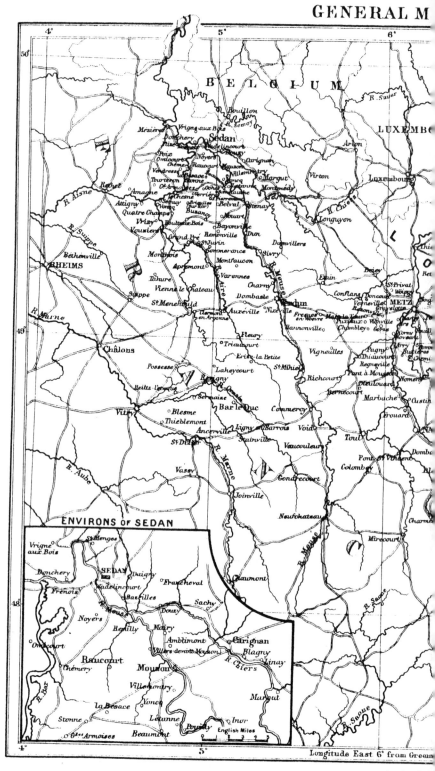

ENVIRONS of SEDAN

English Miles

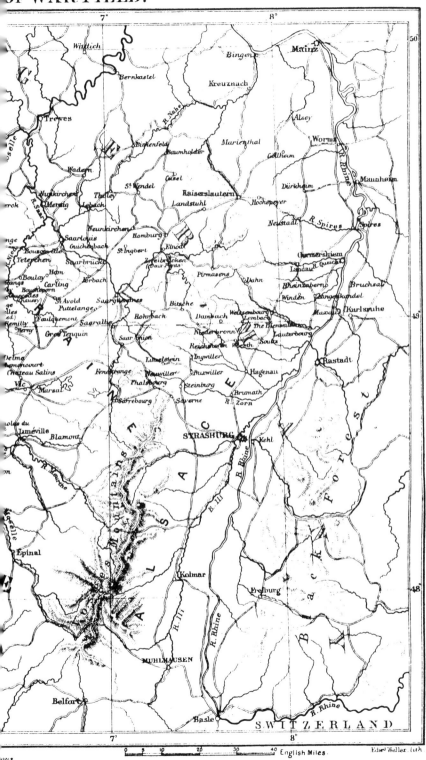

Worley Publications

NAPOLEON AND KING MURAT

by ALBERT ESPITALIER

A facsimile reprint of the English
edition of 1912.
Pages, XVI, 510.
Frontis., 16 Illustrations.
Hardback (21.5 x 14cm).
Published January 1998.
Price £25.00.
ISBN 1 869804 48 1.

Marshal Murat, King of Naples. Everything there recalls his image to our minds; the splendid bay where Caroline dreamed
her dreams; the river of Chiaia where the king used to review his troops with the English bullets singing overhead. Joachim
it was who cut the beautiful road which leads to Posilippo and that other which runs out to Capo di Monte. *A.E.*

OTHER TITLES AVAILABLE

To order your copy or for further information about these and future books, please write (or telephone) to:-
Worley Publications & Booksellers, 10 Rectory Road East, Felling, Tyne and Wear, NE10 9DN
Telephone: (0191) 469 2414.